JIM BRIDGER

JIM BRIDGER

JIM BRIDGER

MOUNTAIN MAN

A BIOGRAPHY

BY

STANLEY VESTAL

William Morrow & Company

NEW YORK

1946

TO
THE MEMORY
OF
MY SISTER
MAY

CONTENTS

PART 3: TRADER

PART 4: GUIDE

PART 5: CHIEF OF SCOUTS

PREFACE

EVER since the days when, as a boy, I raced Indian ponies and swam in a Western river with the Cheyenne lads, I have felt the lack of a satisfying portrait of Jim Bridger. The intervening years permitted much research, but somehow the books about Bridger never seemed to do him justice. In his own time he was a legend, and since his death historians have been content for the most part merely to pile up facts around these retold incidents. There has been no adequate biography to bring the man to life.

Few men have been so misrepresented.

On the one hand, he was represented in fiction and on the screen as a drunken, loutish polygamist and liar, in a caricature so monstrous that his outraged relatives brought suit to recover damages. The court ruled that no one could confuse this caricature with the real Jim Bridger, and denied the suit.

On the other hand, Jim Bridger's real achievements have been ignored or neglected by writers, who have tried to represent him as an Injun fighter with all the dash and daring of Kit Carson, as a wag with all the wit and love of fun of Joe Meek, or as a crusty, ignorant hillbilly, unable to hold his own in the society of civilized men. His real work as one of the greatest of American explorers has been too often overlooked.

But Bridger's glorious memory needs no false glamour. The man was greater than his legend. His true character requires no defense and no apology. Few men in American history have been more uniformly trusted and respected, or have shown themselves more hospitable or generous, more companionable or more agreeable in manner. Wherever he went Bridger inspired confidence, and usually performed what others about him considered sheer impossibilities. That gray-eyed, rawboned, six-foot frontiersman has never been painted to the life.

The earlier biographies are all out of print. It is time for a new attempt.

I have found considerable new and neglected material, particularly with regard to the meaning of Bridger's Indian name, his knowledge of the Indians, his part in the treaty of Laramie and the defense of Fort Phil Kearney, and his days at Fort Bridger. With all this I have presented, I hope, a truer interpretation of his character and motives than has been offered heretofore.

Living in troubled times, twice suffering the loss of everything he owned and even the profession he followed, he stuck to his beloved Mountains and lived to see them tamed and settled by the men who followed his trail. His skill and knowledge opened the way for the trappers, the missionaries, the soldiers, the railroad men, the cowboys, and the settlers. If ever a man earned that title, Jim Bridger may be called a pioneer.

Jim Bridger's fame wears well. Here is his story.

Stanley Vestal

JIM BRIDGER

PART

1

TRAPPER

I

ENTERPRISING
YOUNG MAN

Jim Bridger was born at the right time—in the spring of
1804, the very year and season when Lewis and Clark set out
up the Missouri River to traverse the Rocky Mountains
which he was to explore so thoroughly.

Jim arrived lean, brown, and dark-haired, and so he remained to the end of his days. His father, after whom he
was named, kept a tavern in the town of Richmond, Virginia,
and also practiced Washington's earliest profession. A surveyor naturally turns where his services are most in demand,
and in those days, when Americans were swarming westward
on the trail of Daniel Boone to take up millions of acres of
new land in Missouri, it was hardly surprising that Jim's
father caught the frontier fever. When the boy was eight
years old, the family loaded their goods into the wagon and
headed west.

That long, leisurely trip over the Blue Ridge, the Blue
Grass, and through the deep woods of half a continent was a
tremendous experience for little Jim, and splendid training
for his after life. All day he was in the open, riding the
spare horse, or peering out from under the wagon sheet, or

afoot and marching along beside the team. At sunset, when the wagon rattled to a stop under a tree, Jim would be first to explore the new campsite, to find the spring or the ford, picking up sticks for the fire, watching his mother at her cooking, going with his father to water and stake out the stock. At night he would comfort the young 'uns when eerie screech owls cried in the treetops, and the paired eyes of wild varmints gleamed from the darkness around the cheerful fire.

When the Bridgers reached the Mississippi, they settled on a farm at Six-Mile-Prairie not far from St. Louis, the metropolis of the West—a town of less than 2,000 inhabitants.

There Jim might have grown up like other young fellows of his time—hunting, fishing, doing chores around the farm, carrying the pole for his father in one hand and a rifle in the other while they surveyed new lands, learning to tree coons, call turkey, shoot bear, and stand off Injuns—until, as the country settled up, he dwindled little by little into a humdrum plowman. What dreams the boy had for his future, what plans his parents made for him, we cannot know. For when Jim was going on fourteen, his mother suddenly died.

While still crushed under the shock of that bereavement, the boy saw his brother, and then his father, swiftly follow her. Only he and his little sister were left. All at once he found himself a heartsick, penniless orphan—and the head of the family! A maiden aunt came to the stricken cabin to look after his sad little sister.

Jim said nothing about his own hopes and plans. Tight-lipped, he threw them all overboard, and pitched in to be a breadwinner.

In those days food was no problem in Missouri. Young as he was, Jim could raise corn and shoot game enough to feed his women folks. But clothes and all other necessities had to be bought for hard cash, and that did not grow on bushes. From the start, young Jim took his responsibilities seriously. He was ambitious. He aimed to give his little sister as good a raisin' as Pappy could have done—or know the reason why. He got a job running a flatboat on the Mississippi, ferrying across all comers, their teams and wagons, between Six-Mile-Prairie and St. Louis.

That was strenuous work for a youngster. The ferry was only a few miles below the mouth of the Missouri, that wild and monstrous river, violent and unpredictable, which rushed down bearing strange gifts from far off unmapped mountains, troubling the clear waters of the Mississippi. Every spring that Big Muddy rampaged down out of the wilderness, hurling an avalanche of driftwood and ice and dead buffalo upon whatever luckless creatures might stand in its path. The lank, half-grown boy found his hands full, what with floods and storms, snags and drifting logs, ice and quicksand. But whatever the weather, Jim was always on duty, subject to the call of any traveler who might board his clumsy craft or beckon from the opposite bank, yelling, "Over!"

The men he met on the river were, if anything, wilder and more violent than the stream itself—rough, tough, hard-drinking, hell-roaring boatmen, who came in their dugouts, Mackinaws, and keelboats down the Mississippi from the Falls or the Ohio, down the Missouri from the Indian towns and fur forts, up from New Orleans. They were reckless fellows, foul-witted, profane, great braggarts, and ready to fight rough-and-tumble at the drop of a hat. Among them the slim lad soon learned to keep his ears open, his eyes skinned, and his mouth shut.

Jim stuck to this hard, ill-paid river job only until his Scotch thrift and industry opened a job for him on shore. He was soon apprenticed to a blacksmith, Phil Creamer, in

St. Louis. There he had a steady job, a chance to learn a trade, and could contribute something to his needy family. The work was hard, the hours from sun to sun. But Jim was eager. It was no small treat for a country boy to live and work in town. To Jim, St. Louis was no mean city.

In winter the town, half French, half American, was quiet enough. Before the Americans came, the French had dubbed it *Pain Court*, because of its short rations, and the French section of the town was still known as *Vide Poche*, from its empty pockets. But our young nation was feeling its oats, and in summer the town came vigorously to life. The Louisiana Purchase, only one year older than Jim himself, had set all men to dreaming of endless opportunities in the uncharted West.

In the blacksmith shop Jim soon became familiar with the crunch of cinders underfoot, the roar of the bellows, the hiss of hot iron in the tub, the clink-clang of his hammer, as he beat showers of sparks from red-hot metal on his ringing anvil. He learned to shoe the heels of restive horses, set wagon tires, make sure-fire beaver traps, and hammer out the great iron grappling hooks used by keelboatmen to drag their boats around an embarras.

But the life in the street outside the open door interested Jim far more. Hundreds of people moved through those muddy lanes, most of them from far-off places: painted Indians in gay blankets, with shaved heads and nodding roaches, jogged by on their ponies; swarthy Mexican muleteers followed their plodding animals through the dust; bullwhackers, bearded and booted, cracked their long whips over the backs of rolling oxen; dragoons, belted with long sabers, clanked along; lean teamsters from the backwoods, in checked shirts and motley homespun, peered out suspiciously from under the brims of their old wool hats; Spaniards from Santa Fe or Chihuahua strolled, proud and deliberate, under their tall, peaked sombreros; French-Canadian *voyageurs* passed, voluble and demonstrative; there came sober farmers and staring, bonneted women under the white tilts of rumbling wagons; naked Indian children played in the ditch; swaggering, brawling boatmen staggered by; and prosperous fur traders passed, in their fancy ruffled shirts, blue coats, brass buttons, and fashionable high-crowned beaver hats.

They all came to the blacksmith shop where Jim worked to have their horses shod, their wagons or carriages repaired, their weapons mended, and to swap horses.

In summer every man in St. Louis became a horse trader, since all knew that any Injun upriver would give everything he owned for a good mount. Not that poor Jim had any horseflesh of his own to swap. But he kept his ears open and his eyes peeled and soon learned the myriad wiles and ways of a man with a horse to trade, all the fine points of that ancient and dishonorable game. Continually thrown with men older and more experienced than himself, the young fellow's naturally keen powers of observation were sharpened, and his native caution soon stiffened into a positive force. The poker-faced deliberation of the horse traders was congenial to the canny Scot in him. He did not forget those lessons. So long as he lived, nobody ever got the better of Jim in a hoss-trade.

In the blacksmith shop, Jim Bridger learned to get along with people of all sorts.

What tales they told! Of the Mountains and the Big Muddy, of buffalo covering the earth—and mountain sheep diving off peaks! Of redskin horse thieves and cutthroats, and the heroes who had gone adventuring among them. Of John Colter who, naked as a jay bird, had outrun hundreds of Injuns to save his skin, the same Colter who claimed to have found all hell boiling up on the headwaters of the Yellowstone; of Manuel Lisa, winner of the famous 1200-mile keelboat race up the Missouri—Lisa, who had kept the Sioux from joining the British in the war of 1812; of Lewis and Clark, the discoverers, going clean over the Rockies to salt water; of the Chouteaus, kings of the fur trade; of Chief Blackbird and his knavery; and of tall Major Andrew Henry, popular hero of the frontier.

There was a man after Jim Bridger's own heart. When Major Henry was not throwing lead at the cussed Injuns, he was digging it out of his mine at Potosi. Up at Three Forks on the Missouri, after most of his company had lost heart and pulled out, Major Henry had refused to quit. He hung on with only a handful of men and fought off whole camps of bloodthirsty Blackfeet. No wonder men pointed him out so admiringly. He was the first American to harvest priceless beaver fur west of the Rockies.

But these heroes of Jim's were not the far-off figures of a dream. Most of them made their headquarters in his home town. There Jim often saw them, shod their horses, listened guardedly as they talked of buffalo robes and beaver plews, of traffic over trails and downriver, of quick fortunes to be made in the beaver trade and in the trade to Santa Fe. And there Jim was—just standing still—stuck in the mud, though spang in the middle of the great rush of the booming fur trade that flowed through his bustling city.

Small as it was, St. Louis kept abreast of the times. Even while Jim was still working the ferry, the first steamboat had reached its wharves. True, that steamboat was only a wretched, gasping, one-lunged craft that had to be poled along by its luckless crew as often as the wheezy engine broke down. But only two years later, in 1819, a steamboat reached the town every few days throughout the season of high water.

One of them, the *Independence*, actually carried passengers and a cargo up the wild Missouri beyond Franklin—the very first steamboat to navigate that savage stream. From then on boats headed up the Missouri in ever-increasing numbers, packed with people dreaming of quick riches, or came down again laden with precious beaver furs and other peltries, buffalo tongues and tallow, all bought from the Indians for a handful of cheap trinkets or a dram of watered rotgut.

Everybody in St. Louis was getting ahead—everybody but Jim! And none of them needed cash as bad as he did. His little sister was getting tall now, growing up, and her new fixin's would cost a pretty penny. Already Jim could barely make ends meet. Yet the more he needed money, the less chance he had to earn it. No matter which way he looked, his trail was blocked. And now he was about to lose his job. His five years' servitude in the shop was nearly ended. Some new apprentice would be taking his place.

There warn't room for another blacksmith's shop in St. Louis—even if he had the tools and iron to start one. He could not become a fur trader on his own hook, for he had no capital. Without book l'arnin' he could not even be a trader's clerk, and after his father died, Jim had dropped all hopes of schooling. He could not even sign his own name. He had been too busy keeping his sister in school.

Yet he *could* not turn his back on the West or head back to the crowded settlements where he had been born. Seemed like no matter which way he aimed to turn, he always ended up facing *west*. Yet he had no mind to hire out as a cussed pork-eater at some trading post upriver, working like a horse for less than his keep, or a half-starved, half-drowned keelboatman, bushwhacking his way up the Missouri on a diet of sodden hominy and rancid tallow.

Something had to be done, and mighty quick at that.

What it might be had Jim stumped. But five y'ar in the blacksmith shop had l'arned him not to strike till the iron was hot.

When that spring morning of March 17, 1822, marked his eighteenth birthday, Jim felt restless and uneasy as a starving coyote in a trap. His time was nearly up.

But Jim had not long to wait. Three days after, a local paper, the *Missouri Republican,* carried this brief notice:

To ENTERPRISING YOUNG MEN. The subscriber wishes to engage one hundred young men to ascend the Missouri River to its source, there to be employed for one, two or three years. For particulars inquire of Major Andrew Henry, near the lead mines in the county of Washington, who will ascend with, and command, the party; or of the subscriber near St. Louis.

(Signed) WILLIAM H. ASHLEY.

II
SET POLES
FOR THE MOUNTAINS

THE RIVER was bank-full. And on that brisk April morning two big keelboats belonging to the Rocky Mountain Fur Company lay tied up, one below the other, along the St. Louis wharf, their sharp prows splitting the swirling muddy current—both being made shipshape for their long voyage to the Great Falls of the Missouri.

The first had been loaded already, its long cargo box amidships, higher than a man's head, packed solid with supplies and trade goods for the expedition, its square sail snapping in the wind on the mast forward, its long cordelle dangling from the masthead to the deck. The boatmen's poles and oars lay neatly stacked on the narrow runways from end to end. The great sweep swung idly in the eddy at the stern, ready for the hand of the steersman.

The keelboat below was still loading. Forty men, busy as beavers, trotted across the narrow landing stages fore and aft, lugging the goods aboard, shoving and heaving to stow the heavy cargo so that it might not shift. Stacks and piles of bundles and bales, boxes and packs strewn along the bank quickly melted away.

Half the population of St. Louis was there to see them start. Some had gathered around Colonel Ashley to watch his men busy saddling up their favorite mounts among the fifty head of restless, half-broken horses which were to accompany the boats overland. Some stood looking on from a distance—among them a lean, anxious woman clutching the hand of an excited young girl.

The more important citizens were gathered about a tall, slender man of commanding presence in buckskins and a beaver hat, who was directing the loading of the boat. A keelboat had to be loaded more heavily forward than aft. Otherwise it might run aground on a sandbar so far that it could never be shoved off. This group on the wharf were laughing at three drunken boatmen, who were being half-driven, half-dragged to the nearest landing stage by a sturdy, red-faced Irishman with a saucy cock's feather in his tall hat. The patroon kicked and roared and shoved them aboard, cursing with all the fluent virtuosity of a seasoned riverman.

While they laughed, a young fellow eased through the group until he reached the elbow of the tall man in the buckskin coat. There he cleared his throat and said, "Major."

Andrew Henry turned at the word and found himself looking into the steady gray eyes of a muscular, dark-haired, upstanding youngster. His earnest face showed the effects of recent vigorous scrubbing with soap and water, his patched homespuns were clean, his boots freshly greased. With the ingrained habit of a military officer, Henry observed with approval that the young fellow's rifle was clean.

"Well, young man, what do you want?" The big man's voice rang with the friendly confidence of the born leader.

"I aim to go to the Mountains with you, Major, if you'll let me. My name's Bridger."

The Major seemed puzzled, perhaps even a little suspicious. "Colonel Ashley has been here right along. Didn't you ask him?"

The young fellow's eyes did not waver. "I reckoned I'd liefer ask you," he explained, shyly.

For a time the Major was silent, frowning a little. Then a sudden grin animated his tanned face. "Of course! You're Jim—the boy in the blacksmith shop. I hardly knew you all cleaned up this way." The Major was serious again. "Our roster is filled up. But," he hesitated, "we could certainly use a blacksmith. You can ride, I suppose?"

"I'd liefer go with—with the boats."

"What do you know about boats?"

"Right smart. I ran a ferryboat afore I was a blacksmith. And I can shoot," Jim added, pressing his advantage.

"Not running away, are you?"

The young man stiffened. "No, sir! My time's up."

The Major smiled, and laid his hand on Jim's shoulder. "All right, Bridger, you can go with the boats—with me. We'll pay you the same as the others."

Jim Bridger lost no time in getting aboard the lead boat. Shouldering his pack and rifle, he crossed the springing planks, set foot on deck, and took his stand out of the way of the boatmen on the afterdeck. There he watched the last bale stowed, watched the last man of the fur brigade come aboard, watched the boatmen pull in the landing stages and cast off the lines. The two big keelboats drifted down and swung out into the current.

Then Mike Fink, King of the Keelboat Men, patroon of the flotilla, scrambled to the top of the cargo box. Lustily he yelled for all to hear: "Set poles for the Mountains!"

Six oarsmen forward of the cabin swung to their oars. Twenty polemen gathered forward, holding their long iron-shod poles. Mike seized the helm with one hand, and with the other raised to his lips the horn hanging about his neck to blow the signal for the start.

But Mike Fink could imitate the mellow moan of a boat-horn perfectly; his lips never touched the horn. At that sound, the oars dipped rhythmically together. The polemen facing the stern dropped their poles into the muddy water, set them against the river bottom, threw their shoulders against the curved sockets at the ends of the poles, and began to push. Leaning with their heads almost down to the level of the running board, they forced their way single file to the stern, pushing the boat forward. Led by the patroon, all hands sang together. When the polemen reached the stern, their patroon gave a shout. All faced about, swiftly ran back to the bow, dropped their poles to the bottom again, and once more shoved manfully against the crutch-like sockets of their poles. Slowly the boats gained way.

As the long low craft came upstream opposite the wharf again, the people on shore waved and cheered. Jim and his comrades waved back. White powder smoke bloomed from the muzzles ashore. Jim and the other hunters snatched up their rifles and fired into the air. Half hidden in smoke, the boats moved on, while around him the guns went on banging, one after another, popping like a string of firecrackers. As the breeze swept that acrid smoke away, Jim swallowed the lump in his throat, snatched off his old wool hat, and swung it round his head in farewell to his little sister and his old aunt. St. Louis and its people dwindled as he watched. His great adventure had begun.

It was already mid-afternoon, and most of the boatmen had been celebrating much too well to work the boats very far upstream that first day. So the Major went up the river only a few miles and lay to—just far enough to keep the guzzlers from walking back to the taverns of St. Louis to celebrate some more. They tied up the boats and swarmed ashore to make camp for the night. In the morning the real voyage to the Mountains would begin.

Making camp, Jim found, was a simple matter. In those days only soldiers and invalids used tents in summertime. Hunters and boatmen took the weather as it came, believing that men who never slept under a roof were in little danger of sickness. Though their clothing might not be waterproof, they knew their skins were. Their only camp equipment consisted of a kettle for each mess, a knife, a cup, and a blanket for each man.

The simplicity of these arrangements did not prevent social distinctions. The French-Canadian boatmen messed by themselves around their own fires on the mush and sowbelly provided by their employers. They were drudges whose sole duty consisted in the heartbreaking labor of getting the boats up those relentless rivers.

But Jim and the other "enterprising young men" who had been hired to trap and fight Injuns, felt themselves quite superior to such pork-eaters, such *mangeurs de lard*. Each group kept to itself.

Jim found that he knew many of his comrades. All the up-and-coming young fellows in town had joined the expedition. Many "had relinquished the most respectable employments and circles of society" to become trappers. They were heading to the Mountains to share in that great gamble for fortunes in fur believed in those days (truly enough) "not to be surpassed by the mines of Peru." Some of them had gone to the Mountains before with Major Henry, or Lewis and Clark, or Manuel Lisa, or the Chouteaus. Others, like Jim, counted themselves lucky to be companions of such great adventurers, fighters, and explorers.

Most were from Virginia or Kentucky or Tennessee. There was Sublette, who boasted that his grandfather had killed Tecumseh. There were Tom Fitzpatrick, rarin' to go, and old Hugh Glass, spry as a spring chicken for all his grizzled whiskers; there were Edward Rose and Jim Beckwourth, the mulattos, adopted warriors of the Crow tribe; Talbot and Carpenter, David Jackson, Robert Campbell, Etienne Provost.

No sooner had the fires been lit, than Jim, eager to make up for time lost in the blacksmith shop, headed into the woods and brought back some rabbits for the mess. Afterward, while men smoked their pipes, he sat and listened. The Major, he heard, aimed to cross the Mountains and hunt on the other side—a country covered with fur, crawling with varmints—and Blackfoot. Terrible fighters, them Blackfoot, but hardly meaner than the Snakes, the Sioux, or the Assiniboines. Jim wondered how he would stack up when he ran into the cussed Injuns. Could he hold his own? Or must he lose his scalp on some lonely beaver stream?

Meanwhile the boatmen, happy-go-lucky as always, in spite of hangovers, fatigue and meager rations, were singing together. But that first evening on the river was not all spent in ease and gaiety and the renewing of old friendships. The crews had to be whipped into shape, and Mike Fink was the man to do it. He had the reputation of being the best rough-and-tumble fighter on the Mississippi. So that night he hopped upon a stump and, flapping his arms like a rooster's wings, crowed at the top of his lungs, challenging all comers to dispute his authority as patroon of the boatmen. He yelled, "I'm a Salt River roarer and I love the wimming and I'm chock full of fight."

That night no one took up the challenge.

The uneven ground was cold and hard under Jim's blanket. The dark trees with their tall stems seemed to him like black rockets soaring up to burst against the paler sky. Jim closed his eyes.

Before he could roll over, he heard the boat horn blow. It was still dark, but it was already morning. Jim and his companions crawled out, stiff and sore, wolfed down the food remaining in last night's kettle, rolled up their blankets, picked up their guns, went aboard. At daybreak the flotilla headed up the river. A favoring breeze filled their canvas. It was plain sailing to the mouth of the Missouri.

They heard the Missouri long before they saw it, a noise as of a mighty rapid, which increased with each stroke of the oars. Yet, strangely enough, as they neared the mouth of that muddy monster, the water below seemed to clear. The placid Mississippi mingled its green waters reluctantly with the chocolate-colored flood from the Missouri; for some distance below the mouth, the two streams flowed side by side in one bed. But after turning their prows up the Missouri, they saw no more clear water. Jim's experience as a ferryman on the Mississippi had hardly prepared him for the violence of the wilder stream.

That violent and clouded water rushed out, carrying great trees with all their roots and boughs and trailing vines, whirling and plunging towards him, mingled with the swollen carcasses of buffalo, dead logs, underbrush, and all manner of flotsam.

As the two boats beat their way upriver, avoiding those dangerous missiles, every man braced himself for the struggle ahead. Some of them knew by cruel experience that there was no harder labor than lugging a laden keelboat up the Missouri. Their sails soon failed them, for the channel of the river was too narrow, too crooked for tacking, even when the wind was favorable. And wherever the channel was narrow, the current proved too swift for their oars. The water was often too deep for poles, and the sandy banks too shifting and temporary to permit a regular tow-path. These banks were overgrown with brush and trees and grass shoulder-high through which the men, pulling on the long cordelle or tow-rope, had to fight or cut a way.

But the tricky water, the treacherous banks, were the least of their troubles. Everywhere the bare, bleached bones of dead trees planted solidly in the mud projected above the surface, all leaning downstream. They had to steer among these dangerous snags—any one of which might gore the boat and send it to the bottom. Sometimes there was *no* way open, and they tied up the boats while men chopped out the snags ahead. Yet even these thousands of snags threatening their voyage were not their worst danger. There were other snags called "breaks" hidden beneath the muddy water, to say nothing of the treacherous "sawyers"—logs which, anchored in the stream by their branches or roots, yet had leeway enough to bob up and down as the current passed over them, surging upward violently enough to overturn a small boat or rip out the bottom of a big one. Everywhere were sandbars, quicksands. But worst of all was the embarras—a "raft" or log jam blocking the current, clogged with sand, bound together with roots and driftwood, forming a regular dam around which the river plunged madly through a narrow spillway at one side.

Jim and his comrades found it quite impossible to pull or row the keelboat up such torrents. They had to throw grappling hooks out ahead, then slowly and painfully turn the capstan until they had warped the boat up to the hook. Then they would cast another hook farther ahead and repeat the toilsome process. Wherever the stream was free from obstacles and snags, it was likely to be too deep or too swift for poles or oars. Then the weary boatmen plunged overside and, seizing the long cordelle fastened to the masthead, waded against the icy current as through a heavy surf, plodding over sandy bars, slipping and falling on the sloping banks, pulling on the rope with one hand and clinging to the brush and branches which drooped from above with the other— "bushwhacking" they called it. With good luck such a crew might make a dozen miles a day. At best, their speed was likely to be about a mile and a half an hour, but often they made no greater distance between sunup and sundown.

At that season rain fell almost every day. Thunderstorms roared and bellowed. Strong gales blew up and down the river even when the wind ashore was not particularly high. As the water rose and fell, it undercut the banks, sending great trees crashing into the stream across the boatmen's path. Sandbars dissolved beneath Jim's feet, chill rains soaked him, hailstones pelted him. For everyone—hunters as well as boatmen—had to lend a hand, and there was no shelter afloat or ashore. At every emergency Mike Fink pranced up and down the cargo box, shouting, leading a song, joking, talking, cheering on his men. A patroon on the Missouri kept as busy as a man killing snakes.

In spite of all these difficulties, they pushed on—past St. Charles on its hill, past the broad Gasconade coming in from the south and the yellow waters of the Osage River, past Point Labadie, Côte Sans Dessein, Cedar Island, Manitou Rocks, and the difficult Wizard's Island. As they entered that evil stretch of the river near the present town of Lexington, Missouri, they saw it "covered with wood," bristling with snags that had to be chopped out before they could proceed.

Fort Osage, established by Governor William Clark not long before, stood not far above—one of those triangular forts he loved to build, high on a bluff, 100 feet above the water, visible for miles up and down the stream. The men all looked forward to reaching it. There they could rest a little, see strange faces, swap for a little tobacco and salt, powder and ball, or eat Injun dog in the loafshaped lodges of the Osages. They reached a point only 20 miles below.

That day Jim Bridger squatted on the afterdeck of the leading keelboat, half asleep in the sun. A few rods below, trailing after him, came Colonel Ashley's boat, having an easy time of it, Jim thought, after Major Henry's boat had cleared the way. Suddenly he saw the boat behind swerve from its course, swing broadside to the current. Swiftly it began to drift downstream, gaining way every moment. The patroon called out.

Now wide awake, Jim stood up, watching the helpless craft. Suddenly every man on it fell to the deck as if swept down by some invisible hand. The big keelboat heeled over. The bow dipped under. By the time the crew had got to their feet again on the sloping deck, she was sinking by the bow. Quickly the crew clambered to the top of the cargo box, but the water rose even faster. Within three minutes where the boat had been there was nothing but the heads and flailing arms of the men beating the water.

Major Henry shouted his orders and let his boat drift back

under control to the struggling men in the water. The Major
was cool and efficient. He saved every man. But the boat,
with $10,000 worth of supplies, had literally, as the trappers
put it, "gone under."

It was a sorry and bedraggled crew which plodded through
lines of staring Indians up from the landing to Fort Osage.
The Rocky Mountain Fur Company had lost half its supplies, half its investment—and half the men had lost their
transportation. It was a long, long walk from Fort Osage to
the Great Falls of the Missouri.

From the Fort, they lugged their heavy boat on, carefully
avoiding snags, until they reached the mouth of the Platte.
Above that, Jim heard, he would see "goats" and buffalo—
and prairie dogs, rattlesnakes, and owls all living together
in the same hole. Woods and hills gave way to plains and
prairies. Now, he thought, he was heading into the real
West. He must be getting close to the Mountains.

That evening in camp he sensed something unusual going
on. It 'peared like the old-timers war a-fixin' to play tricks.
Jim saw them whispering and grinning together. Suddenly
one of them let out a yell. Four of them grabbed Jim by the
arms and legs, swung him three times, and tossed him out
into the muddy water. Jim came up gasping and swam for
shore. They ducked him plenty before they let him out. By
that time the air and the water were full of greenhorns.
Every one of them was soused in the river.

When they had all clambered out, panting and dripping,
the leader of the old-timers made them a speech. The Platte,
he said, was the beginning of the Upper River. From the
earliest times it had been the custom to initiate greenhorns
here on their first trip up the Missouri. Now, he said, they
had washed off some of the green, and it was time for a
celebration. Every greenhorn had to set up drinks for all

the old-timers—or they would shave him bald as a buzzard.

The Major supplied the extra cheer for the men who would pay. But most of the young men, not having yet received any wages, preferred to part with their hair. That was the last haircut Jim Bridger had for many a long year.

Cheered by the fun, the horseplay, and the liquor, the outfit pushed on past Fort Lisa—so important in the fur trade of those days; past the famous Council Bluff where Lewis and Clark had smoked with the cussed Injuns about the time of Jim's first birthday. They passed the last military post, Fort Atkinson, and Blackbird's Hill, on top of which the grave mound of the Omaha chief was visible for miles along the winding river. Here the bottoms stretched away from the bluffs on the west side far into the lowlands on the east. The channel was so crooked that after a three-day voyage of fully 30 miles, they still made camp within a thousand yards of the hill from which they had started. Getting out of this maze, they passed Floyd's Bluff, where Lewis and Clark had buried Sergeant Floyd. Beyond White River they saw the beginnings of Fort Kiowa.

While the weary boatmen dragged the keelboat 40 miles around Great Bend, Jim and the other hunters strolled about a mile across the neck. Soon after, they reached Cheyenne River, "the Fork," safely passed the dangerous stretch about the mouth of Moreau River and reached the mouth of Grand River. Above it twin Ree villages perched on their curving bluff above the island—villages which looked like a mass of huge mud igloos, defended by a circle of tall pickets and a ditch. The Rees seemed friendly enough.

All this time the outfit's horses traveled overland under guard, keeping as close to the boat as the lay of the land allowed. Colonel Ashley was in charge of this cavayard. He knew well enough how great a temptation to the redskins a good horse was, since among them all success in war or hunting buffalo depended upon the speed and wind of a man's mount.

He generally made camp close to the river, and at night picketed his horses near the water with the men further inland, camping behind a breastwork made of their packs. On the march his scouts rode out ahead, behind, and on the flanks. With such precautions the Colonel felt sure he could cope with any Indian enemies.

But the Colonel overlooked the danger from Indian "friends."

One morning on the boat Jim heard the cry "Injuns!" He saw five horsemen suddenly appear from behind a ridge just beyond the horse herd. Old-timers on the boat quickly identified the redskins as Assiniboines, friendlies.

The five warriors, riding in line, came down the slope at a walk, singing and shouting, making a great noise—their usual way of demonstrating peaceful intentions—for hostiles generally sneaked up, not making a sound.

Not to be outdone, the horse guard emptied their guns in a salute to these few visitors. The Assiniboines, mingling with the guard which followed the herd of loose horses, shook hands all round and hugged everybody without dismounting. Then they jogged along with the white men, laughing and gesturing, making sign talk with all the good will of a cat about to swallow a mouse.

This friendliness went on so long as the horses were within rifle range of the boat. But by a strange coincidence the channel at this point swung gradually to the opposite side of the riverbed. As the boat sailed on, the distance between it and the horse herd steadily increased. By the time the boat had passed long rifle range, galore of Injuns suddenly showed up, riding down to join their fellows with the horse guard, until the white men were completely submerged in this horde of redskins.

The loose horses, already restless at the smell of Indians, quickening their gait, broke into a trot.. Not to be left behind, the Indian riders kicked their ponies forward and so managed to get in between the loose horses and following guard.

Suddenly Jim heard a sharp yelp. At that signal all the Indians laid quirts to their ponies' flanks, whirled their buffalo robes around their heads, and yelled like devils. The Colonel's horses stampeded on the dead run in a great cloud of dust. Before the horse guard could reload and set their triggers, the thieves had swept the herd over the ridge and away. In no time at all the Company had lost its animals, the precious horses which were to have carried its goods around the Great Falls to Three Forks.

Jim and his disgusted comrades plodded on to the mouth of Yellowstone River, and went into camp. Jim dropped his pack, leaned on his rifle, and looked at the river, the bluffs, the wooded points in the bottoms. So here he was now in what they called the Mountains. And nary a mountain in sight!

III
HIVERNAN

AFTER supper that night, Major Henry made a speech. The Major reckoned everybody already knew that his plan had been to winter at the Three Forks of the Missouri. But after losing the keelboat and half their supplies, he and Colonel Ashley had decided that it would not be smart to venture too far among the hostiles. He had then decided to make headquarters at the Great Falls of the Missouri. But now that they had lost nearly all their horses, even Great Falls was too far into Blackfoot country. It wasn't likely they could get another string of good horses from the Indians in a hurry. They would have to hole up and winter at the mouth of the Yellowstone. "We'll fort here."

Next morning the Major selected a site for his fort on high ground near the river above the mouth. All about in those broad river bottoms points, or patches of standing timber, were plenty. Logging parties scattered into the woods and kept their saws whining and their axes ringing from daybreak to dark. With so few horses, the men had to snake logs to the fort by sheer grit and elbow grease.

Meanwhile Jim and his helpers brought the anvil and bellows ashore, rigged a temporary blacksmith shop under a brush arbor, and then went to work beating out hinges and hasps and fire irons, ran bullets for the hunters and kept the grindstone whirling to keep knives and axes sharp. Jim had staked everything on becoming a hunter and trapper in the Mountains, but now it looked as if he was stuck in the blacksmith's shop again, same as ever.

Jim helped hew out the dugout canoes in which Colonel Ashley and half a dozen men set out down the Missouri River for St. Louis, there to organize another band of trappers, to build new keelboats, and buy supplies to fill them. Jim relaxed with relief when he was not told to go back with Ashley. The Colonel reckoned he would be back again next summer for the march to Three Forks . . .

The fort was a simple affair: two parallel rows of log cabins facing each other, with a stockade of upright logs connecting the ends of the buildings, thus forming an open yard between. Here the men could corral their horses—if they could ever get any. It did not take long to cut the logs, notch them, lay them up, chink the cracks, adze out planks for doors, and lay a flat roof of poles covered with sod. There war heaps of stone in the breaks around with which to build chimneys. The beaten earth served for a floor.

That autumn the weather was fine. As soon as the fort was built, the men scattered to hunt and trap in the neighborhood, where nearly every critter known to the Plains abounded. Jim had never hunted buffalo horseback, and probably had better luck stalking them than he would have had green in the saddle. He and his friends killed galore of elk, deer, goats (antelope), and water fowl, besides bobcats, rabbits, wolves, and other small fur-bearing animals.

Sometimes a band of curious Injuns turned up to trade, and camped around the fort in their taper smoke-browned tipis. Then Jim had a chance to stare at the painted faces of giggling Injun girls shyly peering from under their shawls, a chance to swap for golden-brown smoked elkskins that smelled enticingly like smoked turkey, or to get some old woman to ply her flying awl and make him moccasins to order.

Sometimes the Major and his men hiked several days' march to distant camps to trade, carrying packs on their backs full of tobacco, buttons, ribbons, handkerchiefs, vermilion, beads, finger rings, steel bracelets, coffee, sugar— and rum. They gathered buffalo robes in plenty, but had not much luck trading for horses. Such trips soon wore out Jim's boots and clothing, and he learned from the Injun gals to dress buckskin and to dry, split, and twist buffalo sinews, moistening the fibres in the mouth, shaping them into fine, pointed threads, and so—with an awl—make and mend his own clothing and moccasins. From the day his old boots wore out, Jim never wore such footgear again so long as he lived in the mountains.

Jim was a careful workman. His years in the blacksmith shop had taught him the value of good tools and craftsmanship. He was "sober and frugal." Once he learned how to do a thing, he remembered how to do it, and thereafter did it well.

By the time winter came on, with sudden blizzards rushing furiously in on a sixty-mile wind, filling the air with smothering ice particles for days on end, the little fort was snug and ready—with firewood, food, and shaggy robes. During those storms, Jim and his comrades huddled in the fort, hardly daring to leave it. If any hunter was caught out in such a storm, Jim and his friends in the fort fired their guns at regular intervals to guide him back. For in that blinding smother a man might easily get lost and freeze to death within a hundred yards of the gate.

Sometimes buffalo white with snow came drifting with the storm to crowd under the lee of the stockade until the blizzard passed. They never left that shelter, either for grass or water. Nothing could drive them away—Jim could kill meat without going outside.

As the skies cleared he could see, from the flat roof of the house, herds of elk, white-tailed deer, and buffalo scattered around the valley, walking over the deep crusted drifts to browse on the bark of willows sticking up through the snow. The ice was nearly three feet thick on the river, and all through the long, cold nights trees popped and exploded like cannon with the frost, jerking Jim wide awake.

In March, when the ice went out with a great grinding and roaring, the valley all around was covered with icy water. Day and night huge cakes of ice came floating down, chopping down dead trees, grinding together, crashing through the timber with relentless force. They tore up full-grown cottonwoods and swept them away like weeds. Still the Missouri went over its banks, the Yellowstone backed water, and the rising flood carried away acres of ice formed earlier in the river bends, ice on which the men could see scores of deer and elk and buffalo, rabbits and wildcats drifting by. It was days before open water appeared again and land began to show its back here and there above the flood. Jim remembered his experience on the Mississippi as a tame affair. The Missouri had been bad enough; but the Yellowstone and the Missouri together were wicked.

Yet Jim Bridger was content. Now he was no longer a greenhorn, but a regular *hivernan*. He had *wintered* in the Mountains! He was a Mountain Man!

After the ice went out, Major Henry led a brigade of picked men, some afoot, some on the boat, some in the saddle, upriver. He had learned there were other trappers stirring in the country, so he lost no time in heading for the beaver streams.

But meeting an overwhelming force of Blackfeet near Great Falls, the Major was forced to retreat.

Mike Fink and his partner Carpenter were in the party, and Talbot, Carpenter's friend. Mike and Carpenter were both marksmen, and when on a spree had the habit of filling their tin cups with whisky and shooting them off each other's heads. Jim Bridger did not think much of that trick, good rifleman though he was. But Mike and Carpenter shot plumb-center every time.*

Then, on the Musselshell, Mike and Carpenter fell out—over a squaw. From that day there was bad blood between them.

* The story of how Mike Fink used to shoot tin cups full of whisky off Carpenter's head during a spree has been narrated in fiction and on the screen with Jim Bridger as the principal. But such reckless and showy behavior was utterly foreign to Bridger's careful, sober character. There was nothing of the braggart, bully, or drunk-

Back at the fort, the survivors celebrated their safe return. Mike Fink, as usual, was drinking. Talbot, fearing trouble, tried to patch up the quarrel between Mike and Carpenter. Mike shook hands on it, and to seal the bargain proposed that Carpenter and he shoot the tin cups. It would be like old times, he said—and proof that neither held a grudge. Carpenter may have distrusted Mike, but, if so, was too proud to show it. He tossed a coin to decide which one should have the first shot. Mike won the toss.

Carefully Mike measured out the fine, glazed Dupont powder from his powder-horn; carefully he selected a Galena lead "pill" and a leather patch, pulled out his hickory wiping stick, rammed them home. Deliberately he stepped off sixty paces, turned, and slowly raised his rifle. Carpenter filled the tin cup and placed it on his head, facing Mike.

Mike set his trigger. His finger curled around it. *Tchow!* Down went the cup, and down went Carpenter, dead, shot through the middle of his forehead.

Mike seemed astonished, claimed it was an accident. But, knowing how well Mike could shoot, Talbot did not believe that. He remonstrated.

Mike coolly answered, "All right, I've killed him. Now I'll kill you, too."

Talbot jerked out his pistol, fired once, and dropped Mike, dead as a doornail . . .

Meanwhile moccasin telegraph brought news that the Blackfeet had cut up a band of trappers under Jones and Immel, men of the Missouri Fur Company, on Pryor's Fork of the Yellowstone, at about the same time they were jump-

---

ard about him, and no instance of his exhibition of any such traits has come down to us on the record. Moreover, all who knew him bear witness to his quiet, steady, sober, and responsible character.

ing Henry at the Great Falls. It came home to Jim that trapping on the Upper River was a mighty risky business.

The men were still talking about this disaster when another blow fell.

Early one morning, when it was getting light, Jim heard a dull pounding on the fort gate. He turned out with the others to see what was up. When the guard opened the gate, a chunky French Canadian slipped in, and after him an apple-cheeked, beardless boy about Jim's age, lank as a bear in spring. The pocket of his hunting coat bulged with his Bible, his buckskin breeches were bagged and frayed about the knees, his moccasins still spattered with dried blood. They were couriers from Ashley. The two of them had hoofed it upriver hard as they could go to bring the news.

When the Major appeared, Jedediah Smith came out with his message. Hundreds of miles below the Colonel had run into trouble at the Ree villages. Eight hundred Injuns had caught him napping, had killed thirteen men, wounded a dozen others, got all his horses. The Colonel wanted help, and wanted it quick. Jed told the Major that the Colonel was asking him to come downriver with all the men who could be spared.

That same morning Major Henry called all his men together in the courtyard of the fort and made a short talk. It would be a hard trip. The two couriers had had some narrow escapes coming up the river, and going down in boats would be even more dangerous. If they got through, there would be a big fight—a regular battle. He was sorry he could not take everybody along, but some men would have to remain to look after the fort, the Company's goods, and the horses they had traded for.

Then the Major pulled a little black book out of his pocket

and read off the names of the men he had chosen for the expedition.

Jim Bridger stood with the others, listening anxiously to the names as they fell one by one from Henry's lips. Would the Major leave him behind? Jim was a good shot, he reckoned, and a hard worker. But he was only nineteen, and so far had missed the fun. Maybe the Major still figured he was too green, too young, for such a big war party. Jim shifted his moccasined feet uneasily, peering over the shoulders of the older men in front. As each name was read out, some man would look around grinning, or silently grip the hand of a comrade who was also among the picked men.

On and on went the Major, and still Jim did not hear his name called. Maybe they didn't have him in that book at all. Maybe he was rated no better than a campkeeper. Jim was just about ready to sneak off to hide his disappointment. It seemed like every man in the fort had been named. The Major was plainly about to put his little book away. Jim stood there, almost alone, red in the face.

The last name called was "Bridger." Then Jim remembered why he came last in the book and grinned. He had been the last to join at St. Louis.

Quickly the men got their plunder together. The Major issued powder and ball. The Mackinaws were launched. They all piled in and, with the Stars and Stripes flying, shoved off into the muddy current. There were eighty of them, and every man loaded for bear.

IV
THE MISSOURI LEGION

It was nearly a thousand miles down to Fort Recovery at "the Fork," the mouth of Cheyenne River. But under Major

Henry's leadership, they made the trip without mishap, slipping by the Ree villages in the night, every man vainly lusting for a chance to count a *coup*. They all joined Ashley about the first of July; it was then nearly thirty days since the Rees had bested him.

The two partners went on down to Teton River where they could buy ponies from the Sioux and hit the overland trail. In this way, Jim was told, they could by-pass the treacherous Rees, instead of having to pole or tow their heavy boats through the narrow channel under the bluffs and the rifles of their enemies.

In fact, it looked as if the Rees had actually furthered the purposes of the partners by forcing them off the river. For now Ashley and Henry had new ideas, new plans, for harvesting the fur. In Canada, where the Hudson's Bay Company monopolized all trade with the Indians and was, in fact, a little kingdom on its own, it was possible to regulate trapping so that the game never played out. But in American territory, where no such monopoly and no such control existed, all the beaver around an established trading post was very soon cleared out, resulting in heavy losses to the company which had financed the costly establishment.

It was Henry's plan—an idea adopted from Manuel Lisa —not to engage Indian trappers, but to hire white men and keep them on the job the year round. Instead of maintaining a fort, the partners proposed to bring their goods on pack animals each summer to some central point in the richest fur district, wherever that might be, hold an annual fur fair or rendezvous there, and then carry the furs back to St. Louis. In this way the company would be saved the cost of permanent forts, could always do business where the fur was thickest, and could make a second profit by selling supplies to the

trappers at mountain prices, since the trappers would never
leave the Mountains to go down to the settlements and outfit
themselves.

This plan was especially useful on the Plains and in the
Rockies, where Indians could easily support themselves on

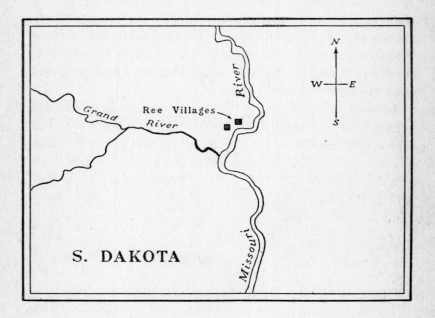

buffalo and other big game and were not under the necessity
of trapping small fur-bearing animals.

During the months when the fur was not in prime condition, Henry explained, the company's trappers could be kept
busy exploring and discovering new beaver streams to be
exploited the following season. This meant year-round employment for Jim.

So far bad luck had prevented the partners from working
out their plan. But once they changed from keelboats to

pack saddles, they would be free from all the hazards of the wild Missouri.

Nevertheless they and their men were determined to punish the Rees. No man knew better than Major Henry the impossibility of trading and trapping among warlike Plains Indians without commanding their respect.

Now, the only credentials to respect among Indians were valor and victory in battle. Jim Bridger did not need to be told *that;* everybody on the frontier knowed it. If ye warn't ready to fight at the drop of a hat, the cussed Injuns hadn't no use fer ye—unless to sculp ye.

So Jim and his comrades were delighted to learn that Colonel Henry Leavenworth, Commandant at Fort Atkinson, had not waited for orders from St. Louis, but was advancing up the river with three keelboats, some artillery, and six companies of the Sixth United States Infantry to join them in punishing the Rees. Also, Joshua Pilcher, head of the Missouri Fur Company, had turned out all available forces to join the expedition and avenge his own men, Jones and Immel. Major O'Fallon, Indian Agent, had appointed Pilcher subagent for the campaign. This authority would enable Pilcher to bring 500 Sioux warriors into the fight.

Jim and his war-minded comrades waited impatiently in camp at Fort Recovery for Colonel Leavenworth and his troops. They were eager to get back upriver and give those treacherous Rees the biggest kind of licking.

When the Colonel arrived, Jim thought he looked glum. On the way up, one of his keelboats had been snagged and sunk with a lot of Government property and 70 muskets. Seven of the Colonel's men had been drowned.

But if Leavenworth was glum, his allies were not. The fur traders quickly supplied him with good rifles to take the place of the lost muskets. Leavenworth announced that he would

organize his forces as the Missouri Legion. He commissioned
a number of the Mountain Men as officers in his command:
Captain Jed Smith, Ensign Edward Rose, Quartermaster
Thomas Fitzpatrick, Sergeant-Major William Sublette, Cap-
tain Henry Vanderburgh, Captain Angus MacDonald, First
Lieutenant Moses B. Carson, Second Lieutenant William
Gordon.

The other Mountain Men were mustered in as enlisted men.
Jim Bridger was one of the youngest of these buck privates.

It seemed mighty queer to be a soldier. Jim and his fellow
recruits received no uniforms—and wanted none. Though
nobody, Jim reckoned, could have taken him and his friends
for soldiers—dressed as they were in nondescript buckskins
and headgear of all sorts, each armed to suit his personal
taste—still Jim and the others took care not to stand in
line too smartly, not to keep step or come to attention too
promptly. They let everyone know they were free men and
volunteers and *not* subject to the slavish discipline of Regulars. They obeyed orders with deliberation, and called their
newly commissioned officers by their first names.

Chief Fireheart led the mounted Sioux. When the command started upriver from Fort Recovery, it mustered almost
800 well armed men. As they marched up the stream, hundreds of Sioux came riding to join the straggling column.
By the time the Missouri Legion reached the Ree villages,
Jim judged that Leavenworth had all of 1100 men—by all
accounts, nearly two to one of the Rees.

But Leavenworth was taking no chances. He avoided Ashley's mistake, and tied up his boats 20 miles below the villages. Then he advanced overland upriver with his artillery
trailing along far behind.

When they came in sight of the two villages perched on
the bluff behind their rickety palisades, Jim had a good look

at the earth lodges, huge mud igloos, the tall medicine pole with its dangling effigy like some great doll rising high above all.

The villages looked to be about eighty yards apart, and the whole shebang stretched along the river for all of three-quarters of a mile. From where Jim stood, they looked like a lot of gopher mounds inside a picket fence. Behind the town, at some distance, were hills; below it open prairie. There were hardly any trees anywhere in sight.

Jim watched Pilcher and his mounted men ride forward and disappear behind the villages to cut off all retreat. Meanwhile the Sioux, eager to do battle, were tying up their ponies' tails, uncovering their shields, painting their faces, chanting war songs, and unlimbering their bows. As soon as all were ready, Fireheart led them charging up the valley in a great cloud of dust to the prairie below the villages.

Then Jim saw the Rees come pouring out from behind their pickets. They tangled with the Sioux on the prairie below the nearest town. Jim could not see much for the great cloud of white powder smoke and dun dust. Faintly he could hear the yelling and the popping of all those guns Ashley had foolishly sold to the Rees.

The Rees stopped the Sioux dead in their tracks. Pilcher came dashing back to call up the troops. Leavenworth shouted a command. The Legion stepped out rapidly along the west bank of the Missouri. Ashley's men marched nearest the river; the Regulars marched in the center. The riflemen marched on the left. Once they got within rifle range, the Rees fell back quick as scat into their towns.

Now was the time. All they had to do, Jim thought, was to charge in after the Rees, chase them out the other side, and then rub them out in the open.

But to Jim's disgust, the Colonel ordered a halt. He said

he was waiting until his artillery came up. According to the book, a town had to be shelled before it could be occupied!

That first volley made a lot of racket and knocked over the big medicine pole.

But after that, Jim could see no results of the cannonading. The Rees kept their heads down, and the cannonballs just silently buried themselves in the heavy sod walls of the lodges.

By the middle of the afternoon, all the ammunition of the artillery was used up, and the Rees had learned to laugh at the white man's big guns.

The Sioux were laughing too, laughing at the Colonel. Said they, "This white chief is just an old woman. He sits away off here shooting into the air. That is no way to fight. If he were a warrior he would ride in, stab or strike somebody, try to capture a weapon or a horse. That is the way of a warrior. You asked us to come and make war on the Rees. But this is not what the Sioux call war. If this is all the fighting you are going to do, we might as well go home."

Major Henry and Pilcher and all the other Mountain Men nodded hearty agreement. The Sioux had uttered their exact sentiments. Jim Bridger watched the Major and the other leaders walk over in a body to put the matter up to Leavenworth. Meanwhile, Jim and his comrades had time to raid the Ree corn patch along the river.

While Jim was munching the particolored ears of runty Indian corn, the contemptuous Sioux came up to join the feast: "*He-han!* Well, well. So you are able to stand up and eat? Look at that Sioux. He is wounded and bleeding. Show me a wounded white man. If you go to the battlefield beside the village, maybe you will find blood on the ground. That is Sioux blood. Maybe you will find a dead man. But he will *not* be a white man. *We* have done all the fighting that was done today. *We* have shed all the blood that was shed. If we Sioux had known that white men were afraid to fight, we would never have come along. We can lick the Rees any day without bothering white men to come along and watch us fight."

That kind of talk didn't go down well with Jim Bridger and his trapper friends. "You talk very brave," they signed back. "But wait until tomorrow. Then you will see how the white man can fight."

The Sioux only laughed—and pointed to what was going on on the prairie. The Ree chiefs were bringing the pipe of peace out of their village to smoke with the Colonel. Astonished, Jim and his friends questioned their leaders. They were outraged to learn that the peace council with the Rees was the Colonel's idea—the Colonel had *asked* them to smoke. Before they could digest their fury at this news, the Colonel demanded that the Sioux and Mountain Men join him in smoking with the Rees!

The Sioux flatly refused to burn tobacco with their undefeated enemies. The Mountain Men, amazed and furious, were almost speechless. Jim watched Pilcher, packing his rifle, walk up and down, up and down, itching for a fight.

The Rees watched Pilcher also, and when Colonel Leavenworth proposed to smoke with them, the Rees refused to make peace unless Pilcher and the angry Mountain Men smoked too.

At that Jim saw the Colonel's face go fiery red. But the next thing Leavenworth knew, Chief Fireheart and his Sioux got on their horses, ready to ride away. The Chief declared, "The white chief talked very brave, but he is afraid of the Rees. I wanted to fight, but the white chief got scared and turned back. We were told that the Indians were the wind, but the white men were the whirlwind. Still the whirlwind

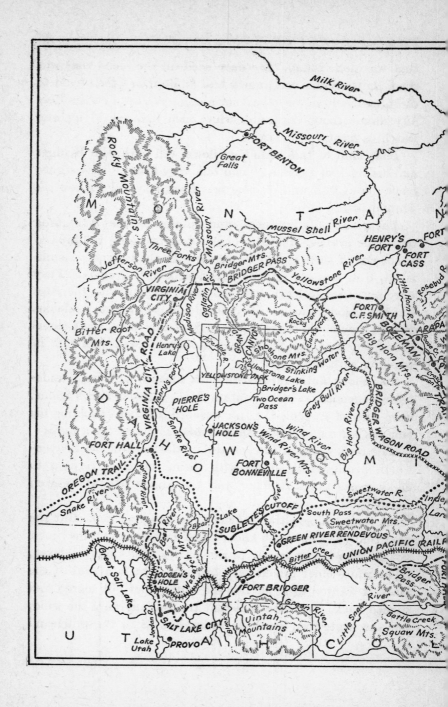

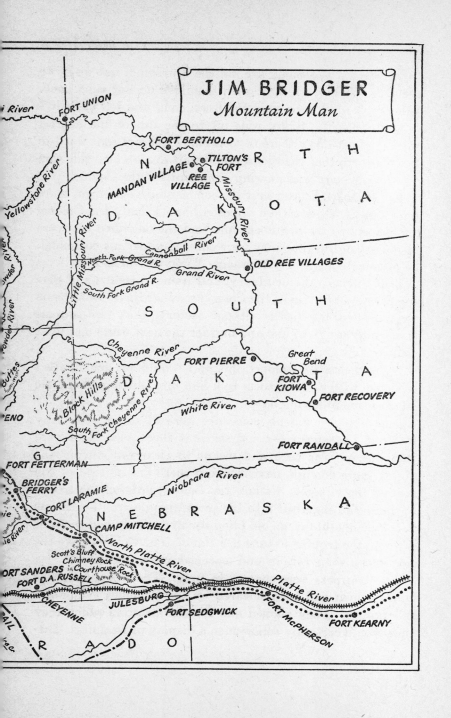

turned back. We Sioux are not the whirlwind, but we go to the Ree villages, we fight with them, we do not turn back. When you white men whip the Rees, come and tell us of it."

With that the Sioux rode off to the top of the nearest ridge and sat down there to look on. Fireheart sent word to Leavenworth that the Sioux would wait to see which side won out. Everybody was showing contempt for the Colonel.

But it looked to Jim as if the commanding officer got more pigheaded the more they opposed him. Finally the Colonel angrily ended the argument and told the outraged trappers in plain English that they were enlisted under his command. "You must obey orders," he said. "You will do as *I* say."

Still Pilcher, Major Henry, and Ashley pleaded and persuaded, trying to make the Colonel see that there could be no appeasement, no peace without victory, that the Indians would only laugh at him and murder the next white man that came their way.

Nevertheless the Colonel, though he could not get the Rees to smoke with him, let them talk him into putting the battle off until the following day.

Jim Bridger and his comrades were fit to be tied. Any fool but Leavenworth could see that the cussed Rees were just playing for time and meant to clear out during the night. Sure enough, next morning there was no sign of life around the villages. Finally the Colonel ordered the troops forward and marched into the town unopposed. There was only one inhabitant, an old blind squaw; nobody had thought it worth the trouble to take her along. The Colonel gave the old woman some rations and marched away downriver.

The trappers were shamed to fury. Their reputation as fighting men had been smeared by the Colonel's vacillation and failure. They blamed him for the disasters which they knew would certainly follow such a display of weakness. Bitter and scornful, but helpless under military controls, they had to do something. A few of them sneaked away and slipped back to set fire to the villages.

Leavenworth called Pilcher on the carpet for that. First he publicly stated that Moses Carson and Vanderburgh were guiltless in the matter of the burning towns; whereupon the two men burst into tears, bitterly shamed by the praise of such an officer.

Colonel Leavenworth's reprimand to Pilcher backfired. Pilcher put his opinions in a letter to the Colonel: "Humanity and philanthropy are mighty shields for you against those who are entirely ignorant of the disposition and character of Indians, but with those who have experienced the fatal and ruinous consequences of their treachery and barbarity these considerations will avail nothing. You came to restore peace and tranquillity to the country, and to leave an impression which would insure its continuance. Your operations have been such as to produce the contrary effect, and to impress the different Indian tribes with the greatest possible contempt for the American character. You came (to use your own words) to 'open and make good this great road'; instead of which you have, by the imbecility of your conduct and operations, created and left impassable barriers."

Bridger and his fellow volunteers were glad to part company with Leavenworth and the military. As the Colonel headed down the Missouri, they headed west—to follow the overland trail up Grand River to Henry's Fort. But every man was thirsting for a chance to l'arn the cussed Injuns a thing or two.

V
HUGH GLASS AND
THE GRIZZLY

IF BRIDGER wanted to fight the Rees, he soon had his wish. On the fifth day out (August 20, 1823) from the Ree village, near the forks of Grand River, the cussed Injuns tore into Henry's party, wounded two men, killed Anderson and Neil.

The whole country swarmed with angry savages driven from their towns, thirsting for the white men's blood, scornful of their peace.

This was Jim Bridger's first hard Injun fight. As soon as the war party had pulled out, Henry and his men made tracks towards Yellowstone.

But they were not to get off so easily.

Along with all the young men in Henry's party was one graybeard, a hunter from Pennsylvania, named Hugh Glass. Glass had been wounded in Ashley's battle with the Rees. He was a wiry, tough old fellow with the beard of a buffalo and the heart of a bear. After seeing their comrades shot down that morning, most of the young fellows stuck close to the main party. But Old Glass went on ahead to hunt—for of course Henry's men had to live on the country as they went along.

Grizzly bears were numerous all along the Upper Missouri, but, perhaps, nowhere more so than on the Grand River.

Many white men and Indians had been torn to pieces by these ferocious beasts, for in those days the bears had not been much hunted, and feared no man. Often they ran in groups of two or three, and would instantly attack or chase any man they saw. Since they were not very keen-sighted

40

animals, the man who was seen by them was generally too near, when seen, to get away. He had to kill or be killed on the spot. Such bears were terrific adversaries, hard to kill. Lances and arrows made little impression upon their thick coats, their tough hides, their iron muscles covered with layers of fat. Bullets were sometimes not much better, and Prince Maximilian tells of a bear which ran away from his party, carrying the lead of fifteen rifles in his carcass. The trappers dignified the grizzly with a title all his own; they called him "Old Ephraim." Indians counted *coup* upon grizzlies as they did on human enemies, and the man lucky enough to kill one proudly wore the claws as a necklace.

On the fifth day out, old Hugh Glass and a companion were hunting in advance of the party. Glass was in the lead, following the stream, and was forcing his way through a dense thicket of plum bushes. The wild plums grow in sandy places, in thick clumps. When Glass came out of the thicket into a small clearing by the water, he found himself within a few paces of a huge she-bear and two sizeable cubs lying on the warm sand.

Old Glass knew that there was no chance to run. He was hemmed in by the dense brush, through which he could only move slowly, while the bear could plow through it as if it were only grass. Everything depended on the single shot in his long rifle. He threw the muzzle forward, crooking his gnarled thumb to set his trigger.

The bear launched herself upon him with a ferocious grunting growl—that dreadful sound imitated by Indian warriors when bent on instant murder. Before Glass could level his rifle, the she-bear had him by the throat, jerked him from the ground, and flung him down, gasping, with a sickening thud. Crouching upon the helpless old man, she caught his thigh in her teeth, tore off a mouthful of his flesh, and turned away to her waiting cubs.

Breathless and bleeding, Glass took advantage of her move to escape that yellow-red terror. He scrambled to his knees. But the moment he moved she was back again, pouncing upon him. Her strong teeth met in his shoulder; she shook her head and rolled him over. Glass threw up his arms to shield his face and throat. She caught them between her teeth, bit him severely again and again through the wrists and arms. He heard, as well as felt, her cruel teeth rasping on his bones.

Hearing the growls of the bear and old Hugh's yells, the other hunter plunged through the hampering brush, tried to help. But the nearest cub, catching the spirit of its enraged mother, rushed on him. He had to jump into the river to save himself. There, standing in water waist-deep, he raised his rifle, shot the foremost cub. Then he yelled for help.

By that time, the main party had heard the cries and shots of the hunters. They charged to the rescue. Man after man burst through the thicket. There they saw the bear, growling horribly through bloody fangs, standing over the torn body of their comrade. Seeing them, she rose and stood facing the intruders—a shaggy fury, six feet tall, waving her great paws set with those long sharp hooks, ready to attack. From all sides rifles cracked. At the first shots, the she-bear tumbled, rolled over, growling and squealing, clawing at her wounds, until at last she dropped dead across the mangled body of her groaning victim.

The trappers dragged the heavy carcass from their comrade's body. Of course there was no surgeon in the party, but it needed no doctor to tell those pitying men that Old Glass had only one chance in a hundred to live. He had been frightfully torn and mauled. They tried to help him up, but he could not stand. He fell back upon the sand, rolling and screaming in agony, covered with blood.

Major Henry and his men made the poor fellow a bed of robes and blankets under the shade of a tree. They pitied him, but there was little they could do. That night they camped on the spot, and all night long old Hugh's groans and writhings disturbed their sleep. Next morning the Major called a council. What to do?

Little was said. Every man knew that the party must go ahead at once. August was already half gone, and, if the beaver fur was to be taken before the animals retired behind their ramparts of ice and frozen mud for the winter, the men would have to hurry. In that region, it was said, there were only three months—July, August, and Winter. The whole success of their year's venture depended upon getting to work promptly. Yet they knew that Old Glass was in no condition to travel.

Had he been only slightly injured, they might have tied him in his saddle. Had he had a broken leg or a gunshot wound, they might have put him into an Injun drag, or travois, and carted him across the prairie, jouncing along under the old nag's tail. Even a very sick man might have been carried in a litter slung between two mules. But everyone could see that Glass was unfit for travel, even in a litter. He could not be moved.

One reason for the success of the Mountain Men was, of course, that they had the habit of adapting themselves completely to the circumstances in which they found themselves. They, like their forebears in Kentucky and Pennsylvania, habitually acted on the old principle: when in Injun country, do as the Injuns do. And so, this time, they stepped right in the tracks of the redskins.

When a Sioux warrior was badly wounded on the warpath

and could not travel, his comrades would generally leave him (often at his own request) in some comfortable spot—a cave, a sheltered thicket—with arms, dried meat, a buffalo robe, and such healing medicines as they might have along, and then go on home, on the chance that he would recover in his own good time and turn up at camp as soon as he could. Many true stories of such exploits are known, and Wounded Knee Creek, in South Dakota, takes its name from such a happening. The Mountain Men, faced by the same conditions as the Sioux braves, adopted their well-tried methods. It was voted that Hugh Glass would have to stay behind and take his chance.

But Major Henry and his men were not hard-boiled enough to ride away and leave that helpless old man to die alone. Mountain Men were, as a rule, as generous as they were brave. And so the Major decided that two men must remain behind and care for Glass until he died—or was able to travel. That meant, to everyone present, *until he died*. Nobody really expected him to recover.

Major Henry called for volunteers.

Naturally, nobody was eager to remain with Glass in that dangerous region. They were still in the heart of Ree country, and nothing would please the Rees more than to catch three white men in such a fix. Moreover, that country was a battleground of all the warring tribes, swarming with hostiles, Injuns to whom any stranger was an enemy. And now, after Leavenworth's failure to lick the Rees, the rating of an American was so low that even the friendly Sioux could hardly be counted as allies.

None of the men hankered for that chore. They knowed well enough that, to the Injuns, a scalp's a scalp, anyways you fix it. Major Henry proposed that every man contribute to a purse to be given to the men who volunteered to stay.

That seemed fair, and every man pledged a dollar. Some writers talk of passing the hat, but it is not likely that many of those trappers had coins in their possession. The year's work was just beginning, and Mountain Men were accustomed to living on credit until they met at rendezvous and were paid their year's wages. Probably Major Henry received their pledges and promised to advance the money, deducting it from the pay of his men. At any rate, eighty dollars was contributed.[1]

The willingness of these men to contribute was the measure of their unwillingness to stay. The Rees were sure to follow their trail, dogging them every step of the way: even then, no doubt, Ree scouts lay behind the rim of the valley watching them, wondering why they had halted, planning— as soon as the white men moved on—to come down and see. . . .

The old man, in dreadful plight, lay there on his buffalo robe, held together by his bloody bandages, his breath rasping with feverish rapidity. His gnarled hands and bony shoulders looked thin and shrunken. He suffered, but he did not plead. Only his eyes—bright as a captive bird's— spoke for him.

For the first time Jim Bridger felt how hard, how savagely cruel, life on the frontier could be. By nature and training he was a shy, cautious lad, silent in the presence of older men. But now, moved by the helpless old man's agony, young Jim cleared his throat. "I reckon I'll stay."

For a moment Jim saw the old man's eyes light hopefully on him. Then those eyes swept on around the circle of faces

[1] Numerals throughout refer to Notes, pp. 310-323.

in mute appeal. Old Glass wanted more than a youngster like Jim by his side.

Even then none of the men answered that appeal. Shamed they might be, but they would not throw away their lives; *too much had happened that day.* There was a long awkward silence. Finally a fellow named Fitzgerald pushed forward. "I reckon I kin stand it for a while, Major, if Jim kin."

The circle broke up quickly. Forty dollars was mighty nigh half a year's wages, but if Fitzgerald war fool enough to swap his ha'r for that, let him. It warn't their funeral— but his'n—and Jim's.[2]

Henry and his men went on. Fitzgerald and young Jim began their lonely vigil by the deathbed of the moaning, mangled graybeard.

Two days dragged by, and old Hugh Glass refused to die. They fed him on soup, dressed his fearful wounds with cold water—their only remedy—and kept the flies away. They hardly dared to build a fire, for fear the smoke or flame should be seen by roaming Injuns. They never dared to shoot, for fear the reports of their rifles should tell some savage of their hideout. There was nothing to do but sit and worry. Forty dollars a head seemed a small price for a life now that the pressure of their comrades' presence was removed.

On the third day, so far as they could tell, Glass was no better—and no worse—than ever. That morning Fitzgerald saw Injun sign. He was frightened. The younger man caught the contagion of his fear. Fitzgerald declared he would stay no longer. "We cain't do no good here," he insisted. "The old man's shore to die, anyhow. If we stick around much longer, we'll lose our hair."

The younger man gave in at last. Both agreed to abandon Old Glass and strike out after their comrades. Glass was hardly conscious; it would be easy to slip away.

But Fitzgerald knew that if he turned up at Fort Henry with word that Glass had not died, the consequences would be unpleasant. On the other hand, if Glass were declared dead, it would be necessary to produce his plunder in proof of it; the Major would naturally expect to have the old man's effects brought in. Probably Glass owed him for them. And so Fitzgerald and the boy stole the old man's rifle, his powder horn, bullet pouch, knife, and flint, and sneaked away that night. They left him utterly defenseless.[3]

Fitzgerald and young Jim hurried fearfully through that hostile land, making good time. They caught up with Major Henry's men about the time they reached the Yellowstone.

At the fort, to their dismay, the party found that Blackfoot and Assiniboine raiders had swept away twenty-two horses from their small cavayard. While they were still smarting from this heavy loss, a large war party of Gros Ventres rushed them, quickly killing Trumble, Decharle, and two others.

They had scarcely buried these dead, when thieves ran off with seven more animals. The cussed Injuns were after Jim and his friends morning, noon, and night. The fort on Yellowstone was too hot for them. They could hardly defend themselves there—much less hunt or trap.

Major Henry turned his toes upriver. He and his men made tracks for the mouth of the Big Horn.

Luckily, on Powder River they ran into a big camp of friendly Crows and traded them out of forty-seven horses. Then, moving on more rapidly, they forted at the mouth of the Big Horn to make their fall hunt.

Here the brigade split up into several parties. Bridger

rode with Etienne Provost, heading up the Powder, over the divide to the Sweetwater, westward thence, and so over the Continental Divide.

All furs came handy to the Mountain Men, but it was chiefly the silky brown beaver that Jim and his fellows looked for. A prime skin, *plus*—or plew—might sell for five, six,—even eight dollars.

At the first sign of the critter—a dam, a slide, a lodge, shavings about a standing tree, or a log cut down—Jim dismounted to make sure that the sign was fresh and plenty. Then, if possible, he set his trap at the foot of the beaver slide on the muddy bank, where the playful animals launched themselves into the water.

Every trapper had his own routine. Jim peeled off his moccasins and waded upstream to the bottom of the slide. From his trap sack he pulled out a steel trap, spread the jaws, set the trigger, and carefully deposited the contraption under water. The chain attached to the trap he fastened to a notched stake already prepared, peeled of its bark, long and smooth. Slipping this stake through the ring at the end of the chain, he planted it firmly in the bottom of the creek. Then he fastened a float or marker to the chain with a long string, so that, if the beaver swam away with the trap, the float would mark its position.

At his belt Jim carried a small horn vial filled with castor. When all was ready, Jim yanked the stopper from this bottle of "medicine," dipped the end of his slender bait stick into the powerful scent, and then stuck it in the ground so that it leaned above the open trap. When he had done all this, Jim waded carefully back downstream to keep from leaving any human odor, climbed on his horse, and moved on to set his other traps.

The beaver, attracted by the scent or playing on the slide,

sooner or later put his foot in the trap. The pain and fright caused him to dive into the water, heading for the entrance of his lodge. This made the ring at the end of the chain slip down the stake and catch in the notch at the end. The beaver, unable to reach the surface, soon drowned, never having a chance to gnaw off its foot and free itself. The beaver died quick—not like poor old Glass.

When Jim's trapline no longer brought beaver, he moved on upstream and set a new line or went over the hill to some other creek. In this way he and his comrades cleaned out all the tributaries of the main streams on which they worked.

Trapping was hard, lonely, and dangerous work, and a man was always wet to the waist from wading in those icy mountain waters. There were grizzlies and hostile Injuns all around, so that the trapper had to keep his eyes skinned and his nose open, watchful and wary as a wild animal. Otherwise he lost his hair, and his comrades would wag their beards and say, "I reckon he's gone under."

In January Bridger went back with the rest to winter at the fort on the Big Horn. In such a winter camp, the men were divided into messes, each cabin having its own mess of six persons—four trappers and two campkeepers. The trappers had nothing to do but take their turns at hunting to supply the camp with meat. No man hunted for himself or his own mess. Whatever he brought in—buffalo beef or venison, prairie hen or quail, Injun dog or painter—he must deposit before the Captain's cabin. All game went into the common larder.

Among the cussed Injuns one of the common causes of strife was dissatisfaction over the distribution of meat. When Indians butchered, they had certain traditional rules as to what parts of the carcass should belong to the man who killed the animal, and to the first man—and second—and third—who came up to help butcher. The trappers too, when away from camp, usually followed this same system. There was little chance of a quarrel over meat on the prairie.

But in an Indian camp, when chiefs distributed the meat, there was often much resentment and not infrequently a bitter quarrel resulting in bloodshed or murder. For not all cuts of beef or venison are equally tasty and filling. In fact, not a few of the Indian tribes on the Plains originated in such a quarrel which led one band to separate from the others and set itself up as an independent tribe.

To avoid all such strife in camp, Bridger and his comrades worked out a system of their own. When all the hunters had come in and deposited their loads before the Captain's door, the Captain would call out his lieutenant to supervise the butchering. Yet another man was chosen to dispense the meat; he took his stand facing the Captain's cabin with his back to the pile of meat. Then the cutters went to work. Poor old Glass, Jim remembered, was—had been—an expert cutter.

As soon as a cut was ready, the lieutenant called out, "Who gets this?"

Then the dispenser, not knowing what the cut might be, called out "Number 5," or "Number 3"—the number of one of the messes. Thus no one could play favorites. Even the Captain's mess took whatever luck provided.

The campkeepers cut wood, grained skins, cooked meals, kept up fires, looked after the horses, and made themselves useful in every way around camp—and, when it moved—on the trail. . . .

All this time Jim Bridger felt more and more uneasy. The memory of Old Glass kept worrying him. Poor old man, left to lie unburied where the wild varmints could pick his bones.

And then Jim began to wonder. Maybeso the old man had *not* died of his terrible wounds; maybeso prowling Injuns had killed him—or white-fanged wolves. These thoughts Jim kept to himself. But they plagued him all the more for that—specially at night. In daytime he could keep busy—but at night!

Then he would dream of the bloody old man, wake up in a cold sweat, and be afraid to sleep again for fear Old Glass would haunt his slumbers.

Sometimes Jim wished desperately he had never been soft-hearted and offered to stay with the dying gray-beard; sometimes Jim wished he had stuck it out and stayed thar with him come hell or high water until the old man was cold and buried. Jim took a strong dislike to Fitzgerald, tried to keep out of his way as much as he could. That guilty secret they shared made Bridger hate the sight of the man. Fitzgerald himself was surly and gruff whenever he spoke to Jim. For days at a time they would not look each other in the eye. . . .

One cold night, coming back empty-handed from a long hunt, Jim put his horse into the corral and headed wearily across the courtyard of the little fort for the flat-roofed cabin of his mess. The stockade was lighted only by a blood-red, malformed moon falling down the sky.

Suddenly Jim straightened. Through the gloom he saw, standing motionless, a skinny figure with a long gray beard and glittering eyes. His heart stopped—Old Glass! The old man's ghost had caught up with Jim at last. Speechless, Jim halted. The apparition advanced, came close. The fierce old man's face, now distorted with rage, leered down at him.

Before Jim could get started and make tracks out of there, that gray ghost quickly stretched out a bony arm to lay its gnarled hand upon his shoulder. Jim shook. But he felt no wraith-like touch, no icy fingers. The lank ghost seized his shoulders in a grip of iron.

Horror gave way to sharp pain, pain to relief that the ghost was a living man. A wave of joy filled Jim's heart. The old man was *alive*—Old Glass was alive and kicking. Jim was heartily glad. He breathed again.

Relief quickly gave way to dismay: his guilty secret was out. And that dismay as quickly yielded to fear that his time had come. Old Glass gave Jim a shove, sent him reeling back against the rough stockade, raised his new rifle, shouted, "Speak up, young-un, quick—afore I kill you."

The old man's voice, raised in anger, filled the quiet little fort, and in no time at all the trappers had piled out of their cabins into the gloom to see what the yelling was all about. Here was Old Glass back from the grave! The men crowded around. "Hiya, old coon! Whar did you come from? We heard you had gone under."

They slapped him on the back, grasped his hand. Jim had time to get his wits together. He decided to stay and face the music.

Suddenly Jim saw the eager men give way to admit the tall commanding figure of the Major to the center of the group. They all fell quiet and waited. Major Henry's eyes swept the group. "What's going on?" he demanded. For a long minute his eyes rested on Old Glass. Then he took one step forward and pushed the barrel of the old man's rifle up. "There'll be no shooting in my fort. The two of you come to my cabin. We'll have this out there."

In a few words Jim told his shameful story, glad to get it all off his chest. He denied nothing. He did not try to defend himself or lay the blame on Fitzgerald. Jim finished and stood waiting for the blow to fall. But the Major, mercifully making no comment, turned to Glass.

Glass had an amazing tale to tell:

When he had come to on Grand River and found his friends and weapons gone, found himself without food, sick and wounded, with only the clothes he wore and the buffalo robe he lay on, he might have despaired. Bitterly he resolved to survive to avenge himself upon the rascals who had abandoned him there to die. There was nobody to help him; he would help himself. His savage anger and lust for revenge gave him strong purpose. Hate cleared his brain and warmed his blood. With nothing to eat, he knew he could not stay where he was. Near the spring he found berries and sucked their juice, gaining strength to creep up to the high prairie which stretched away endlessly off to the southeast toward Fort Kiowa, the nearest place where he could count on finding white men. The fort lay some two hundred miles away. Old Glass started to crawl to that fort.[4]

On the open prairie any Injun who might see him would think it fun to kill the helpless old man and take his hair; nevertheless Glass crept out upon that prairie.

Luck favored him. After some time he saw a pack of wolves pulling down a buffalo calf. He lay low until the wolves had killed their victim, then crept up, scared off the wolves, and squatted by the torn carcass. Having no knife, Glass gnawed off the meat he needed and, after stuffing his shirt front with gobbets of raw flesh, crawled away refreshed. So he kept on, gaining strength, nursing his wrath, until he stumbled into sight of Cheyenne River, followed it down to the Missouri, hobbled down the Missouri to the fort. There he rested—but only until a boatload of trappers passed, heading upstream. The scarred old man could not wait for his revenge. He joined the party.

As they neared the Mandan village, Glass, not yet strong enough to help work the boat around the bend, went ashore to lighten it and cut across. All alone, he blundered upon two Ree squaws, tried to hide himself. The squaws called their warriors to kill him. Glass could not run.

But two Mandans rushed out on their ponies and carried him off to Tilton's fort nearby.

There he learned that the Rees were hovering all about. They had just killed all the men in the very boat in which Glass had been traveling.

But vengeful Old Glass would not even stay the night there. After dark he left the fort alone on foot, heading up the Missouri to the Yellowstone, up the Yellowstone to the Big Horn, going thirty-eight sleeps among savage tribesmen and more savage bears. Yet all that seemed simple to him now that he had a knife, a rifle, flint and steel. Those little fixin's made a lone man feel right peart.

Now his relentless purpose had brought him a thousand miles to Henry's fort. . . .

While telling the story of his sufferings to the Major, Old Glass ignored Jim completely. From Jim's story, he must have concluded that the young-un was not altogether to blame. He did not look at Jim, but proclaimed his pardon briefly in the words, "Whar's Fitz?"

The Major explained that Fitzgerald had taken his wages and gone to Fort Atkinson, far down the Missouri, near the mouth of the Platte—many a long, long mile below Fort Kiowa. The Major offered Glass his old employment.

But that sturdy avenger could not wait. Said he, "So thar he is? I'll git him yit."

Learning that the Major was sending letters to the settlements, Glass offered to carry them down; but Henry sent four other men along with him. That was the end of February, 1824.

Jim carried a heavy load of shame and was glad to see the old man go. Neither the Major nor his comrades said anything. If Old Glass, the injured party, could forgive Jim, they saw no reason to hold the boy's action against him. After all, none of them had had the nerve to stay with Glass even as long as Jim and Fitzgerald. Probably they rather welcomed the story Old Glass told, as showing that Jim and Fitzgerald were no braver than the rest of them. In that rough world where every man was a law unto himself, such deeds were soon forgotten.

But Jim could not forget. Always before he had been under orders, responsible to older men, having only to think of their wishes, their commands. Now such reliance on Fitzgerald had led him astray, had shamed him before the only world he knew, had made him despise himself. He was still the same shy, cautious youngster as before; but henceforth he would use that caution not for himself, but for others. From that day on he was his own man, responsible *for* others but responsible only *to* himself. He had learned the hardest way that a man's wisest plan is to follow duty, not selfish interest; for every man knows where his duty lies, but no man is smart enough to see the way to his own best interests.

All the rest of his life Jim Bridger looked out for other men, until his nickname—"Old Gabe"—became a synonym for courage, unselfishness, generosity, looking out for others less capable or more reckless than himself. The similarity in sound of his nickname "Old Gabe" to "Old Glass," the name of the man he had wronged, always kept in Jim's mind the memory which was the reason for his new behavior.

Sometimes a bad mistake in early life proves to be the making of a man—*if* he has the makings of a man. . . .

Afterward Jim heard that the Rees had ambushed Glass and his comrades on the Platte, killing two of them. But the old man, armed only with a knife, had reached Fort Atkinson along in June. There was Fitzgerald. There was that "ornery skunk." Now Glass could kill him.

But he found Fitzgerald in uniform, a soldier in the Army. It might be a serious matter to kill a soldier. Like as not some misguided folks would call it "murder." Glass conferred with the commanding officer.

That gentleman used his authority to right the wrong, compelled Fitzgerald to make good the old man's loss, then talked Glass out of shooting the rascal.

Glass shook the officer's hand. Said he, "I reckon the skunk ain't wuth shootin' after all."

PART

2

BOOSHWAY

VI
BLANKET CHIEF

WHEN Major Henry's men left the fort to make their spring hunt—that is to say, their spring trapping expedition—Jim Bridger went along.

But it was not the same Jim Bridger. Young as he was, barely twenty and only a hired hand unable to write his own name, Jim had set up a new goal for himself.

Twice, while obeying the orders of other men—Leavenworth and Fitzgerald—Jim had come to shame and trouble. It was clear to him now that he must become his own man, taking orders from no one and making all his own decisions.

For him this meant to become a "free trapper." Jim set his heart on going into business for himself just as soon as his contract with Henry and Ashley expired. He was encouraged to find that several of his comrades shared the same ambition.

To be a free trapper meant that Jim must be a master of his trade. For a poor trapper with no booshway (bourgeois) or boss to pay him wages and tell him what to do could not last long in the mountains. Jim determined to become a master trapper: before he was through, he would bring in more beaver plews than any man in the outfit!

Of course, this resolve did not imply any dissatisfaction
with his treatment at the hands of Major Henry. On the
contrary, Jim secretly aspired to emulate his hero.

And so, when he became a free trapper, he continued to
bring his furs to the company, taking in return the goods he
needed or a draft on St. Louis which would help care for his
little sister in the settlements. Jim was able enough to pay
his debt for equipment, salt away his wages, and have a little
left to buy a few blankets to trade to the cussed Injuns.

But Jim Bridger soon found that working on his own
hook as a free trapper was not the simple business he had
imagined. So long as Major Henry was his booshway, it
was up to the Major to find the beaver; all Jim had to do
was to trap them. But now, with no booshway to give orders,
Jim saw that he must find his own beaver as well as trap
them, or utterly fail, helpless as a cat in hell with no claws.

Yet it would not do for Jim to find only enough beaver to
fill his own packs—that was clear. For no free trapper
could safely work alone. At the very least he needed one
partner and a campkeeper or two—if by some miracle such
a handful of men could keep the Injuns out of their hair.
But Jim Bridger was not a man to look for miracles, and few
of his comrades cared to operate by ones and twos. So the
free trappers organized into groups or brigades, each under
the leadership of a partisan chosen for his skill and character. It was clear then that, without a booshway, Bridger
must either rely upon his comrades to find the beaver for
him, or else lead his comrades to the fur himself. Naturally
the trappers liked to work with men they knew and trusted.
Most of the free trappers in Bridger's brigade were old
hands of the Ashley and Henry outfit.

At first, of course, it was a question who should lead these
brigades. There was plenty of competition. Bridger was no

more ambitious than the rest, and nearly every one of his comrades—most of them older men—had some striking advantage over Jim. Bill Sublette was a better businessman; Kit Carson a more dashing Injun fighter; Tom Fitzpatrick more original and enterprising; Jim Beckwourth better at wangling favors from the cussed Injuns; Etienne Provost at least Jim's equal in judgment; Jed Smith had his book l'arnin'; while as for marksmanship, horsemanship, and general efficiency, Jim ran neck-and-neck with the others. He came to realize that, though he could hold up his end, he could never be a booshway over such doughty men merely by excelling them in trapping, hunting, fighting, and trading with the Injuns. True, he could do what other Mountain Men did—pack a mule, break a horse, run bullets—and was always hell-bent to do it better. But Jim saw that such skills, though useful and even important, could not in themselves lead him to the top.

But to his surprise and secret pleasure, as time passed Bridger gradually became aware that he possessed one qualification more important in the fur trade than all these, and that he had it to a degree that none of his comrades (and indeed few men in history) had ever approached; *he was a born explorer.*

And suddenly, to his intense satisfaction, he also realized that *exploration was the principal part of the fur business.* Any of the boys knew how to clean out a beaver colony— once he found it. But to lead a big brigade of trappers through strange, wild country in such a way as to keep them all profitably busy, required not only executive ability of a high order, but most unusual gifts—the gifts of a born explorer.

It is one thing—a rather simple thing—to paddle up one river and down another, as Lewis and Clark did; or to fol-

low a guide along beaten trails across country, as Frémont
did. But it was quite another to explore all nooks and corners of a vast region and for years after *hold in mind* the
detailed lay of the land of the whole northwestern quarter
of our continent. *That incomparable feat Jim Bridger was
equipped to accomplish.*

It all began simply enough: as a free trapper, Jim had to
know the country he worked in.

Moreover, his knowledge of the country was not merely
that of a map-maker or topographer, who knows which way
the rivers run and where the mountain ranges lie. He must
know far more than that; he had not only to know the country, but how to *live* in it. He had to know where the mountain passes lay, how they could be approached at every season, and during what months of the year they were open.
He had to know where streams could be forded, how much
water, grass, and fuel were available at every possible camping ground, what valleys were likely to be comparatively free
of snow in winter and where the drifts lay deepest. He had
to know the trails which laced the country—Indian trails,
game trails, trails over which a wagon might be made to
pass—which parts of which streams were navigable, where
hostiles and friendlies, beaver and buffalo were likely to be
found, and where the unmarked boundaries of tribal lands
lay. His livelihood, his safety, and those of all his comrades
depended upon the accuracy of his knowledge of all these
things.

Only a man with extraordinary and relentless powers of
observation, only a man with an utterly reliable memory
could possibly gain and retain exact knowledge of the
mighty welter of mountains, the endless tangle of streams
and valleys which formed Bridger's vast hunting grounds.

Of course he could not possibly have observed or remembered such a huge quantity of interlocking detail unless he had been keenly interested in the country. No man could have achieved what he did as explorer unless he had been passionately in love with the wild beauty of the region.

Those were magnificent ranges, draped with forests, crowned with everlasting snows, with sapphire lakes like jewels about them, laced with rushing torrents, with their lone bare mountain meadows above timberline, their sheer cliffs, and snug parks below. Such magnificence, such space and wide horizons got under Jim's skin, into his blood and his character—making the man bigger, stronger, cleaner and more independent than the shy boy in the blacksmith shop. That high, dry, crystal air—air like wine—iced sunshine—cleared his brain, lifted his heart.

But for Jim Bridger the mountains were not just pretty scenery or a springboard to emotion. *He loved them for what they were*, not for what he might dream up about them—loved them so that every detail he could observe was treasured in his memory as lovers treasure remembered intimacies.

It is not surprising, of course, that the surveyor's son should grow into an explorer, especially when successful exploration was the rock upon which his own career must stand. But Jim Bridger had been a lonely lad—all the more lonely for having belonged to a large family which was suddenly snatched from him—a lonely lad to whom his remaining relatives were primarily responsibilities, since, though he provided for them, he did not see them for years at a time and could neither write nor read letters.

He was also a man of strong, self-reliant, and independent character, seldom requiring the support of friends to make his way. Though generous and hospitable, admired and respected by all the leading men in the West, it does not ap-

pear that Bridger was fond of company. The men he lived
and worked with were comrades rather than companions,
partners rather than friends, protegés rather than beloved
persons. Jim disliked and distrusted strangers, though his
early-developed strong paternal feeling made him kind always to women and children. But there is no evidence in the
record that he ever experienced a romantic passion or a devoted friendship. *Jim Bridger loved places better than people. That is why he was such a great explorer.*

He loved the earth and all that grew out of it, loved the
creatures that lived on it, even loved the pesky Injuns because they lived so close to it.

Some would have it that Jim was unimaginative, utterly
practical. But there is a higher kind of imagination than
that which seizes upon some bit of experience and blows it up
into something utterly unlike itself. Jim Bridger understood
fiction and could tell tall tales as well as anybody. But for
his own satisfaction he used a more exacting type of imagination—that imagination which identifies itself with reality,
lovingly exploring every nook and corner of *things that are,*
thinking the thoughts of our Creator after Him.

No doubt Jim's long and intimate association with the
Indians helped confirm him in this habit of mind. For the
Indian—even in his poetry—used no metaphor, no simile.
When the redskin was inspired to compose a song about a
buffalo, he was imagining *that buffalo*—not using it to re-
mind himself of something else. . . .

Of course Jim profited by other men's explorations. For,
when the day's ride was over, or when scattered trappers
gathered again at rendezvous or winter quarters, many a
long evening they spent comparing notes, discussing trails
and passes, camps and beaver streams. The trappers have
been represented as spending all their spare time drinking

and gambling. But the fact is that during long months of the year they had nothing to gamble and nothing to drink. When they got together, it was to talk about the country they worked in. Many a map Jim drew with a stick in the sand by the light of a campfire.

But of course he did not depend entirely on the trappers' observations. The Indians knew that country first, and Jim missed no chance to learn from Crows and Flatheads. And so, as time passed, Jim gathered his matchless lore of mountain geography.

He soon had outstanding discoveries to his credit. . . .

In the spring of 1824 Crow hunters told Fitzpatrick that if the white men wanted beaver, they had only to follow a plain Indian trail to South Pass. Beyond that Pass, said the Crows, "you can throw your traps away and kill all the beaver you want with clubs." After that, Tom and Jim could hardly wait to make tracks out of winter quarters.

The ensuing discovery of South Pass,[1] in which Bridger had a part, opened the door of fortune to his employers—and also opened an easy road over the Continental Divide for hosts of emigrants who, in later years, were to follow up that trail to Oregon and California.

Over the Pass they went and found the Crows were right. Bridger and Tom trapped many a pack of beaver. After rendezvous on Sweetwater, Fitzpatrick put his furs into skin boats, which suffered shipwreck at the mouth of that stream. Though all the men dived for hours for the lost furs, they recovered only just enough to pay their debt to Ashley. They made no profit on that year's hunt—except their explorations.

Bridger and Fitzpatrick had found South Pass with the help and counsel of the Crows. But in the fall of '24, Bridger made an equally important—and much more startling—discovery, quite without help from anybody.

The trappers were in camp in Cache Valley, and during one of their unending discussions of mountain geography, got into an argument as to where Bear River went. Bets were laid, and they had to send somebody to settle the bets. Already Bridger's reliability and skill in exploration were well known; they asked Old Gabe to go.

Accordingly Jim built himself a bullboat.

To do this, he killed a buffalo, skinned it, and stretched the rawhide over an openwork basket of willow sticks thick as his wrist, lashed together with strips of green hide. In this leather tub he set out down the canyon of that turbulent stream. Below the canyon he climbed a hill.

Far away to the south he saw a great body of water. Jim hurried down to the river. The bullboat carried him on for another 25 miles through marshes to the mouth of the stream. There, finding his craft more buoyant than it had been in the river, Bridger dipped up some of the water, tasted it. It was brine!

Jim left his bullboat on the shore, and turned his toes up-river.

Back at camp all the men stared at each other with a wild surmise. Salt water! Old Gabe war some punkins, sure enough. He could shine in the biggest kind of crowd, and you kin lay to that. "Hell, Jim," they swore, "you done found the Pacific Ocean!"

Actually, Bridger had discovered Great Salt Lake.

Jim always felt peculiarly possessive of Salt Lake Valley. No wonder. He had found it; he loved it; it was *his!* It might well have been called Bridger's Hole. . . .

There was much to do after the discovery of South Pass and Salt Lake: further explorations of the valleys and mountains which led out from them. So it was not until much later that Bridger explored the Fire Hole River, Yellowstone Lake, and other wonders now included in the Yellowstone Park.

But it was not these great *discoveries* which made Jim Bridger foremost in his arduous profession. Any other Mountain Man might have blundered into such discoveries. Jim's great achievement was the *detailed reconnaissance* of the whole mountain region—a job so well done that all who afterwards came into that country turned to him for guidance.

By the time Ashley (now independently wealthy) retired from the mountains in 1826, Bridger was already a partisan of free trappers working with the company. His colleagues were Thomas Fitzpatrick, Jedediah Smith, Etienne Provost —worthy comrades and competitors for any Mountain Man —each captain of his own brigade of trappers.

Captain Bridger maintained an almost military discipline among his men, and held regular inspections to see that their weapons and equipment were clean and in working order. If he found a dirty gun, there was trouble for the man who owned it.

One day when Jim was out alone, some Blackfeet jumped him, shot his horse before he could fire. The horse, feeling their arrows, reared and bucked. Bridger lost his grip on his gun. It fell to the ground.

With a whoop, one of the warriors snatched it up. Jim quickly got control of his mount, kicked it into a dead run, and so got safe home with his scalp.

Next day Bridger went round his camp inspecting the arms of his men. Maloney's rifle was dirty.

Bridger was stern. "What would you do," he demanded, "with a gun like that if the Injuns war to charge this camp?"

Maloney grinned impudently. "Begorra, I would throw it to thim and run, the way you did!"

Without a word, Bridger walked off. It was a long time before Jim felt like inspecting Maloney's gun again. . . .

Meanwhile the Hudson's Bay Company in the British Possessions was not sitting on its hands. In 1827 Bridger and his friends ran afoul of Peter Skene Ogden and his Canadian trappers. The prolonged contact between these rival outfits, though not warlike, was none too friendly. The Americans, offering better prices for beaver than the Hudson's Bay Company, tried to trade Ogden's men out of their furs. Ogden, secretly forbidding anyone of his command to make snowshoes for the Americans, kept them from supplies they needed as winter came on. Both parties were ready to fight for each other against the cussed Injuns, but—when it came to beaver —it was dog eat dog.

"Accompanying Mr. Ogden's trading party were a party of Rockway Indians, who were from the North, and who were employed by the Hudson's Bay Company, as the Iroquois and Crows were, to trap for them. Fitzpatrick and his associates camped in the neighborhood of Ogden's company, and immediately set about endeavoring to purchase from the Rockways and others the furs collected for Mr. Ogden. Not succeeding by fair means, if the means to such an end could be called fair,—they opened a keg of whisky, which, when the Indians had got a taste, soon drew them away from the Hudson's Bay trader, the regulations of whose company forbade the selling or giving of liquors to the Indians. Under its influence, the furs were disposed of to the Rocky Mountain Company, who in this manner obtained nearly the whole product of their year's hunt. This course of conduct was naturally exceedingly disagreeable to Mr. Ogden, as well as unprofitable also; and a feeling of hostility grew up and increased between the two camps.

"While matters were in this position, a stampede one day occurred among the horses in Ogden's camp, and two or three of the animals ran away, and ran into the camp of the rival company. Among them was the horse of Mr. Ogden's Indian wife, which had escaped, with her babe hanging to the saddle.

"Not many minutes elapsed, before the mother, following her child and horse, entered the camp, passing right through it, and catching the now halting steed by the bridle. At the same moment she espied one of her company's pack-horses, loaded with beaver, which had also run into the enemy's camp. The men had already begun to exult over the circumstance, considering this chance load of beaver as theirs, by the laws of war. But not so the Indian woman. Mounting her own horse, she fearlessly seized the pack-horse by the halter, and led it out of camp, with its costly burden.

"At this undaunted action, some of the baser sort of men cried out 'shoot her, shoot her!' but a majority interfered, with opposing cries of 'let her go; let her alone; she's a brave woman: I glory in her pluck;' and other like admiring expressions. While the clamor continued, the wife of Ogden had galloped away, with her baby and her pack-horse." [2]

Yet after all the machinations and underhanded deals of the fur men, there was little enough profit when the first summer came. The Americans had not traveled 15 miles from their encampment when Blackfeet attacked them, killing three, running off 40 horses, and getting away with most of their goods *and* $4,000 worth of beaver! . . .

By this time the Crow Indians had given Bridger the name Casapy [3] or Blanket Chief. The name, the Crows say, indicated a man in charge of some blankets—probably on some trading expedition to their camps. Yet, though so unpretentious in meaning, the name came to be a proud one. For, as season followed season, Bridger's qualities impressed all men in the mountains. He had the four great Indian virtues—bravery, fortitude, generosity, wisdom—and the white man's spunk and commonsense besides. Everybody respected him. There was for Jim Bridger only one rung more to the top—to be Booshway!

By this time Major Andrew Henry, Colonel W. H. Ashley and Bill Sublette had had enough of the mountains—enough fun, enough danger and hardship—and wealth enough. So in August, 1830, James Bridger, Thomas Fitzpatrick, Milton Sublette, Henry Fraeb, and Baptiste Gervais became joint owners of the company, thereafter known as before, as the Rocky Mountain Fur Company.

So, in just eight years, James Bridger climbed from apprentice in a blacksmith shop to the power and position of his hero, Major Henry. *Wagh!* Now Jim was booshway—with all a booshway's trouble and worry. Before long Jim began to savvy why Henry had sold out and quit the mountains.

The competition of the Hudson's Bay Company made trouble enough. But now here came Drips and Vanderburgh with goods and men galore, sent out by the rich American Fur Company to steal Bridger's trade.

Vanderburgh and Drips moved right in. They admitted they were green at the business and did not know the country. *But*, they declared, bold as brass, that did not matter—they would simply follow Bridger and his partners around and that way find all the beaver they wanted. Vanderburgh and Drips made no bones about that.

Furiously, Bridger and his partners hightailed it out of that camp on Powder River, over South Pass, Green River, and finally went into winter quarters at the forks of the Snake.

The summer rendezvous was to be held in Pierre's Hole, famous for its scenery, rattlesnakes—and Blackfeet! Jim Bridger called it "the finest valley in the mountains!"

VII
THE BATTLE OF
PIERRE'S HOLE

EARLY in the year 1832 the partners of the Rocky Mountain Fur Company let it be known that they would hold their annual rendezvous in Pierre's Hole. And so, when the spring hunt was over, Bridger and "Broken Hand" Fitzpatrick led their trappers towards the Hole or, as it is now called, the Teton Basin.

They had chosen that basin on the headwaters of Snake River for their fur fair with good reason. Few valleys in the mountains can equal it. Open, level prairie—bare of trees except along the wooded river and the rushing mountain rills which lace its grassy levels—it offered plenty of forage for their horses, good water, enough timber to give cover in case of a fight, and ample fuel for their fires. The Hole extends for nearly thirty miles and is, in places, nearly half as wide—a beautiful valley overhung by the magnificent range of the snow-capped Tetons. With all its beauty, it was wild country; the groves of tall cottonwood trees towered above tangled growths of underbrush, willows, and creepers, dense as a jungle. Pierre's Hole was also close to the richest fur country in the Rocky Mountains, the country of that most implacable of tribes, the Blackfeet.

Of course Jim and his partners realized that the site of the

rendezvous was also known to their detested rivals, Drips
and Vanderburgh, partisans of the American Fur Company,
who were undoubtedly heading for the Hole to get as much
of the trappers' beaver as they could. In fact, when Jim and
Tom Fitzpatrick rode in to make camp, they found their
rivals already there.

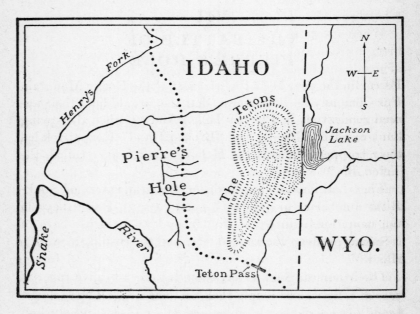

William Sublette, who was bringing goods for the trade
from the States, had not arrived. It seemed likely that the
American Fur Company would get all the business, as soon
as Fontenelle showed up. Here was a pretty pickle. Jim and
Tom held council and decided to offer to divide the beaver
country with Drips and Vanderburgh. But their rivals, ignorant of the region and distrustful of the wily Broken Hand,
refused to compromise. So Tom Fitzpatrick, impatient to
begin the trade, in spite of danger from the Indians swarm-

ing all around, saddled a fast horse and, leading another, set out alone to meet Sublette and hurry him up. Jim Bridger had his doubts about the wisdom of that, but Broken Hand felt sure he could get through. A man with a led horse could cover his trail and, by changing mounts, make fast time.

But that summer was an eventful one in the annals of the fur trade. Jim and his trappers were heading into as bitter a battle as Mountain Men had ever fought.

When Captain William Sublette arrived, early in July, bringing with him a party of sixty men and the year's supply of goods, he found hundreds of friendly Flathead and Nez Percé Indians encamped in the valley, and also—to his intense disgust—those inescapable interlopers, Drips and Vanderburgh, of the rival American Fur Company, already on the ground. Fortunately, their colleague Fontenelle, who was bringing their trade goods from Fort Union, had not yet pulled in. The valley also contained the camps of Sublette's trappers, employees of the Rocky Mountain Fur Company, to the number of nearly two hundred men, besides scattered lodges of free trappers.

Sublette's first words were a question: "Whar's Broken Hand?"

The Mountain Men shook their beards. They could not tell. Fitzpatrick had not come in. "Gone under, maybe," was all Jim could say. Like as not the American Fur Company had set the redskins on him.

William Sublette, who had had a sharp brush with the cussed Injuns himself only a few nights before, and whose brother Milton had been severely wounded earlier that season, was mightily discontented with that news. He was secretly afraid that the Blackfeet, among whom he included the even more hostile Gros Ventres of the Prairie, had taken the scalp of his missing friend and partner in the fur business. But that business could not be postponed; the trappers were ready and eager for trade, half starved for a swig of the likker in Sublette's flat kegs. Besides, Fontenelle might come along now any time, and throw his goods upon the market. And so Sublette opened his packs.

"Maybeso the old coon will turn up again after all," he declared, comforting himself. "He knows a thing or two, I reckon."

The trade began. Then Sublette, having first seen to it that every one of his own men was outfitted for the coming season, opened his kegs. He soon had all the beaver in sight —one hundred and sixty-eight pack. The camps were full of carousing trappers, who spent their days gambling, pony-racing, quarreling, chasing Indian women, and so made the most of their annual holiday, their one release from the strict vigilance and unrelenting hardship of their dangerous lives.

In the middle of this wild revelry, Antoine Godin and another Iroquois hunter rode into camp. Behind one of them, clinging to the cantle of the Spanish saddle, rode a white man, thin as a rail, red-eyed and ragged, and—what was simply amazing in those days—unarmed! This emaciated scarecrow claimed to be Fitzpatrick, and told a harrowing tale of how he had been stripped of everything by the cussed Blackfeet, how he had barely survived on a meager diet of roots and rosebuds, until his luck turned and he ran into those Iroquois. For a while his partners could hardly recognize him, for his long hair had turned as white as snow. From that day Fitzpatrick was commonly known as White Head.

Within a week's time the trappers' beaver was all gone, they were sober again, and the rendezvous began to break up. On July 17 Milton Sublette led a party out, heading towards Snake River and the country north of the Great Salt Lake. This small brigade consisted of fifteen trappers belonging to the Rocky Mountain Fur Company, Sinclair and his fifteen free trappers, and Nathaniel Wyeth's dwindled band of eleven Yankee greenhorns, who—unable to handle a long rifle or pack a horse, and mightily alarmed by the dangers of Indian warfare—trailed along with the Mountain Men to save their scalps.

Milton Sublette's little party started late, and moved only eight miles that day. They were sluggish after their week's debauch, and their leader ordered a halt before they were out of the Hole. That night a few Flatheads, led by a minor chief, joined the party. The Flatheads wished to travel with the Mountain Men in such dangerous country; their tribe had been decimated by the Blackfeet.

But if the men in that camp had dreamed how dangerous the spot was, they would have pushed on all night. A horde of hostiles were heading straight for Milton Sublette's camp, a party of the same redskins who had attacked William Sublette on his way to the Hole and had run off some of his horses.

These Indians were not, strictly speaking, Blackfeet, but Atsena, or Gros Ventres of the Prairie, close allies of the Blackfeet. Since their own language was difficult and little known, they generally talked to strangers in the tongue of the Blackfeet, with whom they fought and hunted. Therefore the Mountain Men lumped both tribes under the one name, Blackfeet.

The Atsena got their name Big Bellies from their habit of stuffing themselves, uninvited, in every tipi where they could find anything to eat. They filled the seats at every feast, and were inveterate beggars. Even the Arapahos, their blood brothers, dubbed them Spongers. And this thieving trait was the first cause of their continual fighting with the

Mountain Men. No other tribe ever gave the trappers so much trouble. . . .

The Gros Ventres were formerly poor in horses, as many northern tribes were, since the best animals were only to be had by raiding the vast herds in the Spanish settlements. About 1825, the Gros Ventres had made their first visit to their kinsmen in the South; in fighting their way north again through the territory of hostile tribes, they were stripped of the horses the Arapahos had given them, and reached home as poor as ever. This bitter experience made them very savage, and they became desperate warriors. It also made them eager to revisit the Arapahos in order to beg more horses, and this they did every two or three years, as a regular thing. In 1832, they had made such a visit, and, in order to defend themselves along the way had got up a large party of several hundred lodges.

On their way back they had attacked William Sublette's party one night on Green River, and had run off some of his horses. Those who had distinguished themselves in this raid, or had captured horses, were naturally eager to get home to dance and show off. As they neared their own hunting grounds, these people became impatient and pushed on ahead of the main camp. They left their heavy baggage and slow horses behind with their relatives, and, taking only a few of the best animals, struck out along the range to the north. Beside the horses, they had some scarlet blankets, abalone shells, and other plunder obtained from the Arapahos who traded at Bent's Old Fort. Parts of two bands made up this party, led by a chief, Baihoh.

In their haste these Indians, all by now well seasoned to the trail, were up and moving much earlier than Milton Sublette's sluggish trappers. And so, when the Indians came pouring down out of the hills on the morning of July 18, they saw the white men still in camp below them.

Chief Baihoh had been told by Kenneth "Red Coat" Mc-Kenzie, bourgeois of the American Fur Company at Fort Union, to be on the lookout for his clerk, Fontenelle, who would be in Pierre's Hole about this time. When Baihoh saw the white men encamped there he naturally thought they were Fontenelle's men, and rode down to meet them. For of course the Blackfeet and all their sponging allies were hand in glove with McKenzie.

That morning Milton Sublette, still sore from his wound, with a pipe stuck into his long, scarred face, stalked about keeping a lookout, while his men made ready to move out. Suddenly he caught sight of some far-off moving objects streaming down from the hills. Sublette guessed they must be the men of Fontenelle's party, which he was expecting, and grinned to think that he had completed the trade before his rivals could reach the rendezvous. Other men thought them buffalo. But Wyeth, true to his training on the Yankee seaboard, pulled out his long brass spy-glass, squinted through it for a long moment, and uttered one ominous word: "Indians."

The men dropped their work then. All eyes were fixed upon that savage cavalcade.

The Indians, most of them afoot, were in two parties. Eagerly the trappers counted heads. Wyeth, staring through his glass, estimated one hundred and fifty. Nobody saw any reason to dispute his calculation.

Concealment was now out of the question. The Indians had already seen them—that was clear. They came down the slopes, yelling and whooping, moved out into the open, and halted just out of range.

At first the trappers could not tell whether they were

Crows or Blackfeet. Their women wore the short skirts of the Crows, but their men affected coarse fringes at sleeve-end and shoulder-seam like the Blackfeet. Moreover, they had no uniform way of dressing their hair. Some wore pompadours or bangs, like the Crows; others had long braids and scalplocks like the Sioux and Arapahos. But when their chief rode forward carrying the long pipe, and yelled aloud across the grass, all doubt was ended.

A dozen Mountain Men muttered the same word together: "Blackfeet!"

Wyeth's Yankee greenhorns quizzed the Mountain Men as to what that meant: "Blackfeet?"

"Injuns—and the meanest kind at that," was the gruff answer. The trappers knew there was bound to be a hard fight.

The Arapahos do not believe that Baihoh was meditating treachery that morning. They say that if the chief had suspected he was confronting McKenzie's hated competitors, he would never have risked his life by advancing alone with only a pipe in his hand, especially as the Indians outnumbered the whites so much. Nor would he have brought his women and children down out of the hills into danger. They say, too, that the noisy approach of the Indians is proof of their friendly intentions, since Indian enemies always try to sneak up on their foes, making as little noise as possible. That is the Arapaho belief.

What Milton Sublette and Wyeth thought has not been recorded. There had been so much bloodshed between Mountain Men and Blackfeet that they could hardly have any faith in truces. To them, the noisy approach of the tribesmen may have seemed the sheer arrogance of overwhelming numbers about to annihilate a few helpless victims, and the offer of the pipe a trick to enable the chief to learn all he could before the battle was joined. They must have known that the mere presence of the Flatheads in their camp would be enough to make enemies of the Blackfeet. Sublette was convalescent, and Wyeth a greenhorn. But, whatever they thought, matters were immediately taken out of their hands.

Among the Mountain Men stood Antoine Godin, the Iroquois hunter, whose own father had been murdered by these very Indians on a little stream, thereafter known as Godin Creek. He stared grimly at the lone chieftain.

"Looks like the cussed Injun wants to talk," someone suggested. Nobody offered to go forward for the parley.

Godin spoke up, grimly: "*I'*ll talk to him."

Turning to the Flathead who stood at his elbow, rifle in hand, Godin snapped out a brief question: "Is your piece charged?"

The Flathead glanced quickly at his Iroquois friend. "It is," he answered.

"Then cock it and follow me," Godin replied.

The two of them mounted and rode out abreast to meet the chief halfway: Godin, lithe and swarthy in his fancy buckskins and wool hat, the stocky Flathead with two eagle feathers in the long black hair which flowed down over the shoulders of his fringed scalp-shirt.

Baihoh must have had misgivings as he saw the Flathead coming forward. But if he did, he scorned to show them. He sat his pony, swathed to the waist in a scarlet blanket, with the broad band of bright quillwork across it. On his left arm rested the long stem of the peacepipe.

Godin rode up on the chief's right hand, the Flathead rode up on his left. Baihoh extended his right hand in friendship. Godin's eyes never left the chief's face. He reached out, grasped the Indian's hand, held it tight. Without looking round he shouted, "Fire!"

Instantly the Flathead threw up his barrel, gloated for a split second over the shock in Baihoh's face, then fired. Baihoh tumbled from his saddle in a cloud of white smoke. The Flathead whirled his pony round and galloped away. A great howl of grief and rage burst from the throats of the Gros Ventres. Their bullets whistled angrily around the Iroquois.

But Godin, in bravado, whooped in triumph, and, leaning from his saddle, snatched the corner of the dead man's scarlet blanket up, dragged it from under him, and loped away, trailing the blood-red trophy. He and the Flathead both regained their own party unhurt.

By that time the Mountain Men were returning the fire of the enraged Indians. And as soon as the redskins had recovered from the surprise of seeing their chief shot down, they scuttled for the nearest cover. This was a wide swamp, caused by beavers' damming the stream. The swamp was overgrown with brush, willows and cottonwoods, vines and weeds, all thickly entangled and matted together. Within this thicket the Indians found cover: the men covering the retreat of the women and children; the women hastily raising a "fort" of logs and branches, and digging trenches with their knives behind that rude breastwork. The Mountain Men, finding the Indians all armed with McKenzie's Mackinaw guns, and good shots, took shelter in a ravine which ran across the front of the Indian position, and kept firing from there into the brush.

The down-Easters with Wyeth were wholly unused to such warfare, and exposed themselves recklessly, without being of the least use. Wyeth promptly got them out of the way. He caught up all his horses, tied them up at a safe distance, under cover and out of sight. Then he made a breastwork of his packs, made his men lie down behind it, and ordered them not to leave their post under any circumstances. He himself took his rifle and went off to join the fray.

Meanwhile, the Flathead chief and Milton Sublette had sent off a number of horsemen, hard as they could ride, to carry the news to rendezvous and bring back reinforcements. They covered the eight miles at top speed, and dashed through the scattered camps, yelling at the top of their voices, "Blackfeet! Blackfeet! Up the valley! Git your guns and come a-runnin'!"

Jim Bridger's best buffalo horse, a flea-bitten grey, was staked out beside his lodge. Quickly he threw a saddle on the animal, peeled off his coat, rolled up his sleeves, pulled the fringed buckskin cover from his rifle, and galloped away to battle. William Sublette paused only long enough to order his packers, Frenchmen from St. Louis, to stay and guard the camp. He knew they would only be in the way in a hard fight. He and Robert Campbell rode side by side after Bridger, shouting to each other to make their wills, each naming the other his executor.

When the Gros Ventres saw these hundreds of enemies swarming across the prairies, they fell back into their fort, which was completely hidden in the brush. By that time many of their women and children had already taken to their heels, and were hitting the trail back to the main camp of their people, or hiding in the timber on the mountainsides. Meanwhile, the Mountain Men had been repulsed. A half-breed had been severely wounded, and the others hung back. They could not see the Gros Ventres, while the Indians had a clear field of fire. Even the cream of the friendly tribes, eager as they were to strike their hated enemies, were reluctant to run across the open and charge blindly into the brush.

When Captain William Sublette rode up, he called for an attack. He, at any rate, would not hang back. He told his

brothers of the will he had just made, and rushed into the
thickets. Robert Campbell went in after him, and also Sinclair, the partisan of the free trappers. Only those three,
of all the men present, dared at first to attack. Godin and
the Flathead chief proved to be as cowardly as they had been
treacherous. Campbell, Sublette, and Sinclair kept going
forward, yelling to their men to follow. After a time, others
advanced.

Struggling through the brush, the three leaders found
themselves facing the open space beyond which the Indians
had entrenched themselves. Their improvised "fort" was simply a breastwork of logs and branches, and its low shelter
was extended upward by a curtain of buffalo robes, scarlet
blankets, and lodge-covers, which concealed, though it could
not protect, the warriors behind it. The brush was so thick
that every movement of the white men disturbed it, and so
the Indians could see them coming.

Sinclair by this time was in the lead, gently parting the
branches as he crept forward. A puff of smoke bloomed from
a crevice in the Indian fort. Sinclair jerked back, shot
through the body. Campbell lay nearest, and Sinclair, turning to face him, begged, "Take me to my brother." Then he
fainted.

Campbell crept forward, caught hold of Sinclair's leg, and
dragged him back. When he reached the men behind, he let
them take the wounded man. They carried him out of the
swamp. Then Campbell rejoined his friend Sublette.

All this time Sublette had been snaking his way to the
front. Made cautious by Sinclair's disaster, the Captain lay
still and studied the Indian defenses, trying to find the loopholes through which the warriors were firing. Suddenly he
saw an Indian eye peeping through one of these. Quickly he
raised his rifle, fired, and struck the Indian square in the eye.

With a grin he turned to Campbell, pointing to the opening. "Watch that hole," he whispered, hastily reloading, "and you'll soon have a fair chance for a shot." He stood behind a cottonwood to ram home the charge.

Before he could reload, an Indian fired. Sublette was hit in the shoulder. He moved his arm up and down, making sure that the bone was not broken. Then he grew faint, and sagged to the ground. Campbell caught him up in his arms and boldly carried him out of the swamp. Strangely enough, the ball that passed through Sublette's shoulder also wounded a man behind him in the head.

Warmed to their work by the courage and by the wounding of their leaders, Jim and the other Mountain Men began to pour a steady fire upon the Indian fort. They surrounded it, firing from every side. Wyeth, who was leading a group of Nez Percés, found himself endangered by the cross-fire of his own comrades. One of his Indian allies was shot down at his elbow—and the bullet had come from the rifle of a trapper beyond the fort. The hostile Indians did not fire often; they were running short of powder: but when they did fire, somebody was hit. They kept doggedly inside their fort; they gave no quarter, and they expected none. All that day the siege went on.

The Flatheads and Nez Percés, seeing their enemies in the fort were doomed, now took courage, and dared each other to count a *coup*. Now and then one of them, to show off his bravery, ran swiftly up to the Blackfoot fort, snatched down a red blanket or a buffalo robe, and ran back, yelling in triumph. In this way the friendly Indians encouraged each other, and gradually reduced the cover of their enemies. But that sort of thing killed nobody; the Blackfeet lay low, protected by their logs and earthworks. And there was so little cohesion among the besiegers that no organized charge was ever made.

Jim Bridger was plumb disgusted. He sneaked over through the dry crackling brush for a word with Sublette. "We'll never clean out the cussed Injuns at this rate. I reckon we better burn 'em out."

Sublette, sweating in the heat, nodded. He sent the squaws of the friendly Indians to gather grass and brush to start the conflagration. The wind was brisk, and once started, the fire would drive their enemies out into the open. "Burn 'em out, boys," he said. "That will fix 'em."

The Flatheads and Nez Percés, however, objected earnestly to that scheme.

"No, no," they said. "Those Blackfeet are rich. They have been visiting, and are bringing back presents. If we burn them out, all those fine red blankets and things will be burned up too. We've got them licked; that loot is as good as ours right now. It would be foolish to burn up our own property."

While the friendlies and the whites argued and wrangled about the matter, the Blackfeet in the fort had seen the squaws gathering grass and brush. They knew what was doing. They were desperate, and being desperate, began to taunt and threaten their enemies. Their chief began to yell.

"While we had plenty of powder and lead," the chief shouted, "we fought you on the open prairie. It was only when our powder ran low that we hid in the brush. We came here to die with our women and children. We are only a handful, and you are many. We know you can kill us all. You can burn us out and shoot us. What do we care? *We have thrown away our bodies.* But, if you are hungry for fighting, just stay beside our ashes here, and you will soon get your belly full. There are four hundred lodges of our brothers headed this way. We have sent for them. They are brave, their arms are strong, and their hearts are big. They will avenge us!"

"What are they yelling?" the Mountain Men demanded.

Then everyone with a smattering of the Blackfoot tongue tried to interpret. The translating went on for some time. It was never very clear, passing as it did through so many Flathead, Nez Percé, and Creole mouths before it was turned into broken English. But out of all that confusion of tongues one statement rang clear: "Blackfeet! Blackfeet comin'! Heap Blackfeet! Heap big fight!"

That news was bad enough. But suddenly someone called out: "The cussed Injuns are thar a'ready. At rendezvous! They're raidin' our camps!"

That struck alarm to the besiegers. Back there at rendezvous were their wives and children, their horses and mules, their outfits for the coming season, their clothes, their tents, their priceless beaver. If the Blackfeet captured those, all would be lost!

It was late in the day. Everyone was tired, sore from the kick of the guns, powder-marked, hungry, and dry. Casualties had been heavy: Sinclair and four other Mountain Men had been killed, along with a half-breed and seven friendly Injuns. There were at least a dozen seriously wounded; it had been a hard fight.

But when the Mountain Men heard that danger threatened their camps at rendezvous they did not falter. Jim and the others threw themselves into their saddles, and rode hell-for-leather to meet those eight hundred savage warriors thirsting for their blood.[1]

When Jim Bridger and his comrades came lashing their lathered horses into camp on the dead run, they found the whole place just as they had left it. Nary a Blackfoot was in sight. And the feckless Frenchmen who slouched out of the tents to hear the results of the battle, reported they had seen no hostiles.

Distrusting the efficiency of the Creole guard, Jim led his Mountain Men on a scout around the camp to look for fresh sign of Injuns.

But if Blackfeet had been in that neighborhood, they had made no tracks, sartin! Come night, Jim rode quietly in and unsaddled.

The Mountain Men kept their eyes skinned that night. If more Blackfoot were coming, it was likely they would jump the camp just afore daylight. But nothing happened. And as the sun rose over the mountains, Jim knew that he and his friends had been fooled. The tricky Injuns, in hopes of getting out of their trap, had sent him on a wild goose chase.

The Mountain Men piled into their saddles and hurried back to the battlefield, hoping against hope that the few men left to watch the fort still held the enemy in their sights.

Circling the silent Blackfoot barricades, the trappers took cover, watching for any movement on which they might draw a bead. Failing that, they began to fire into the fort. Still all was silent. No redskins were stirring. Their fire was not returned. Finally Jim went boldly forward to take a look. He saw nine Injuns in the fort—all dead—and twenty-four dead horses. But the garrison had skipped.

Now that there was no danger, the Flatheads came running from the brush to scalp the dead and gather in the loot. They found no plunder, no red blankets, no white shells—not a single pack! The enemy had cleared out with all his belongings.

At any rate, these Blackfoot were in the open now *somewhere* on the trail—maybeso all strung out, each one riding or running, devil take the hindmost. The Flatheads and Nez

Percés lit out on the enemy trail, bloodthirsty as so many wolves. With them rode not a few of the Mountain Men, eager to strike a *coup,* avenge a comrade, and destroy the forces of the implacable Gros Ventres.

As they plunged on, they picked up lame ponies, abandoned packs, or paused to strike the body of some warrior left to die of his wounds.

Not far from the fort they came upon a squaw. Her leg had been shattered by a bullet. Washington Irving's is the classic account of this incident:

"As some of the trappers and their Indian allies were approaching the fort, through the woods, they beheld an Indian woman, of noble form and features, leaning against a tree. Their surprise at her lingering here alone, to fall into the hands of her enemies, was dispelled, when they saw the corpse of a warrior at her feet. Either she was so lost in grief as not to perceive their approach, or a proud spirit kept her silent and motionless. The Indians set up a yell, on discovering her, and before the trappers could interfere, her mangled body fell upon the corpse which she had refused to abandon." [2]

As the pursuers pushed on, they soon caught up with another enemy woman, running for all she was worth. The Flatheads screeched and laughed and struck her down. Their tribal wars never ended, and so they never spared the mothers of their enemies. Before their horses began to give out and so ended the chase, Jim had counted sixteen Blackfeet dead. He felt sure that other bodies had been carried off horseback. But the trail led towards the main body of the Blackfeet and so, when they had destroyed the stragglers, Jim, the trappers, and their Indian allies headed back to camp. They did not need to look for trouble. The hostiles would be sartin sure to provide *that* plenty soon enough.

VIII

ᛁ SHOT IN THE BACK

CAPTAIN WILLIAM SUBLETTE had his wounds dressed by Nathaniel J. Wyeth's doctor and rested a few days in camp before he headed back for St. Louis with the beaver belonging to the Rocky Mountain Fur Company. The fur harvest in that rendezvous amounted to almost $170,000 at St. Louis prices. It was the biggest haul of the fur trade in the Northwest. Washington Irving, who saw Sublette's brigade on the march, reports: "Their long cavalcade stretched in single file for nearly half a mile. Sublette still wore his arm in a sling. The mountaineers in their rude hunting dresses, armed with rifles and roughly mounted, and leading their pack horses down a hill of the forest, looked like banditti returning with plunder. On the top of some of the packs were perched several half-breed children, perfect little imps with wild black eyes glaring from among elf locks. These, I was told, were children of the trappers; pledges of love from their squaw spouses in the wilderness."

Before Bill Sublette started, a few of his men impatiently set out ahead of the main party. They ran into the Blackfoot and several were killed in Jackson's Hole.

Milton Sublette, with Joe Meek and his other trappers, hit the trail again for the Southwest, taking Wyeth and his down-Easters along.

At the same time Jim Bridger and White Head Fitzpatrick headed north, northwest towards Henry's Fork of the Snake River, planning to cross the divide to the headwaters of the Missouri, that hotbed of Blackfoot hostility.

Jim and Tom rode off in high spirits, leaving their rivals Vanderburgh and Drips biting their nails in Pierre's Hole, frantically awaiting the coming of Fontenelle and the trade goods with which they had hoped in vain to get their share of the beaver at rendezvous. After Jim and Tom were gone, they went on fidgeting until they learned or guessed that Fontenelle had reached Captain Bonneville's fort on the upper Green River. Then they hit the trail, found him there, hastily equipped their men from his packs, and lit out as fast as they could march on Jim Bridger's trail. This was about the end of the first week in August.

It wasn't long until Jim Bridger's scouts informed him that his rivals were pushing hard to overtake him. Jim was plumb disgusted at being dogged by those greenhorns—more especially after they had refused to divide the fur country with him. Jim and Tom held brief council. They decided to slip away. Surely they could fool those greenhorns in strange country.

So they went to work, covering their trail, marching through water, leading their men over stretches of bare rock, heading out into the grassy prairie away from the stream they were following, there scattering like quail through the grass, every man by himself in a dozen different directions, to meet next day at a prearranged rendezvous. They traveled fast and sometimes sent a whole bunch of riders off at a tangent to make a plain trail and so lead their followers on a wrong scent. They passed across the head of traveling buffalo herds so that the hooves of the animals might obliterate their trail. They used all the tricks they had learned in years of scouting on the plains and in the mountains.

But the greenhorn Vanderburgh, though ignorant of all that country, was wide awake and never rested. He was ever on the alert, ever wary, and threw his scouts far forward and on the flanks. Probably he had one or two good Indian trailers to help him, and he was ready and willing to learn. And so, to the utter disgust of Bridger. and his party, Vanderburgh stuck to their trail. They could not stop to trap or hunt. Their rivals followed as relentlessly as their own shadows.

Jim and Tom now lost all patience. Their plan had failed. But, if they could not shake off these persistent greenhorns, they decided to make a new road. Rather than share the fur with rivals, they resolved to let the beaver alone and lead Vanderburgh on a wild goose chase. So, heading away from the mountains, they followed the old Blackfoot trail down the Missouri River, and for some time kept doggedly on, never stopping to set a single trap.

Vanderburgh and Drips took after them fast as their flagging horses could carry them, at the same time keeping a bright lookout for beaver dams. But in time even these greenhorns realized that they were being fooled, that the country they were heading into contained few fur-bearing animals. They had lost their chance to buy the beaver at rendezvous in Pierre's Hole. Now it seemed that they were to be given a run-around until the hunting season ended and all fur was worthless.

And so Drips and Vanderburgh also held council, gave up the chase, divided their forces, and explored for hunting grounds of their own. Vanderburgh, taking about fifty men, headed straight into the heart of Blackfoot country. He was new to Indian warfare.

It wasn't long until his scouts found Indian fires burning, surrounded by the carcasses of buffalo just killed. They hurried back to warn their leader. Taking nine men, Vanderburgh recklessly galloped off to reconnoiter. He found everything as they had reported it: fires still smoking, buffalo half-butchered.

Bold as he was green, Vanderburgh followed the Indian

trail—squarely into an ambush. The first volley mortally wounded his horse, which fell and pinned him to the ground. He called to his men to help him up. But before anything could be done, one was killed and scalped at his side. The others ran for their lives. Vanderburgh fired and killed one of the Indians, but they soon split his skull with a hatchet. His party made no attempt to recover his body, but rode night and day until they reached a camp of friendlies.

Meanwhile Jim and Tom settled down to trapping, keeping their eyes skinned for Injuns. They were not easily caught napping or hurried into an ambush. They brought in all the horses before sundown, picketed them in the camp, posted a guard. At the first streak of dawn Jim would mount and ride at full speed out from the camp about half a mile, then circle to cut any Injun trails which showed that savages had approached his camp, lurking in the night. Jim scouted every gully, every thicket. Then, having assured himself that no Injuns lay in wait in the neighborhood, he would return. The horses would be taken out to graze under guard.

On the march scouts rode in advance and along the ridges on either side.

It was impossible for the cussed Injuns to surprise Jim Bridger.

But one day Jim saw a large band of Blackfeet heading into the prairie—yet warily hugging the rocky hillside. Both parties kept their distance. The Indians made signs of friendship. The trappers replied in kind.

A small party of Indians then rode out, holding high the long-stemmed pipe of peace. It was clear from their gestures that they wished to smoke with the Blanket Chief and White Head.

Bridger and Fitzpatrick were willing enough to have peace —if only the peace could be made to stick. But they were doubtful whether to smoke with the Blackfeet after what had happened. The Blackfeet had killed their own trader, Vanderburgh; it warn't likely they would stop at tricking his rivals. The two trappers hesitated.

Then a young Mexican, Loretto, a free trapper who was traveling with them, spoke up. Loretto had a wife, a handsome Blackfoot girl. She had been captured by the Crows. Loretto had ransomed her and made her his wife; their baby boy was perched on his mother's back. Loretto told Bridger and Fitzpatrick not to be afraid. "I know those Indians," he declared. "They are my wife's relatives."

White Head Fitzpatrick nodded, and turned to Bridger. "Well, Jim, you heard what the Spaniard said. Reckon I'll go and talk to 'em. You stay here with the packs and the men. Keep your eyes skinned. Maybeso the cussed Injuns will try to play tricks. Happen you see anything queer, holler."

Bridger agreed. Loretto grinned. Fitzpatrick went forward, trailed by seven lank, brown trappers, their buckskin fringes whipping through the grass. Chief Sun came forward with seven braves to meet them. He had everybody sit down first, and *then* shake hands, so that the peace would be *firm*. That done, the long pipe was lighted, passed, smoked. The palaver began; it went on and on.

Meanwhile, Loretto's wife, staring at the Indians across the way, suddenly uttered a cry of joy: "There's my brother!" Putting her small son into her husband's arms, she ran across to her own people. They welcomed her with open arms and many caresses, as one returned from the grave.[1] It was their first reunion since she had been taken by the Crows. And when they learned that one of the trappers had rescued her, their hearts warmed and softened towards the white men. All the Blackfeet came swarming to greet her, making a commotion.

One of the braves in council saw the movement among his people, and signaled to learn what had happened. One of the young warriors rode quickly out to the council to explain it.

Seeing this move, Jim Bridger became suspicious. The young warrior on the horse had a bow in his hand. Therefore Jim mounted his own horse, and taking his rifle rode out to make the numbers at the council even. His rifle rested across the pommel of his saddle. When Bridger rode up, Chief Sun got to his feet to shake the white man's hand.

Bridger, whose eyes were on the young warrior on the horse, saw that he had four arrows in his bow hand. Knowing how rapidly an Injun could shoot, Jim thumbed back the hammer of his rifle, in order to be ready for trouble.

The chief reached for Bridger's hand. But when his ears caught the click of Jim's rifle, the memory of how Chief Baihoh had been murdered flashed through his mind. With lightning quickness the chief grabbed the barrel of Jim's rifle, pushed the muzzle down. In that tense moment, Jim's finger automatically pressed the trigger; the charge exploded into the ground between the chief's feet.

Before the men on the ground could gain their feet, the young warrior on the horse had loosed two arrows into Bridger's back. Reeling from the pain and force of those sharp points, Jim found himself helpless against the strength of the outraged chief. Sun wrenched the rifle from his hands, swung it high, and brought the stock hard against Bridger's ear and neck with crushing force. A sheet of flame soared up before Jim's eyes, and he went down into darkness.

The chief jumped into Jim's saddle and galloped away to rally his people.

There followed a time of wild excitement. Each side rushed to cover among the rocks. Women ran, dragging screaming children after them. Men jumped back and forth like dancers, dodging the bullets of their enemies. War-whoops and the crack of rifles answered each other. The battle had begun.

Poor Loretto was thunderstruck. His Indian wife was with his enemies—he was with hers. He could see her struggling with her brother's people, trying to get away and run back to him. But they held her, they stopped her, they dragged her screaming away. He "saw her struggles and her agony and heard her piercing cries. With a generous impulse he caught up the child in his arms, rushed forward, regardless of Indian shaft or rifle, and placed it in safety upon her bosom. Even the heart of the Blackfeet chief was reached by this noble deed. He pronounced Loretto a madman for his temerity, but bade him depart in peace. The young Mexican hesitated: he urged to have his wife restored to him, but her brother interfered, and the countenance of the chief grew dark. The girl, he said, belonged to his tribe —she must remain with her people. Loretto would still have lingered, but his wife implored him to depart, lest his life should be endangered. It was with the greatest reluctance that he returned to his companions." [2]

Come night, the shooting ended, as each party pulled out under cover of the darkness. There was no victory, as there had been no reason for the fight. But from then on the Blackfeet and their allies the Gros Ventres saw little reason to hope for peace with the whites. And the trappers had no hopes of peace with them. Three Mountain Men had been killed, and six horses.[3] . . .

When Jim Bridger came to, he found the battle over, the Blackfeet gone, the trappers in camp. Tom Fitzpatrick squatted beside him, grinning solicitously. "Well, old coon," Tom was saying, "when we found you lyin' thar stuck full of arrers as a porkypine, we reckoned you war gone beaver. How air ye now?"

Lying on his face as he was, Bridger turned his head to answer Tom. But the pain of the movement made him dizzy, and he sank back, closing his eyes. His head was one great ache, and it seemed as though his neck were broken. When the spasm passed, Jim opened his eyes again and, to reassure himself and Tom that his heart war still strong, growled *"Wagh!"* *

Then, without raising his head, he tried to roll over. Tom seized his shoulders. "Hold on, old hoss, lay still till I quit them arrers out of your hump-ribs."

"Go ahead," Jim urged. "They tickle my fleece a mite too sharp for comfort."

Jim knew well enough that Indian arrowheads were only

* Considering the violent life he led, people have often wondered how the Indian got along with a language which contains no cuss words, no profanity, and some idealists have supposed that the absence of such words from his vocabulary indicated a moral character much superior to the white man's. But the Indian had his own way of expressing feelings which a white man would have expressed profanely. In this, as in many other things, he imitated the wild animals about him. In particular the Indian—and the trapper after him—had a trick of mimicking the blood-freezing snarl of a grizzly bear about to attack at close quarters. This bear grunt or "brave grunt" was uttered in hand-to-hand conflict as a threat or warning, corresponding to the war whoop or primitive view-halloo in fighting at longer range. Trappers, like Indians, often used this brave grunt in place of more civilized oaths. And no wonder—for no more ferocious sound could be made by the human voice. In old books recording trapper language, that sound occurs frequently, represented by the word *wagh*.

three inches long, flat, triangular irons, with beveled edges
and a notched shank which fitted into a slot in the end of the
stick and was fastened to it by wrappings of fine sinews. But
those points in his back felt as big and sharp as butcher
knives.

While Jim bit on a stick, Tom tugged at the arrows—first
one, then the other. They would not come out. While he
sweated, Jim had a wild notion for a moment that Tom might
shove the arrows on through him, cut off the points and yank
the sticks out backwards. But Tom would not risk pushing
the arrows through Jim's lungs. "I'll have to butcher them
out, boy," he warned.

Jim lay still while Tom worked on him, probing and cutting. Jim could feel the blade of Tom's Green River knife
press into the wound flat against the arrow point, feel it
work back and forth, widening the gash. Finally he heard
Tom sigh. "Thar's one, anyhow."

Then Tom turned to the other arrow. He cut and probed
and tugged and pulled and sawed the arrow back and forth,
fairly lifting Jim off the ground—but all to no purpose.
"I'll swear," he complained. "This hyar arrow is headed
with a fish-hook—wedged in the bone or bent round it somehow. Looks like you'll have to carry this one, Jim—least-
ways till you meet up with a doctor somewhars."

"Well," Jim grumbled, "I don't aim to carry the stick
too. Work it loose and let me up."

By that time the blood had softened the sinews which
bound the point to the shaft. With a little manipulation,
Tom was able to separate the two and throw the shaft away.
He slapped a handful of beaver fur over Jim's wounds, fastened the dressing on with a strip torn from Jim's shirt tail,
and let him sit up.

Then he led up Jim's horse and helped him into the saddle. They all hit the trail for the beaver streams.

IX

DEVIL TAKE THE HINDMOST

ON THE way to Three Forks, where he was shot in the back, Jim Bridger and his partners had trapped with their usual success up the Yellowstone River. They had moved across what is now Yellowstone Park, had seen the cliffs and crashing waterfall at the Grand Canyon, had passed the wide blue levels of Yellowstone Lake and, probably for the first time, had admired the delicately tinted terraces of the bubbling hot springs. From Three Forks they rode to winter quarters at the forks of the Snake.

It was not a happy encampment. Bridger's wounds were the least of his troubles. He and his partners had plenty to worry about. The affairs of their Rocky Mountain Fur Company were going rapidly from bad to worse, and this was not because of any lack of beaver fur or any lack of skill and success in taking it. Fur was still plenty and brought a good price in the settlements. But the hazards and overhead of the company were very great. It cost a heap of dollars to pack trade goods to rendezvous all the way from St. Louis, and to pack the furs from rendezvous back again. The hostile Injuns were always making trouble and causing losses. Though there were never more than about a thousand trappers in the fur country, an average of about one Mountain Man was killed every ten days, year in and year out. And there were too many companies in the field trying to hamstring each other.

Thus the Rocky Mountain Fur Company in two years'

time took 210 pack of furs worth $80,000. During the same
two-year period they had bought two outfits of goods, each
costing Bill Sublette at St. Louis $6000, and for each outfit
they paid Bill at rendezvous a cool $30,000. On top of that,
they paid Bill another $8000 to carry their furs back to
market. So the five partners—Jim Bridger, Tom Fitzpatrick, J. B. Gervais, Henry Fraeb and Milt Sublette—
actually received only $12,000 among them—a great part
of which had to be paid out in wages to those of their employees who were not paid in goods. This, according to the
Yankee Wyeth, finally left them "with little property except
their horses, mules and traps, and a few goods."

Yet Bridger's outfit was an efficient one, much the best
organized, equipped, disciplined and skilled outfit in the
mountains.

So the partners were not happy in winter quarters; moreover, there was so little grass for the horses at the forks of
the Snake that Bridger's favorite race horse, Grohean, which
had been bred by the Comanches, was soon as lean and ribby
as an old squaw's pack-horse. Along in January (1833)
they all had to move camp through the snow to the mouth of
the Pocatello to find forage. They were half frozen on the
way. When they arrived, they found little wood for their
fires, scanty game for their larder, and bitter cold weather.
The men subsisted as best they could on bear, beaver, and
coyote, following the practical maxim of hunters in that day,
"Meat's meat."

Kit Carson and a compañero dropped into that starving
camp early in the spring. Soon after, their hardships were
aggravated by a sudden attack of Blackfoot horse thieves,
who got away with most of their stock, including Bridger's
horse, Grohean. As soon as the loss was known, Bridger led
thirty picked men, including Kit Carson, after the thieves.

They plodded wearily through the deep snow, and at last caught up with the Blackfeet—who had sent the stolen horses on ahead and were waiting for them, fresh and full of fight.[1] There was a useless parley followed by a sharp fight.

In this scrap, Kit Carson, seeing an Injun drawing a bead on his friend Markhead, shifted his aim from the redskin opposite to save Markhead and was himself shot through the shoulder—a wound which left his right arm useless for some time to come. The Blackfeet soon drove the Mountain Men to cover and kept them there through a wretched freezing night, unable to stir or even light a fire. In the bitter cold morning they plodded back to camp with five broken-down horses which the cussed Injuns had not thought worth taking home.

Back at camp Jim quickly organized another moccasin posse and again hit the Blackfoot trail, but could not overtake the mounted thieves. So Bridger had to buy new horses —always a difficult and costly task—from some Nez Percés in the neighborhood.

After that, the trappers scattered for their spring hunt. Bridger and Fraeb worked across Green River into northwest Colorado, on towards the Medicine Bow Mountains and Platte River. There the Rees—Jim's old enemies—stole all the expensive horses he had just bought from the Nez Percés. Finally Bridger turned up at Captain Bonneville's fort on the Salmon River, where rendezvous was held that summer of 1833.

Bridger's men had only fifty-five pack of beaver—more than any other outfit, at that—but all of them were hard up, short on horses and equipment.

Some three hundred trappers assembled with all their Indian relatives and allies, including a band of Shoshones, for a nine-day spree. Here too was the wealthy Scottish sports-

man and baronet, Captain Sir William Drummond Stuart.
"He made them stare. He sported white shooting-jackets
full of pockets and of dandy cut, trousers of shepherd's
plaid, a Panama hat! He carried a two-shoot fowling piece
slung across one shoulder! The mountain men almost busted
themselves laughing at the poor greenhorn's equipment.
But worse was to follow: he had wagons—wagons loaded
with tins of preserved meat, bottles of pickles, brandy, porter, fine wines, coffee, tea. He dined off hams and tongues,
had flour by the barrel, real sugar, and his table service
staggered the minds of the simple trappers, whose whole outfit consisted of a skinning-knife and a tin cup.

"But before long the trappers changed their tune. Sir
William was a splendid horseman; he could shoot with the
best of them; and the way he made 'em come in the first Indian skirmish showed what fighters the Scotch could be.
Moreover, he was as liberal with his strange food and fancy
drinks as the most open-handed of mountaineers. He soon
had the trappers eating out of his hand." [2] Dr. Benjamin
Harrison, son of General William Henry Harrison, was also
in camp. Even in those days Bridger did not lack distinguished company.

By this time Wyeth had realized where the money lay in
the fur business, and though he was without capital at the
time, persuaded Tom Fitzpatrick and Milt Sublette to sign
a contract giving him the right to deliver to their company
three thousand dollars' worth of merchandise the following
summer. Jim Bridger and the other two partners did not
sign—perhaps never saw—the contract. It was not like Jim
to sell out his old compañero, Bill Sublette.

Wyeth went off hugging himself at having bought, as he
supposed, a monopoly. Though he wrote home "an honest

opinion" that "there is here a great majority of scoundrels," he was confident he could cope with the Mountain Men.

After the rendezvous of '33, Bridger, Tom, and Milt Sublette, Wyeth and some free trappers, following the same route Colonel Ashley had taken in 1825, found very little fur as compared with the great harvest Ashley had made eight years earlier. They trapped Wind River, Grey Bull River, the Stinking Water, and loaded their furs into bullboats as soon as they reached the Big Horn. On the way, one of their heedless men, asleep on duty, had seven horses stolen from him; he came in gunshot with his own rifle, and with an arrow sticking in his back. Bridger thought the man lucky to be alive.

Below the mouth of the Big Horn on the Yellowstone River they found Fort Cass, a new post of the American Fur Company, which was extending itself in all directions. Here the party divided. Captain Stuart rode with White Head Fitzpatrick.

From Fort Cass, Fitzpatrick headed for the Crow camps on Tongue River, to get permission to trap in Crow country. He reached the Tongue early in September with only twenty or thirty men. The Crow chief urged him to make camp with the Indians—a startling proposition.

Fitzpatrick, too wary for that, made camp a few miles away, and then went alone to pay his respects to the chief in person.

While Tom was gone, a pack of young Crow warriors visited his camp. They carried off one hundred horses, all his goods and beaver and traps. To add insult to injury, when they met Fitzpatrick on the way home, they took his rifle, stripped the capoté from his back—even took his watch. He reached camp wearing only a gee-string and moccasins—and his scalp. After that, there was nothing to do but hoof it out of Crow country as fast as his men could travel. McKenzie, bourgeois of the American Fur Company, gloated in a letter to his partner Pierre Chouteau, that Fitzpatrick's party "can consequently make no hunt this fall."

White Head, boiling with rage, charged the American Fur Company with instigating the robbery. But the only satisfaction he could get from the rival company, which had purchased the stolen beaver, was a letter from McKenzie.[3] He coolly wrote, "The 43 beaver skins traded, marked, 'R. M. F. Co.,' I would in the present instance give up if Mr. Fitzpatrick wishes to have them, on his paying the price the articles traded for them were worth on their arrival in the Crow village, and the expense of bringing the beaver in and securing it. My goods are brought into the country to trade and I would as willingly dispose of them to Mr. Fitzpatrick as to anyone else for beaver or beaver's worth, if I get my price. I make this proposal as a favor, not as a matter of right, for I consider the Indians entitled to trade any beaver in their possession to me or to any other trader."

Old Gabe, trapping the Big Horn, was not with Tom and Stuart when the Crows robbed them. But when he learned of the theft, he went to work to repair the damage and get on with the hunt. The stolen beaver, of course, was a total loss. Jim could divide his own traps, weapons, powder, lead, and flints with Fitzpatrick's men. But that, Jim knew, was not enough; without horses, Tom's trappers could make no hunt that season. Somehow, Jim had to get horses.

Now buying good horses from an Indian on the Plains was no easy matter. A warrior's success in the hunt and on the warpath was in direct ratio to the number, speed, and stamina of his ponies. Without them, he could win no honors in battle, he could not feed his family or make feasts for his friends, he could make no presents, buy no women, take part in no parades, belong to no society of warriors, win no races:

in short, without a first-rate running horse, trained to hunt buffalo and carry his master in war, the Plains Indian was a pauper, a celibate, and a nobody, and his life—since he could not keep up with his mounted fellows—was not worth a month's purchase.

Moreover, the strength and success of the whole band depended upon the fleet steeds its members owned, so that a warrior who sold a fast horse out of the camp was likely to feel the bitter resentment of all his friends and relatives, and to be called a fool. And so it was the ambition of every warrior to have as many horses, and as good horses as he could steal, beg, or purchase. He might live in a ragged leaky tent no better than a hovel, he might go half-naked, and never give such matters a thought. But to give up his horse was a tragedy—it was to lose his standing, his capital, and the tools of his profession. Often it meant losing his life. It was easier to buy an Indian's wife than to get him to part with a fast horse.*

Old Gabe, quite as well as McKenzie, realized the great difficulty of buying horses—even from friendly Injuns; and there were no friendly Injuns anywheres near. Even had there been any in the neighborhood, Bridger—after dividing

---

* The great distances to be covered on the Plains enforced such a habit of mind. Later, the cowboy felt the same, valuing his horse past the love of woman, as is shown by the fact that your cowboy never was a marrying man.

The strength of this tradition may be measured by its projection into the present day culture of the Plains—for the white men have carried it on. Thus, on the Plains today, you can generally identify a man reared in other regions by the fact that he builds a substantial house and drives a low-priced car; whereas your truebred Plainsman may be content with a bungalow or cottage, but always prefers a high-powered, expensive automobile.

his supplies with Fitzpatrick—had hardly anything left to buy them with. And he needed all of a hundred head.

No doubt Captain Stuart, who had likewise suffered the loss of his horses and goods, would have been glad to use his ample wealth to stake the trappers to a new outfit. He was open-handed as any man on the Plains, and on one occasion had provided Killbuck and La Bonte, starving and reduced to eating rattlesnakes, with complete new outfits,[4] from horses to gun-flints—all "on the prairie," absolutely free. But Captain Stuart was powerless to help; wild Indians would not accept money or drafts on St. Louis.

Old Gabe knew he could not lay his hands on any more goods until Sublette turned up at the summer rendezvous. The trapping season was passing. Time pressed. He must act at once, or McKenzie's gloating prophecy would come true. In that case, he and his partners would owe Sublette to the tune of $15,000—and no beaver to pay it with—or have no equipment next year.

Now McKenzie was one of the most successful, experienced, and canny men in all the West—a truly great executive by any standard; when *he* thought Bridger's situation hopeless, it was no wonder that the trappers in Fitzpatrick's camp despaired.

But McKenzie had crowed too soon. He underestimated Old Gabe's spunk and gumption.

"Wal, boys," Jim said, "if we cain't help ourselves, I reckon thar's no help this side of hell. We're too pore to buy horses—and not strong enough to steal 'em." They waited, hoping against hope. Jim went on. "Maybeso the American Fur Company would quit in a fix like this. But we ain't licked yit. They'll have to git up earlier in the git the best of us. Thar's still one trick left in my —and hyar goes."

In the silence, they could hear the steady hammering of a woodpecker on a cottonwood down the creek. Tom Fitzpatrick shifted his moccasined feet. "Wal, old coon? Out with it."

Bridger grinned, "I aim to git them horses from *the Crows*."

Tom rared back. "We cain't fight 'em. They're too many. If we war lucky enough to beat the cussed Injuns now, they'd rub us out afterwards one by one while we war scattered all over their country trappin'."

"Who said anything about fightin' 'em?" Old Gabe protested. He turned to Newell, beckoned, and then headed for his lodge. Newell followed. Once in the privacy and half-gloom of the big taper tent, Jim thrust his thumb towards a pallet. Newell sat down, and Jim explained his plan.

"You're a slick trader, Doc. You know them Injuns. I'm sendin' you to smoke with 'em. If any man this side of hell kin swing it, you kin. And the quicker, the better."

Doc Newell took his rifle, mounted, and hit the trail to the Crow camp. . . .

The talk was held, according to custom, in the big council lodge, "and the usual amount of smoking, of long silences, and grave looks, had to be participated in, before the subject on hand could be considered. Then the chiefs complained as usual of wrongs at the hands of the white men; of their fear of small-pox, from which some of their tribe had suffered; of friends killed in battle with the whites, and all the list of ills that Crow flesh is heir to at the will of their white enemies. The women too had their complaints to proffer, and the number of widows and orphans in the tribe was pathetically set forth. The chiefs also made a strong point of this latter complaint; and on it the wily Newell hung his hopes of recovering the stolen property.

" 'It is true,' said he to the chiefs, 'that you have sustained heavy losses. But that is not the fault of the Blanket Chief. If your young men have been killed, they were killed when attempting to rob or kill our Captain's men. If you have lost horses, your young men have stolen five to our one. If you are poor in skins and other property, it is because you sold it all for drink which did you no good. Neither is Bridger to blame that you have had the small-pox. Your own chief, in trying to kill your enemies the Blackfeet, brought that disease into the country.

" 'But it is true that you have many widows and orphans to support, and that is bad. I pity the orphans, and will help you to support them, if you will restore to my Captain the property stolen from his camp. Otherwise Bridger will bring more horses, and plenty of ammunition, and there will be more widows and orphans among the Crows than ever before.'

"This was a kind of logic easy to understand and quick to convince among savages. The bribe, backed by a threat, settled the question of the restoration of the horses, which were returned without further delay, and a present of blankets and trinkets was given, ostensibly to the bereaved women, really to the covetous chiefs." [5]

Bridger's movements just after that are not fully recorded. Apparently, after trapping Powder River, he moved on to the Green River, where he ran into Bonneville—who had also been robbed—and certainly some of his men trapped west of the Rockies during the next months, some of them going all the way to Arizona, and even to California.

But one thing is certain. With their new outfit, scanty though it might be, he and Tom kept going, hell-bent to outwit, outfight, and outtrap every skunk in the business. The

men of his brigade were proud of their Booshway. Old Gabe
was *some punkins*, and you kin lay to that!

X

ARROW BUTCHERED OUT

MEANWHILE Nathaniel J. Wyeth, now that he had his contract with Bridger's partners to bring out goods to rendezvous
next summer, hit the trail for the settlements. He embarked
his packs in boats at the mouth of the Big Horn and floated
cheerfully down to Fort Union at the mouth of the Yellowstone. With him traveled Mr. Cerré, one of Captain Bonneville's agents. The bourgeois at Fort Union was Kenneth
"Red Coat" McKenzie, widely known as King of the Upper
Missouri. McKenzie was a great executive, the most successful fur trader in the employ of the biggest company in the
business in American territory—the American Fur Company. Fort Union was the largest fur trading post in the
West, and there McKenzie lived and ruled like a monarch.

When Wyeth and Cerré arrived, McKenzie made them
welcome, and entertained them with his usual lavish hospitality, though of course well aware that they represented rival
companies. He showed them over his admirable establishment, perhaps to make them realize the competition he could
offer them—and even let them see the hidden distillery in
which he manufactured whisky for the Indian trade.

Now, Wyeth and Cerré were well aware that the Act of
July 9, 1832, prohibited the importation of liquor into Indian country. At the same time they shared McKenzie's conviction that the fur trade could not profitably be carried on
without it. McKenzie may have gloated a little over his success in violating the spirit of the law while technically following it to the letter.

But when his guests undertook to do business with him and asked to purchase some of his liquor (for reasons best known to themselves), McKenzie suddenly became the shrewd trader. He willingly supplied them with goods, but gave no discounts, selling everything to them at exorbitant

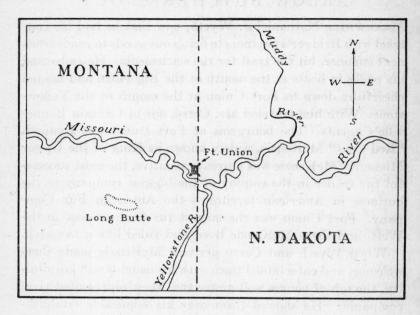

mountain prices. As for liquor, he would not let them have a drop.

Wyeth and Cerré resented such treatment, so, though belonging to competing companies, became quite chummy on the way down-river to the settlements. At Fort Leavenworth they made affidavit against McKenzie, alleging that the American Fur Company was "making and vending whisky in quantity."

At that time the American Fur Company had a reputation for hard dealing and was bitterly hated, not only by its competitors but even by its own employees, and the public believed the company would stop at nothing to monopolize the fur trade. The scandal caused by this affidavit, therefore, was a heavy blast against McKenzie and ended his career in the fur trade. His employer, however, was not seriously disturbed, for already, two weeks earlier, on June 1, 1834, canny J. J. Astor had sold the American Fur Company.

After this smashing victory, it is hardly surprising that Wyeth set out in high confidence with the goods he had contracted to deliver to the Rocky Mountain Fur Company. The rendezvous was to be on Hams Fork.

With Wyeth rode Milt Sublette, upon whose long friendship with the partners Wyeth counted to make the contract stick. Unfortunately for Wyeth, Milt's leg became seriously infected and he had to turn back. Wyeth went on alone. . . .

At rendezvous Bridger and his partners awaited the coming of supplies from the settlements. But when the first pack train rolled in, it was not Wyeth's. Bill Sublette had been too smart for the clever Yankee, and by lightening his packs and traveling overtime, had managed to gain two days' march on Wyeth. Bill opened his packs, grinning at having got the best of the would-be monopolist.

Only two of the five partners of the Rocky Mountain Fur Company had signed the agreement with Wyeth. Perhaps the other three repudiated it; details are lacking. But at that time the partners had more important problems to worry about.

In twelve short years the Rocky Mountain Fur Company had had a great career. It had trapped the mountains with its own men, instead of trading for furs with the redskins. The company had shipped more than a thousand pack of beaver to the settlements, valued at some $500,000—but most of that had gone into the pockets of Ashley and Bill Sublette.[1]

Moreover, during its operation the company had lost property to the tune of about $100,000, and men to the number of seventy—all of whom met violent deaths.

The company, however, had produced great benefits for the nation. Its hard experience had disciplined and trained some of the greatest adventurers and Indian fighters known to history. Its men also had performed important services to science.

Their discoveries and explorations included the greatest rivers of the Northern Plains and the Rocky Mountains, the Great Salt Lake, South Pass, and Yellowstone Park. They had broken the trail to Southern California, traversed the deserts of the Great Basin, and moved up the Pacific coast clear to the Columbia River. Yet the company's greatest service to the nation was the schooling in the fur brigades of the great guides and scouts—men like Jim Bridger, Kit Carson, and Tom Fitzpatrick—who were the pathfinders for later official explorers and military expeditions in the winning of the West.

But all that public service had put no dollars in the possible sacks of the five discouraged partners. Glumly they talked things over, and on June 20, 1834, executed a dissolution of partnership.[2]

When Wyeth arrived at rendezvous, ten days later, there was no Rocky Mountain Fur Company to buy the goods he had brought out to sell them. No excuses Bridger and his partners may have offered could satisfy the indignant Yankee. And it is hardly surprising, after the way he had knocked out McKenzie, that Wyeth felt able to handle Bridger and his friends. Stung by disappointment and anger, his quick intelligence immediately hit upon a solution that would not only make good his losses but also afford him sweet revenge.

Wyeth smiled thinly. "Gentlemen," he declared, "I will roll a stone into your garden that you will never be able to get out."

So Wyeth packed up his unsold goods and hit the trail for Snake River. No doubt Jim and his partners were glad to be rid of him. His threats probably gave them no worry; what could the little greenhorn Yankee do?

They soon found out. On Snake River Wyeth built Fort Hall to house his goods, and at once opened negotiations with the Hudson's Bay Company, to whom he sold the fort and all its contents—thus bringing powerful British competition into the very region which Bridger and his friends had made their own.

Meanwhile a new company, in which Tom Fitzpatrick, Milton Sublette, and Jim Bridger were the partners, took the field.

After that starving rendezvous of '34, Jim Bridger's company ran into more and more trouble, no matter where they turned. In later years, when Jim served as guide and scout, everybody was impressed by his wariness and caution. It is no wonder he developed such useful qualities, considering what he and his friends went through in those unsettled times when the beaver trade was swiftly sliding to its end. Jim learned in a hard school. . . .

Wyeth still had trappers in the field under the leadership of Joe Gale, who had formerly worked for Bridger. Gale had been whipped and robbed by the Blackfeet. One day Kit Carson and Joe Meek and about a dozen others left Bridger's camp and rode over to visit Joe Gale's outfit. Jim Bridger thought it a bad time to go visiting. He savvied Injuns well enough to know that, having once bested Gale, the Blackfeet would soon come back to rub him out.

But if Jim said anything to Kit and Joe Meek, they probably put it down to his dislike for Gale, who had gone over to the rival company. At any rate, they rode off.

When, soon after, the Blackfeet jumped Gale's camp, his men were so ill-armed that they could do no more than hold the horses, and would all have been wiped out but for the fighting spirit of their visitors. Kit and Meek set the Blackfeet back on their haunches, and then took cover in a patch of brush at one end of the grassy bottom.

The Blackfeet, not caring to charge that nest of expert riflemen, simply set fire to the dry grass, which burned furiously right up to the thicket, driving the trappers into the open. There their horses were soon shot down. Forting behind the kicking carcasses, they held off the Blackfeet as best they could.

When Bridger heard the shooting he knew what was up, jumped on his best buffalo horse, and raced to the rescue at the head of a thunder of plunging hoofs, all the men in camp riding at his heels. They charged in, yelling and firing from the saddle, scattering the Blackfeet.

Somehow that was what everybody had expected. Jim had been helping trappers out of fixes so long that it had got to be a habit. Whenever some reckless Mountain Man found himself in a scrape, his first thought was "Whar's Old Gabe? He'd know what to do."

By the spring of '35, Bridger saw that Ashley's old plan of having no permanent forts in fur country was pretty nigh played out—like the fur itself. So when he and Tom Fitzpatrick rode down to Fort Laramie—the new post, built the fall before by Bill Sublette and Robert Campbell for the Sioux and Cheyenne trade—they put their heads together, struck a bargain with the owners, and bought the place. It was the first time in a dozen years that Jim had slept regularly under a roof.

That summer of '35 the rendezvous was held on Green River, at a great camp of several thousand Indians and some two hundred trappers. The season had been bad. Furs were not abundant, though liquor was. But most of the Mountain Men were too hard up, too badly in need of new equipment, to indulge freely.

Here Jim saw Kit Carson out-shoot the bully Shunar in a duel and so win the Arapaho girl who became Kit's first wife.[3]

For some days Dr. Samuel Parker and Dr. Marcus Whitman, the missionaries, camped with the trappers. When Jim learned that Whitman was a surgeon, he asked him to butcher out the arrowhead in his back, which he had carried now for three uncomfortable years. The wound had closed and healed over, but the sharp iron often hurt Jim—especially in cold weather.

The whole camp gathered to watch the operation. Jim stripped off his shirt and sat quietly while the wondering Indians stood round, wedged in a packed ring, staring over each other's shoulders open-mouthed, while Dr. Whitman got out his surgical instruments and went to work.

The operation took some time, but Jim was prepared for this, remembering how Tom had been unable to get the point out when the wound was fresh. Now, Whitman told him, the arrow was bent and hooked at the point, having struck a large bone, and cartilage had formed around the hook.

But Jim Bridger never flinched. When Whitman finally extricated it, he found that the point measured fully three inches long.

That operation made Dr. Whitman's reputation among the Redskins. From that hour he was continually pestered by savages demanding his professional services.

Quit of his arrowhead, Jim Bridger felt unusually cocky. Up to this time, so far as our record goes, he had remained a bachelor. But now—at thirty years of age—he decided to step right in the tracks of Kit Carson, who had womaned a few days before. So Jim also trapped a squaw, as the Mountain Men put it, marrying the daughter of a Flathead chief.

When rendezvous broke up, the family of the bride and all their relatives moved out with Bridger along the trail towards the buffalo range. On the way Bridger camped for a while in Jackson's Little Hole near the Grand Teton while his men trapped in the neighborhood. There he regaled Dr. Parker with stories of Blackfoot battles which had taken place thereabouts.

This peaceful stay in the Little Hole was prelude to another Injun scrape in which Jim Bridger played the leading part. Joe Meek had come along with Jim's party, heading toward the Yellowstone. On the Rocky Fork, Meek found himself in a pretty fix.

XI
OLD GABE
TO THE RESCUE

TRAPPING was not a business which could be carried on profitably by large parties of men. Though the main camp might contain many campkeepers, squaws, children, packers, and horse guards, the men who harvested the fur had to operate in small groups or alone. When Jim Bridger's brigade moved over from the headwaters of Snake River to

Yellowstone country, Joseph L. Meek went on far ahead alone.

On the fifth day out from camp, a large war party of Crows caught up with him. They were on the prairie and Meek was forced to skip to the creek bottom, quirting his mule for all he was worth with the swarming Indians hard on his trail, yelling and firing a random shot now and then as they closed in on him. Unfortunately the beaver had drained the water out of the creek and made dams, and Meek's mule mired down in the swamp.

By the time the Indians were within about two rods' distance, he was ready for them and brought old *Sally*, as he called his rifle, up to his face, ready to fire his last shot. As he puts it: "I knew it war death this time unless Providence interfered to save me: and I didn't think Providence would do it."

The Crow chief was in the lead, but when he found himself looking down the muzzle of Meek's gun, slowed up and yelled to him, "Lay down your gun and you will live."

Meek's state of mind was easily understood: "Well, I liked to live,—being then in the prime of life; and though it hurt me powerful I resolved to part with *Sally*. I laid her down. As I did so, the chief picked her up, and one of the braves sprang at me with a spear, and would have run me through, but the chief knocked him down with the butt of my gun."

So far, so good. They led Meek out to the high prairie south of the stream. There they all halted and turned him over to the three squaws while the warriors sat down in a circle to smoke and decide on his fate. Meek, however, never lost his nerve. While they debated, he coolly counted them. There were 187 warriors, 9 boys, and the 3 squaws guarding him.

They puffed and palavered for what seemed three long

hours. Then the head chief, named The Bold, summoned Meek into the ring. He said, "I have known the whites for a long time, and I know them to be great liars, deserving death; but if *you* will tell the truth, you shall live."

Meek thought to himself: *They will fetch the truth out of me, IF thar is any in me.*

The chief went on, "Tell me where are the whites you belong to; and what's your captain's name."

Meek looked the chief in the eye and said proudly, "Bridger is my captain's name; or, in the Crow tongue, Casapy, the Blanket Chief."

That gave the Crow chief something to think about. He thought for quite a while. Then he demanded, "How many men has he?"

Now Meek knew that Bridger's camp contained some 240 men—enough to lick the hindsides off the Crow war party. But he also knew that, if he told the truth as to their numbers, the Crows would high-tail it out of there and take him with them—or kill him. His chances of seeing Bridger again would be almighty slim.

On the other hand, if he lied to the Indians and so encouraged them to go looking for Bridger's camp, it was sartin the Crows would want to kill him when they found he had lied to them. But Meek was one of the bravest of the Mountain Men. He answered: "Forty."

The Crows relaxed. The chief laughed. "We will make them poor," said he, "and you shall live, but they shall die."

Meek thought "Hardly," but kept a poker face and said nothing.

When the chief asked him where he expected to rejoin Bridger's camp, Meek gave him an honest answer and told him how many days before Bridger would reach the appointed place. Meek *wanted* the Crows to find that camp.

So then the Indians began to hustle around, packing up for the march to meet Bridger. Two of them mounted Meek's mule, and the women loaded him down with packs of moccasins stuffed with dried meat. A war party always carried its pemmican packed in new moccasins to save weight, for as fast as the ration was consumed new moccasins were needed to replace those worn out on the march.

Scouts preceded the party. Seventy warriors formed the advance guard. Meek marched with the women and boys in the middle, and the rest of the warriors followed. To amuse themselves, the squaws prodded their captive with sticks to keep him moving, saying over and over again with much laughter, "White man very poor now." Meek was glad there were only three women along to keep poking him.

They traveled till late that night, then camped. The Indians slept in a circle with Meek in the center. He did not sleep very well. All next day they marched in the same manner, Meek keeping his temper with difficulty and saying nothing. That evening they put him to cooking for the party, and again on the third and fourth days.

On that last day, Meek was feeling pretty bad. Bridger was bound to show up soon, and if anything went wrong, he knew the Crows would rub him out.

On that last day the Indian scouts left their horses on the slope of the ridge ahead and crept up to peer over. Right away one of them came running back, mounted his horse, and rode rapidly in a large circle—to indicate a big party of enemies over the ridge. All the warriors sat down, but immediately after the scouts signaled that the white men were going to camp.

Meek could only trust to luck. He understood the signals of the scouts perfectly; now the time had come. They all rode to the top of the hill overlooking the Yellowstone River and the vast plains beyond. About three miles away Meek recognized Bridger's big camp with hundreds of horses grazing about it. His heart beat double-quick about that time, and every once in a while he put his hand to his head to feel if his scalp war still thar. Then Meek saw Bridger's horse guard make the signal which indicated that he had discovered the Injuns. It was the showdown.

Says Meek: "I thought the camp a splendid sight that evening. It made a powerful show to me, who did not expect ever to see it after that day, and it war a fine sight anyway from the hill whar I stood. About 250 men, and women and children in great numbers, and about a thousand horses and mules. Then the beautiful Plain, and the sinking sun; and the herds of buffalo that could not be numbered; and the cedar hills, covered with elk,—I never saw so fine a sight as all that looked to me then!" When he turned his eyes on that savage Crow band and saw the chief standing amazed with his hand over his open mouth, saw the warriors' tomahawks and spears glittering in the sunlight, his heart shrunk up to about half its right size. The chief turned on him with a terrible scowl: "I promised that you should live if you told the truth; but you have told me a great lie."

All the warriors gathered round with their weapons in hand. But Meek knew better than to show any weakness. He kept his eyes fixed on Bridger's horse guard, who was riding up the hill to drive in the horses. This movement distracted the chief and his warriors, and when the horse guard had come to within about 200 yards of the Crows, the chief ordered Meek to yell to him to come to them.

Meek stepped forward and yelled as loud as he could: "Keep off, or you'll be killed. Tell Old Gabe to try to talk with these Injuns and help me get away."

By that time the horse guard was between the Crows and

Bridger's horses. He headed them back to camp on the dead run.

When Jim Bridger got the word that his old compañero Joe Meek was a captive and in danger of death, he wasted no time. After a few questions, he called his leaders together, gave instructions, caught up his rifle, and mounted his big white horse. Then Jim rode out alone until he was within about 300 yards of the war party. There he reined up. Scanning the line of Injuns on the ridge, his eyes caught a familiar figure.

"What tribe are they, Meek?" he shouted.

Meek's yell came, "Crows."

Then Bridger knew how to go ahead. He shouted, "Tell the big chief to send one of his little chiefs to smoke with me."

Jim saw Meek turn to The Bold to translate the message. After a little thought, the Crow chief beckoned Little Gun to go forward and smoke with the Blanket Chief.

Meanwhile Jim, scanning the line of Injuns on the ridge, could see all the warriors openly preparing for a fight, shaking out their war bonnets, which had been carried in taper rawhide cases, stripping the covers from their round shields, painting their faces, straightening their best arrows, loading their guns.

Then Jim saw Little Gun coming, and dismounted. Jim knew the Crow rules of warfare; he began to strip off his clothing. He threw down his hat, pulled off his long-tailed hunting coat, shed his shirt, and kicked off his buckskin leggings until he stood naked in moccasins and breechclout. Little Gun also halted and undressed, laying his weapons ready on top of his buckskins. Then both men, holding their open palms high, walked forward to meet—both naked, so that neither could be carrying a concealed weapon.

As Little Gun came on, Jim saw that he was a big ugly fellow with long hair hanging to his heels and a stiff pompadour smeared with red paint standing high over his painted forehead. Little Gun was strutting. He felt sure that Jim had no heart to attack him, for then Meek would be gone beaver.

When the two men met, they lowered their arms to hug and kiss each other, according to custom. But as they embraced, Bridger took care to stand so that Little Gun's back was turned toward a gully which cut through the ridge a little to one side.

"*Sho-da'-gee,*" said Jim, in hearty welcome—how hearty Little Gun hardly guessed. That Crow war greasy and sweaty and smeared with paint. But Jim kept on hugging him and kissing his ugly face—all the time looking anxiously over the Injun's shoulder, keeping his eyes glued to that gully. It seemed to Jim that he would have to hug that lousy Injun all day before he caught sight of his five armed trappers, who suddenly showed themselves at the end of the gully within easy rifle-shot. Little Gun was cut off and held prisoner. *Wagh!* Bridger did not need to hug him any longer. He turned the Injun loose and quickly stepped back.

The tricked Crows on the ridge howled their anger and dismay, and began to mount their horses and line up for a charge on the five trappers to recover their naked chief. Little Gun heard the yelling, looked round, and saw how he was trapped. Angrily he turned towards Bridger. Jim thought he might try to grab him and use his body as a shield against the bullets until his warriors could ride the trappers down. But before Little Gun or his friends could do anything, one hundred Mountain Men popped out of the gully and came trotting towards Bridger, forming a line to repel the charge. The milling Indians on the ridge hung poised.

The iron was hot. Bridger struck, yelling to Meek, "Tell the chief to send you to me and I will let Little Gun go."

Jim saw Meek turn to the scowling chief. He knew The Bold would give in. Sullenly the Crow said, "I cannot afford to give a chief for one white dog's scalp." Bridger saw Meek making tracks away from the cussed Injuns.

When Meek had safely passed Little Gun's clothes and weapons, Jim gave the Crow the signal to be on his way. Meek and Little Gun kept their eyes skinned, and gave each other a wide berth. And when Meek came up, thar was some *real* huggin', sartin sure. . . .

That evening the Crow chief with forty of his warriors came peacefully into Bridger's camp to make a truce for three moons. The chief explained very plausibly that the Crows had formerly been at war with white men. "But now," he said affably, "we want to be friends with your camp, so that we can all fight together against the wicked Blackfeet, who are everybody's enemies." To make the truce firm, the Crows brought in Meek's mule, his gun *Sally*, and all his plunder. Old Gabe and his Mountain Men sat in a ring with the Crows and gravely smoked that pipe of temporary peace.

But before the Crows left Jim's camp, their chief walked up to Meek, gazed fixedly into his eyes, and said, "Today I give you a new name—*Shiam Shaspusia*, for *you* can out-lie the Crows." [1]

XII
INJUN SCRAPES

WHEN cold weather sent Bridger and his men into winter quarters in the autumn of 1835, they settled down to the usual relaxations. They had nothing much to do but keep their larder full of meat. It was a big camp—more than 500 persons, with all their many horses and mules. Some Delaware Indians camped with them.

One day the Delawares found sign of Blackfoot horse thieves prowling around. The Delawares grinned. They saw a chance to take a scalp or two.

But they had no horses of their own. Without consulting Bridger, they talked some of his men into lending them two good horses, and staked these animals out as decoys to the Blackfeet. Then, lying hidden close by, the Delawares waited. When the thieves crept up to steal the horses, the Delawares shot them, and so got the scalps they were after.

When the Delawares came whooping in with the scalps, bragging of their smart trick, Jim knew there was hell to pay. Quickly he and his men felled trees and built a temporary fort and a corral for their animals. Scarcely had the trappers fortified their position before more than a thousand painted Blackfoot devils appeared, hell-bent to rub them out. For two long days and nights the fight went on. But because of Jim's preparations, and the quality and number of his well-disciplined men, the trappers fought them off successfully with little loss.

When at last the Blackfeet pulled out, Bridger wiped his brow. But his troubles had only begun. He knew that neighborhood was certain to be mighty unhealthy the rest of the winter. The hunters dared not go out to kill meat, and they and their families would starve sitting inside the fort all winter. So, cold as it was, they threw their packs on the mules and their saddles on the horses and moved out from the Big Bend of the Yellowstone in January—much earlier than Bridger had intended. He led them upriver to Crow country, trusting more to his superior fire-power than to his unstable truce with that tribe. To keep the Crows in good humor while he trapped their streams, he made presents to the chiefs and traded with the warriors.

In most communities women set and maintain social standards, and as all women in the trapper camp were Indians, the Mountain Men inevitably conformed in most things to the ways of the squaws. In fact, most of them took pride in their close adaptation to life in the wilderness and were mighty pleased whenever a greenhorn took one of them for a genuwine Injun.

Yet, in spite of this, they were white men with American traditions. Some of them still had at heart a chivalry unknown to unromantic redskins, and pampered their wives in a manner that made Indian women think them far the most eligible men on the Plains. In fact, if there had been enough Mountain Men to trap all the squaws, nary an Injun could have womaned.

Bridger's friend Joe Meek was particularly fond of his handsome Snake woman, whom he called the Mountain Lamb, and spared no beaver when it came to providing her with *fofurraw*. She could have all the fine horses, scarlet cloth, and beads he could lay hands on, and Joe tolerated no affront to her—though she was, in truth, pretty well able to take care of herself.

The trappers governed their camp by very similar rules to those enforced by the Indians in their own camps. One of these rules was that no man should fire a gun within the camp.

One day a bunch of Crows rode in, bringing shaggy buffalo robes to trade for the white man's powder and ball and blood-red nor'west blankets. For some hours the bargaining went on agreeably enough. Then one cheeky young brave, strutting about camp to be admired, passed Meek's squaw sitting outside her lodge, beading a moccasin for her husband. He paraded up and down, hoping for a glance from her. But she, proud wife of a Mountain Man, went deftly on with her embroidery and paid the conceited young Crow no heed. Angered by her indifference, he wished to display his scorn of women in general and of her in particular; he struck her with his quirt.

Meek was in her lodge and saw the blow struck. His gun was handy. A second later he pulled the trigger: *tchow*— and the warrior fell dead.

Confusion swept the camp. Women and children scattered, taking to the brush. The men ran, grasping their weapons, taking cover wherever they might find it. Indians and whites fired back and forth among the tipis. Two or three Crows went down; one of the trappers was killed.

Finally Bridger, by heroic efforts, asserted his authority and managed a truce; the angry Crows pulled out, the camp was quiet.

Disgusted, Old Gabe went round to Meek's lodge. "Well, you raised a hell of a row in camp," Bridger complained.

"Very sorry; but couldn't help it. No devil of an Indian shall strike Meek's wife."

"But you got a man killed."

"Sorry for the man; couldn't help it, though, Bridger."

Jim shook his head. The fat was in the fire. Like as not the Crows would gather reinforcements soon and come yelling back to avenge their dead warriors. Again Bridger struck camp and hit the trail.

They followed the Big Horn and the Little Big Horn, on through Wind River Valley and South Pass to Green River.

There a few Nez Percés turned up. They complained to Bridger that the Bannocks had stolen their horses. They asked his help.

Old Gabe knew well enough that he must cooperate with

his Injun allies, and without delay granted the request, manned an expedition, and recovered the stolen animals.

The Bannocks were on a hunt at this time. When they learned that the horses they had appropriated were now in the camp of the Blanket Chief, they lined up, fired a few guns, and charged through it. Indian enemies ordinarily sneaked up in silence, but friendly Indians always came yelling and emptying their guns in token of peaceful intentions. This time, apparently, the Bannocks had a divided mind. They wanted to reconnoiter the camp and see if their horses were in it as well as to show off their own courage and, if possible, intimidate Bridger's men.

Alert to the danger, Jim stepped out of his tipi and stood there with his rifle on his arm, holding his horse by its lariat, ready to mount, and also to keep it from being stampeded by the yelling savages.

The horse was a fine one; the Nez Percés had given it to him for his help in recovering their stolen stock.

When the Bannock chief rode into the trapper camp and saw Jim holding the very horse which he himself had taken from the Nez Percés, his resentment got the better of his judgment. Quirting his warhorse forward, he insolently urged it over the lariat, jerking that out of Jim's hand.

Jim might have let the challenge pass, not wishing to have another fight in the middle of his camp; but his Negro cook, furious at that insult to his Booshway, instantly threw up his rifle and shot the chief dead.

In the fracas that followed, one of the Bannocks put an arrow through the heart of Meek's wife.

Startled by the fall of their chief, the Bannocks were all in confusion. Jim lost no time in taking advantage of that. He and his men quickly mounted and drove the Bannocks before them back to their own village, through and out of it, herding them onto an island in the river. Then, surrounding the island, the trappers kept up a hot fire until dark. All night they hung round listening, not without satisfaction, to the continual wailing that came over the water.

As soon as it was light, they saw an old woman walking out of the brush, holding aloft a peace pipe. "You have killed all our warriors," she said; "do you now want to kill the women? If you wish to smoke with women, I have the pipe."

Well, there was no use fighting any longer—and no point in smoking with women. The trappers mounted and rode away. They had taught the Bannocks a lesson. It would be a long time before those Injuns would meddle with the Mountain Men. . . .

At rendezvous Jim learned that Fitzpatrick, bringing supplies from the settlements, had already reached Independence Rock. Captain Stuart and Dr. Whitman with two white ladies were in the party. The coming of two "real white women" caused a great sensation among the Mountain Men, many of whom had not seen a white woman in ten years' time. They put on their best bib and tucker and rode out Indian-fashion, charging the camp of the newcomers in line and firing their guns—but politely carrying a white flag in order not to alarm the ladies by this military demonstration.

All the while Mrs. Spalding and Mrs. Whitman were in camp, they were the center of attention, and no work was done until they had departed on their way to the Columbia River. . . .

As early as 1833 John Jacob Astor had foreseen the decline of the beaver trade. He wrote at that time from London, "I very much fear beaver will not sell well very soon unless very fine. It appears that they make hats out of silk in place of beaver."

As we have seen, Astor sold the American Fur Company to some gentlemen in St. Louis about the time Wyeth's affidavit put Kenneth McKenzie out of business. The new owners still called Astor's firm by its old name, the American Fur Company.

It was reorganized to compete with the Hudson's Bay Company, which was now—thanks to Wyeth—firmly established at Fort Hall.

Jim Bridger and his comrades in the mountains probably could not know the reason for Astor's retirement from the fur trade, but they already had a hunch that the beaver trade was going to the dogs. Beaver were not so easily found as before; prices were steadily going down. It seemed best to combine forces with the American Fur Company, and about this time Bridger and his partners merged with the St. Louis outfit. They were all a little humiliated by having to work for their former hated rivals. It was decided that Bridger and Fontenelle would be the partisans leading the fur brigade in the mountains; Drips took over the job of packing out the goods from the settlements to rendezvous and carrying the furs back to St. Louis.

Bridger's men had another scrape with the Blackfeet on their way to the headwaters of Yellowstone River, at Hell Gate Pass, but about Christmas they encamped on the Powder River.

That camp on Powder River was a wild one. According to Meek, "there never was a winter camp in the mountains more thoroughly demoralized than that of Bridger during the months of January and February. Added to the whites, who were reckless enough, there were a considerable party of Delaware and Shawnee Indians, excellent allies, and skillful hunters and trappers, but having the Indians' love for strong drink."

After the Indians had drunk themselves into poverty, they were naturally enraged with the traders who had sold them the liquor. The Mountain Men, too, were well liquored up and up to no good.

Nearby was a fort belonging to Captain Bonneville which had been left in charge of Antoine Montero.

Bonneville had unwisely indulged in sharp criticism of the Mountain Men, their character and ways. Now they were in a mood for revenge. Bonneville's company was in competition with Bridger's men. The trappers set out to make life miserable for Montero, his employee.

The first thing was to get rid of his livestock. Using an old Indian trick, the trappers herded their own animals to graze close around Montero's fort until all the grass was gone there. Montero was forced to send his own horses and mules to a distance to find pasture, and it was then no trick at all for the Mountain Men and Indians to stampede them, run them off, and leave Montero afoot. Having got away with his animals, they all went to work on what remained of the property. When the winter was over, Montero had little more left than the clothes he stood in. His handful of Frenchmen did not care to risk their skins to save the goods in Bonneville's warehouse.

The Mountain Men thought Montero had only got his just deserts, but while they were running wild on Powder River, their partisan Fontenelle went down to Fort Laramie. There, perhaps inspired by their saturnalia on Powder River, he committed suicide, so Meek says, "in a fit of *mania a potu!*"

When spring came, Bridger was glad to leave the Powder. He headed for Blackfoot country to trap the headwaters of the Yellowstone. There, in the high altitudes, winter hung on into the spring and beaver fur remained prime much later than in other regions. Near Henry's Lake he found the trail of a large Blackfoot camp, traveling fast—a trail marked at frequent intervals by the bodies of dead or dying Injuns, stricken with smallpox. The Blackfeet were running away from that dread scourge.

Following the trail, Bridger's advance party ran into a Blackfoot rear guard of 150 men. Beyond it they could see a big camp. They jumped the Injuns, but were outflanked and driven off.

That night Bridger laid his plans. Somehow or other he had to get round that big Blackfoot village. They were enemies, and their camp was full of smallpox. It was impossible to make peace. These Injuns, Jim discovered, were members of the Siksika tribe—close allies of their numerous kinsmen, the Piegans and the Bloods.

Next day Jim's main camp caught up with the advance guard. The fight was renewed.

But this time the Injuns were far more numerous, having fallen back nearly to their own main camp.

Bridger's problem was to keep the warriors busy in the valley while he led his pack train along the high bluff overlooking it. Bridger's mounted men charged the Blackfeet furiously, but the Indians had been reinforced, and the battle surged back and forth. Riding to and fro, they broke up their lines into little groups. It was every man for himself and the devil take the hindmost. At times the Indians swept the trappers back; at others the trappers had the Indians going.

When Cotton Mansfield's horse fell, he dropped his rifle; the horse lay on his leg, while half a dozen Indians ran yelling to get his scalp. He gave himself up for lost and yelled out, "Tell Old Gabe that old Cotton is gone!"

Kit Carson heard, turned, fired, and dropped the leading

warrior, frightening the others off. Kit saved Mansfield, who dashed away.

A moment later Kit's horse threw him. His single-shot rifle was empty. Kit was ready to holler himself, but Cotton was nowhere to be seen. Luckily, White rode past, reached out his hand, and swung Kit up behind his saddle.

Doc Newell shot a warrior and rode up to scalp him. Jumping from the saddle, he grabbed the Indian's long thick hair in one hand and, pulling out his knife with the other, made a pass at the scalp. Just then the dead Indian jumped up and pulled his own knife. It was a question of whose scalp would be taken.

Newell was ready to settle for a place in his saddle and let the scalp lock go, but the Indian's hair was decorated with gun screws and somehow these tangled Doc's fingers in the hair so that he could not let go. The Indian had both hands free and a butcher knife ready in one of them. But Doc was quick-witted. He saw that his only chance lay in running, dragging the Indian after him by the hair. In this way he finally got the best of the Blackfoot, stabbed him, and took his scalp.

"Still the fight went on, the trappers gradually working their way to the upper end of the enclosed part of the valley past the point of danger." [1]

It was in this fracas that the famous painter of Indians, John Mix Stanley, saw Meek firing from the saddle, a scene he afterwards made the subject of that well-known painting The Trapper's Last Shot.[2]

In reality, after firing his last shot, Meek kicked his horse into top speed and overtook his comrades.

But the Blackfeet were still unsatisfied with the result of the contest. They followed after, reinforced from the village, and attacked the camp. In the fight which followed, a Black-

foot woman's horse was shot down, and Meek tried to take
her prisoner: but two or three of her people coming to the
rescue, engaged his attention; and the woman was saved by
seizing hold of the tail of her husband's horse, which, setting
off at a run, carried her out of danger.

"The Blackfeet found the camp of Bridger too strong for
them. They were severely beaten and compelled to retire to
their village, leaving Bridger free to move on." [3]

Having safely got around the big Blackfoot camp, Bridger
scarcely had time to catch his breath before he discovered the
village of Little Robe, one of the Piegan chiefs, lying squarely
in his path.

Little Robe held parley with the Blanket Chief and made
a long speech full of complaints, blaming the whites for the
smallpox which was destroying his people.

But Bridger had the answer to that charge. He told Little
Robe how Jim Beckwourth, a mulatto who had been adopted
into the Crow tribe and become one of their chiefs, had done
this evil thing. Beckwourth, Jim said, had traded two infected blankets from his Mackinaw boat to the Blackfeet—
blankets brought up from St. Louis. That was how they
caught it. Bridger pointed out with emphasis that Beckwourth was not only a chief of the enemy Crows, but he was
a Negro, and therefore *not* a white man.

Little Robe gravely considered the words of the Blanket
Chief and found them good. "I take your words," he said,
and offered to trade. He had horses and buffalo robes; and
so, when the swapping was over, the two camps parted ami-
cably.

But Jim's unhappy men were growling and grumbling.
Their partisan Fontenelle had gone under, and so the annual
supplies had been delayed. There was not even one small
plug of tobacco in the whole hankering camp.

The trappers had long ago stopped dreaming of bread and butter. They could go without sugar and coffee and liquor on the trail. When game was scarce they could starve for meat two or three days, tighten their belts, and let it pass. But the honing for tobacco was not so easily conquered, not so easily forgotten. Everybody, including Jim Bridger, was in ill humor because of this critical shortage of their greatest luxury. Even the French trappers, usually so cheerful, were now sullen and savage. Their hearts were bad.

Next day Bridger's brigade camped astride the trail which ran along the river. That evening Jim was resting while his wife put her kettle on the little cooking fire outside the small traveling tipi when he heard a commotion among the lodges. Men were swarming out of them, running towards the river trail, all of them packing their rifles, there to form a milling mob. Jim jumped up, mounted his horse, and kicked it into a run to see what was up.

As he neared the crowd, he could see the heads of mounted Indians and the crossed ends of the poles of a travois raking the sky above the shoulders of a pack-horse.

It was a lone Blackfoot warrior, followed by his wife and daughter, his pack-horses and lodge poles, his slinking dogs. There they sat, these three enemies, rigid with fright, spang in the middle of the trapper camp.

"The damn fool," someone was saying, "he sure put his foot into a trap this time."

"Keel heem, keel heem," yelled a Frenchman, setting his triggers.

"Save the women," one laughed, and was promptly answered, "To hell with the women! Maybeso he's got some *tobacco*."

Jim forced his horse forward, shouldering through the crowd until he was alongside the Blackfoot. He saw then what had happened. The foolish Blackfoot, seeing Jim's tipis on the trail, had headed in among them, supposing they belonged to his own tribe. When he realized his mistake, it had been too late to run, and so he had hurried on into the middle of the camp—thus throwing himself upon the mercy of the Mountain Men. He must have hoped that they had rules such as the Blackfeet had against killing people in camp.

Jim knew there was scarcely a man in his camp but had a personal grudge against the Blackfeet, hardly a man but had lost comrades to their arrows; not a man but had often been forced to run for his life from them or lie awake all night in hiding, or been put afoot when his horse was stolen. To them this helpless enemy was like a beaver in a trap, something to be knocked in the head. The Blackfeet had killed their women. Moreover, their captive was packing a long, fringed pipe bag. *Tobacco!* Here was sweet revenge.

Before the killers could act, Old Gabe called out, "Joe, Kit, Doc—git around these yere Injuns. I reckon we'll have no killin' in my camp."

As Carson, Meek, and Newell rode to his side, surrounding the frightened Blackfeet, Jim ordered the crowd to disperse. "Git back now. These folks came into camp in peace. If you want to shoot Blackfeet, thar's plenty of 'em not so fur away."

His eyes ranged over those hundreds of angry faces. He added, slapping the butt of his rifle, "If you want to kill these yere Injuns, you'll have to kill me fust!"

The crowd stood silent, motionless—uncertain. Before anyone could speak out, Bridger signed to Meek to take hold of the bridle reins of the woman's horse. Kit took those of the man, and the two of them headed out of camp, the scared girl following closely. Bridger rode behind, never deigning to look back at the angry, disappointed mob.

On they rode past the last tipi, on along the triple lodge trail. Nobody had anything to say. When they had convoyed the Blackfeet out of rifle range safely away from camp, Bridger halted that little cavalcade. Kit and Joe returned the reins of the horses to their unwilling guests. The women raised and lowered their open palms in the stroking gesture of blessing.

Then Meek, with one eye on the Blackfoot's long, fringed pipe-bag, plied his fingers in the graphic sign language, demanding, as some little return for saving the cussed Injuns' lives, a present of tobacco. He hoped for the whole bag.

Maybeso that Blackfoot warrior was ashamed of being rescued, ashamed of his folly in riding into an enemy camp— something he would never hear the last of. Maybe he was as stingy as he was foolish. He was not in a position to argue the matter, but still he would not surrender the bag. Very grudgingly he shared his tobacco with the three Mountain Men.

Old Gabe and his compañeros were plumb disgusted. All they got for their bother was hardly enough for two chaws!

XIII
THE LAST RENDEZVOUS

TRAPPING in and around Yellowstone Park, Jim made his spring hunt and then led his men through Two Ocean Pass to the valley of Wind River for the rendezvous that summer of '37. It was a pretty slim affair. Few of the trappers had much beaver to trade, and the camp was quiet, with much less drinking and gambling than had been usual at fur fairs in the mountains.

However, it was much enlivened by the coming of Dr. W. H. Gray, a missionary to the Flatheads, who came bringing four white women—also missionaries. And every night the Shawnees and Delawares danced their great war dance before the tents of the missionaries, while the trappers joined in, *hi-ya*-ing and prancing in the best Injun style.

Sir William Drummond Stuart, back from St. Louis with a new outfit, was also in camp. He was a veteran of Waterloo, an officer of the Guards, and had brought with him his cuirass and helmet—curious equipment for Indian fighting. Joe Meek, inspired by the presence of the ladies, borrowed Sir William's armor and paraded about the encampment on horseback; the shining cuirass and the tall helmet with its dangling horse-tail made him the admiration of the Indians —if not of the ladies.[1]

Sir William's artist, Alfred J. Miller, made many spot sketches in watercolor and afterward several large romantic paintings of the scenes on the trail and at this rendezvous * —not forgetting the irrepressible Meek and his warlike habiliments.

The following winter Jim camped with the Crows' on the Powder, and in '38 again made tracks for the Yellowstone and the headwaters of the Missouri. He was irresistibly attracted to that high beautiful country so rich in furs. He wintered on Green River.

Early in '39 Jim went to St. Louis. There he found little to please him. He had been too long in the mountains. Store

* A portfolio of these sketches, in color, was recently (January, 1944) published in *Fortune*. Miller's sketches, journal, and notes will shortly appear, I understand, between the covers of a book (Houghton Mifflin Co.) compiled by Mrs. Clyde Porter and Bernard De Voto. One of these sketches shows Bridger, mounted, on a hill overlooking the rendezvous at Green River.

clothes were stiff, itchy, and uncomfortable after his soft buckskins, his long hair felt hot tucked up into the crown of his beaver hat, and the store boots with which he had replaced his moccasins "choked his feet like hell." Before the end of May he was on a steamboat with nearly a hundred others and his young friend Jim Baker, heading for the mountains. A further journey by keelboat brought him to a landing where he packed his goods in carts and put out up the South Platte to the Laramie Plains.

There Jim Bridger ran into the cussed Injuns "thick as bees" and was repeatedly held up by big bands. But every time he talked them out of fighting and went on his way. Baker records: "Thanks be to James Bridger for our safety, because I learned then and later of his great knowledge of, and ability to treat with, the redskins, which was never excelled by any scout of the Plains."

Crossing South Pass, Jim moved on to Horse Creek and made camp on Green River, that clear, rippling streamlet full of trout, just two miles above the mouth of Horse Creek, and not far from Captain Bonneville's fort.

Jim must have felt in his bones that this would be the last rendezvous of trappers in the mountains. He was only thirty-five years old, yet the beaver trade was finished. His occupation gone, he must have felt a nostalgic pleasure in this last reunion of his kind.

The tipis of the trappers and the Indians extended up and down the right bank of the river for about a mile on the edge of a three-mile plain of sandy loam, a grassy bottom, long familiar to all Mountain Men.

There he could stretch out beside the fire, smoking his pipe, dreaming of the past—and of the uncertain future. Squaws, riding discreetly in pairs, dressed in their best garnished and fringed buckskins, with red blankets, and silk kerchiefs on their heads, on rawhide saddles with high curving pommels and cantles, passed by with chinking, clashing sleighbells on their saddlery. But these, for all their finery, were none the less able to pitch a tent, saddle a pack-horse, or roast the sizzling *boudins* on the hot coals. Some old herald would be stalking among the tipis, stretching his lungs to sound off in his high-pitched, far-carrying crier's voice, broadcasting news, orders of the chiefs, jokes, and moral lectures. Old men smoked under the trees, children played in the river, old women scraped hides or carried firewood on their stooping shoulders, young lovers stood conversing on the prairie, wrapped in the anonymity of a borrowed blanket.

There were plenty of old friends of the Blanket Chief in camp—Snakes, Flatheads, and Nez Percés—and old compañeros of the beaver trail in their blackened buckskins fringed with Indian hair. These brought their scanty packs of furs to trade, only to find that prime beaver had gone down from $6.00 to $4.00 the plew or less—though goods from the settlements still sold at the same outrageous mountain prices:

Meal, one pint	$. 50 to $1.00
Coffee beans, one pint	$2.00
Cocoa beans, one pint	$1.00
Sugar, one pint	$2.00
Diluted alcohol, one pint	$4.00
Chewing tobacco, one plug	$2.00

More essential commodities such as guns, powder and ball, flints, bear traps, beaver traps, blankets, handkerchiefs, and all kinds of *fofurraw* sold at enormous profits. They were all paid for with those hairy bank notes furnished by the elusive beaver. And this at a time when the best dinner in the States could be had for fifty cents!

In the old days at rendezvous trappers had lived like lords while their beaver lasted—feasting to the sweet aroma of coffee and boiled chocolate, delicious inhalations of honeydew tobacco, heady fumes of alcohol. In the old days Jim had often seen a single trapper blow a thousand dollars. But now the days of their glory were past. Beaver were scarce, prices were going down. Too many companies were in the field, too many trading forts, too many free trappers, too many hostile Injuns—too many cussed silk hats in the settlements!

At that last rendezvous there was little drinking of spirits and almost no gambling or pony racing. Even the greenhorns realized that the day of the trapper was over.

Only the Indians had the heart to gamble, chanting together as they played the hand game—that primitive version of *Button, button, who's got the button.* All night they played, singing their lusty, taunting tunes, trying to guess in which of the weaving hands of their opponent the button was hidden.

Jim had heard those songs until he could have sung them himself. In many a camp he had heard that thump of tom-toms and that *swish-swish* of rattles where some group of men were singing songs to give them success in hunting or on the warpath. All that was familiar enough to his ears.

He saw the traders lay out everything in their packs for inspection by their customers. When all was ready, Injuns gathered to bargain for powder and lead, for Green River knives, plug tobacco, vermilion, gay silk handkerchiefs and cotton bandanas, pocket mirrors, beads and bells, until their horses and hides and robes had all been swapped. Then the warriors had nothing to do but lie in the shade on their faces, with their heads in the lap of a wife or grandmother who devoted herself by the hour to scouting through her loved one's hair to catch the lice and crack them with her yellow teeth.

The trappers' pony races, the games of Old Sledge played for high stakes, the shooting-matches and carousing—it was all the old thing which Jim had seen a thousand times and now would see no more.[2]

For the next three or four years, Bridger wandered around, trying this and that—restlessly uncertain what his future work might be. Sometimes we lose sight of him altogether, or catch mere glimpses of him in camp on Henry's Fork, or at the fort of his old compañeros Vasquez and Sublette on Cache la Poudre, or on the trail with White Head Fitzpatrick.

If ever he visited the site of some former rendezvous on Wind River or Green River, he found it lonesome and deserted.

We know from the letters [3] of Father Pierre Jean de Smet that Bridger saw him on Clark's Fork. De Smet, marveling that Jim could for years have carried an arrowhead in his body, asked him if the wound had been long suppurating. The good Father records Jim's humorous reply, "In the mountains meat never spoils."

It began to look as if Jim's days in the mountains were numbered—a prospect which made him uneasy as a gutshot coyote. The mountains war whar he belonged, and you kin lay to that. That war his idee. But gnawing at the back of his brain with all the painful persistence of an iron point buried in his flesh was the question whether or not a man of his responsibilities and ambitions could afford to stay there. He had his daughter's schooling to pay for, his kinfolks in Missouri to think of. Jim was no pork-eating Frenchman, willing to work for less than his keep. He had been a chief and a partisan too long for that.

He saw how it would be. Each year he would go back to

the settlements—each year to stay a little longer—until at last
he'd have put his foot square in the trap and could never
get loose at all! Yonder in the settlements he could go back
to blacksmithing or run one of them newfangled ferryboats.
Maybeso. But the notion of settling down once for all and
sleeping under a roof with nary a taste of buffalo marrow
made him sick all over. Jim's stick simply wouldn't float
thataway. *Wagh*!

But for the present, he had little time to worry. Irrespon-
sible friends and hostile Injuns kept Old Gabe plenty busy.

Sioux and Cheyennes from east of the mountains were on
the warpath in Snake country, boastfully determined to wipe
out all white men and enemy tribes. The smallpox scourge
along the Missouri had almost annihilated the village tribes
in 1837-38, had decimated the Blackfeet, and crippled other
savage nations to the east and north. Now the Sioux and
their allies were free to turn their full force against the mountain tribes to the west. That summer of '41 buffalo were
scarce on the Plains. Sioux, Cheyenne, Arapaho, had strung
their big camps along Yampa River and were busy making
meat, getting ready for the war to follow.

Bridger's old partner, Henry Fraeb, went boldly to those
hostile camps, trading contraband whisky for Sioux jerky.
It war a turrible spree. Therefore, though not getting enough
meat for his own camp, Fraeb quickly made his getaway,
heading for the buffalo pastures, leaving a few white men
with their Injun wives and children and a parcel of Shoshone
warriors at his camp on the Little Snake.

After their debauch, the Cheyenne and Sioux found all
their hunting had to be done over again. Their meat was
gone, and all they had for their labor was a mean hang-over.
They blamed Fraeb for their poverty. Now that he had
escaped them, the horses left in his camp offered compensa-

tion for the loss of their dried meat. Besides, those Shoshones were enemies.

This was all the excuse needed. The fact that a few white men were in the camp was hardly considered. Indeed, as in most Indian wars where white men were involved, the tribesmen, consumed with hatred of their ancestral enemies, hardly gave the white men a thought.

Soon after, the men in the Snake camp went off hunting. The Sioux and Cheyenne attacked and ran off all the horses without the loss of a man. The women and children saved themselves by taking to the brush at the first alarm. . . .

When Bridger learned of this raid, he sent Jim Baker and a few others to warn Fraeb. By the time they caught up with the "Dutchman," a scouting party brought news of another brush with the same Indians.

Old Gabe advised Fraeb to clear out of that dangerous region and join forces with him on Henry's Fork. "Too many Injuns" was the word.

But Fraeb was stubborn as he was confident. He bared his yellow teeth: "Ve vill see who dis country belongs to yet."

Of course Fraeb had been in the mountains with Old Gabe too many years not to respect his warning. He sent his women and children into hiding on Squaw Mountain, and then started to build a fort or corral of logs to protect his men and animals. Next day, the 21st of August, the hostiles charged his camp, shooting down his horses, while his trappers rallied and tried to hold them off.

Jim Baker said, "It was the hardest fight I was ever in."

It lasted all day. Baker reports: "The Indians made about forty charges on us, coming up to within ten or fifteen paces every time. Their object was to draw our fire, but old Frapp * kept shouting, 'Don't shoot till you're sure. One at

* Fraeb.

a time!' And so some of us kept loaded all the time. We made breastworks of our horses and hid behind stumps. Old Frapp was killed, and he was the ugliest-looking dead man I ever saw, and I have seen a good many. His face was all covered with blood, and he had rotten teeth and a horrible grin. When he was killed, he never fell, but sat braced up against the stump, a sight to behold." [4]

Finally the Sioux rode away. Over a hundred head of horses had been lost in the fight, and of the forty-five head left alive, only five were unhurt. Fraeb and three white men had been killed and at least as many Snakes. Baker and the other trappers brought in their women and children from Squaw Mountain, hastily cached their belongings on the battlefield, and hit the trail for Old Gabe's camp. It had been one of the fiercest fights in all the bloody history of the mountains.

Old Gabe must have been tempted to say, "I told you so." Instead he gave his friends a new stake, doctored their wounds, made room for them in his crowded lodges. Then he led a pack train to the battlefield and brought home the meat and property they had cached there.

Next spring Fraeb's men and White Head Fitzpatrick hit the trail for Fort Laramie. Bridger rode with them—back towards the cussed settlements, away from the mountains he loved. Everything seemed to be pushing him eastward, while every inch of the man ached to head west.

Once the mountains had been all his, full of beaver and sport and good living, comradeship, authority, wealth. Once he had owned hundreds of horses, had been booshway of great camps, had been—in fact—a great chief, feared, loved, admired.

Now he was poor, lonesome, and—if he went on thisaway —he'd be lucky if he didn't turn up sick, too. Just about everything that could plague a man was on his trail, and he couldn't see nowhar to make tracks to. Like a man caught in a prairie-fire, he was plumb surrounded. For a long time Jim had worried over the collapsing business of the American Fur Company.

But now he fretted about a far more urgent problem: since the fur trade had played out, *what* could he do with *himself?*

3

TRADER

XIV
FORT BRIDGER

CAREFUL as always, however troubled in his mind, Old Gabe led the party by a roundabout route through the Black Hills, and so avoided the Sioux war parties.

On the North Platte, Bridger's outfit ran into part of Colonel John C. Frémont's expedition under the command of Charles Preuss, Frémont's topographer. As Bridger's men rode over the ridge, they threw a big scare into those greenhorns, who at first mistook them for raiding Sioux.

That evening the two parties camped together. Frémont was about to head into the country from which Bridger and White Head had come. So Preuss invited Jim to supper, and after the tablecloth was removed, listened with eager interest to his account of the Mountain Men's adventures.

While Bridger was answering questions at his host's table, White Head and the other trappers were being cross-examined by Frémont's men. What the trappers told them kept those poor greenhorns up all night, sitting uneasily around their campfires, smoking, stretching their ears to hear about terrifying Injun scrapes, all narrated with great particularity of bloody detail. The trappers' stories fairly shook their hearts.

What Bridger himself had to tell was bad enough. Sioux, Cheyenne, Gros Ventres were scouring the upper country in great force. Even now they lay encamped directly in Frémont's path—at Red Buttes. Old Gabe said the cussed Injuns had declared war on every living critter west of the Buttes. But mainly they aimed to jump a big camp of whites and Snakes on Sweetwater. Jim offered to guide Preuss and his men to the head of Sweetwater. Jim's eyes shone—that war back towards the mountains! But as Frémont, the booshway, was not on hand, Preuss could not accept the tempting offer. Bridger wished Preuss and his booshway luck.

Next morning it looked as though Frémont were going to need it. His men were all in low spirits. Green as they were, they had no heart for traipsin' into hostile Sioux country. That very spring, they heard, two other small parties had been cut off by the Sioux: one in the Black Hills; the other on the trail from Crow country. It all added up to a terrifying prospect . . . Most of them were "strongly disposed" to turn back.

Bridger found Frémont at the fort.

Fort Laramie was, in those days, the principal trading post on the Oregon Trail—a quadrangular building of adobe bricks, with walls fifteen feet high surmounted by a wooden palisade. These outer walls formed the back of ranges of rooms surrounding a courtyard some 130 feet square. All doors and windows, of course, opened into this yard. At the rear there was a small postern. Opposite this was the main gate under a square tower with loopholes where a brass cannon mounted guard. At two opposite corners of the fort blockhouses projected boldly from the walls so that defenders there could sweep all four sides of the fort. That summer of 1842 Bordeaux was in charge, with two clerks and sixteen *engagés*.

Of course, as a member of the American Fur Company, Bridger made himself at home in Fort Laramie.

In summer the courtyard was none too cool. And so the trader and his clerks sat all day in the shady, floored entranceway, a sort of dog-run or tunnel 15 feet long under the great tower, through which the breeze swept constantly.

There Bridger warned Frémont of the dangers ahead. Kit Carson, Frémont's guide, fully supported Jim's opinion of the dangerous state of the country, and openly declared his conviction that they could not escape without some sharp encounters with the Indians. It looked to Bridger as if Frémont war a leetle mite mad at Kit for speaking out thataway. But when Kit Carson up and made his will, Jim saw that Frémont war gettin' his dander up sure enough. For when Kit Carson made his will, all Frémont's Frenchmen were skeert half to death.

It hardly surprised Bridger when Frémont hired Fitzpatrick as his guide for next year!

While Jim sat in the gate advising Frémont, he had an experience which was to change the whole course of his life, mark an epoch in Western history, and create a brand new industry which still flourishes all over the mountains. To the men in the fort it was nothing out of the way—only a big nuisance. But Bridger had better eyes than most men, and what he saw set his moccasins on a new trail.

His experience was closely parallel to that of Francis Parkman on the same spot four years later. Let Parkman tell it:

"We were sitting, on the following morning, in the passage-way between the gates, conversing with the traders Vasquez and May. These two men, together with our sleek friend, the clerk Monthalon, were, I believe, the only persons then in the fort who could read and write. May was telling a curious story about the traveler Catlin, when an ugly, diminutive Indian, wretchedly mounted, came up at a gallop, and rode past us into the fort. On being questioned, he said that Smoke's village was close at hand. Accordingly only a few minutes elapsed before the hills beyond the river were covered with a disorderly swarm of savages, on horseback and on foot. May finished his story; and by that time the whole array had descended to Laramie Creek, and begun to cross it in a mass. I walked down to the bank. The stream is wide, and was then between three and four feet deep, with a very swift current. For several rods the water was alive with dogs, horses, and Indians. The long poles used in erecting the lodges are carried by the horses, fastened by the heavier end, two or three on each side, to a rude sort of pack-saddle, while the other end drags on the ground. About a foot behind the horse, a kind of large basket or pannier is suspended between the poles, and firmly lashed in its place. On the back of the horse are piled various articles of luggage; the basket also is well filled with domestic utensils, or, quite as often, with a litter of puppies, a brood of small children, or a superannuated old man. Numbers of these curious vehicles, *traineaux,* or, as called in the bastard language of the country, *travaux,* were now splashing together through the stream. Among them swam countless dogs, often burdened with miniature *traineaux;* and dashing forward on horseback through the throng came the superbly formed warriors, the slender figure of some lynx-eyed boy clinging fast behind them. The women sat perched on the pack-saddles, adding not a little to the load of the already over-burdened horses. The confusion was prodigious. The dogs yelled and howled in chorus; the puppies in the *traineaux* set up a dismal whine as the water invaded their comfortable retreat; the little black-eyed children, from one year of age upward, clung fast with both hands to the edge of their basket, and looked over in alarm at the water rushing so near them, sputtering and making wry mouths as it splashed against their faces. Some of the dogs, encumbered by their load, were carried down the current, yelping piteously; and the old squaws would rush into the water, seize their favorites by the neck, and drag them out. As each horse gained the bank, he scrambled up as he could. Stray horses and colts came among the rest, often breaking away at full speed through the crowd, followed by the old hags, screaming after their fashion on all occasions of excitement. Buxom young squaws, blooming in all the charms of vermilion, stood here and there on the bank, holding aloft their master's lance, as a signal to collect the scattered portions of his household. In a few moments the crowd melted away; each family, with its horses and equipage, filing off to the plain at the rear of the fort; and here, in the space of half an hour, arose sixty or seventy of their tapering lodges. Their horses were feeding by hundreds over the surrounding prairie, and their dogs were roaming everywhere. The fort was full of men, and the children were whooping and yelling incessantly under the walls.

"These newcomers were scarcely arrived, when Bordeaux ran across the fort, shouting to his squaw to bring him his spy-glass. The obedient Marie, the very model of a squaw, produced the instrument, and Bordeaux hurried with it to the wall. Pointing it to the eastward, he exclaimed, with an oath, that the families were coming. But a few minutes elapsed before the heavy caravan of the emigrant wagons could be seen, steadily advancing from the hills. They gained the river, and, without turning or pausing, plunged in, passed through, and slowly ascending the opposing bank, kept directly on their way by the fort and the Indian village, until, gaining a spot a quarter of a mile distant, they wheeled into a circle. For some time our tranquillity was undisturbed. The emigrants were preparing their encampment; but no sooner was this accomplished, than Fort Laramie was fairly taken by storm. A crowd of broad brimmed hats, thin visages, and staring eyes appeared suddenly at the gate. Tall, awkward men, in brown homespun; women, with cadaverous faces and long lank figures, came thronging in together, and, as if inspired by the very demon of curiosity, ransacked every nook and corner of the fort. Dismayed at this invasion, we withdrew in all speed to our chamber, vainly hoping that it might prove a sanctuary. The emigrants prosecuted their investigations with untiring vigor. They penetrated the rooms, or rather dens, inhabited by the astonished squaws. They explored the apartments of the men, and even that of Marie and the *bourgeois*. At last a numerous deputation appeared at our door, but found no encouragement to remain.

"Being totally devoid of any sense of delicacy or propriety, they seemed resolved to search every mystery to the bottom. . . .

"The emigrants felt a violent prejudice against the French Indians, as they called the trappers and traders. They thought, and with some reason, that these men bore them no goodwill. Many of them were firmly persuaded that the French were instigating the Indians to attack and cut them off. On visiting the encampment we were at once struck with the extraordinary perplexity and indecision that prevailed among the emigrants. They seemed like men totally out of their element; bewildered and amazed, like a troop of schoolboys lost in the woods. It was impossible to be long among them without being conscious of the high and bold spirit with which most of them were animated. But the *forest* is the home of the backwoodsman. On the remote prairie he is totally at a loss. He differs as much from the genuine 'moun-

tain man,' the wild prairie hunter, as a Canadian voyageur,
paddling his canoe on the rapids of the Ottawa, differs from
an American sailor among the storms of Cape Horn. Still
my companion and I were somewhat at a loss to account for
this perturbed state of mind. It could not be cowardice: these
men were of the same stock with the volunteers of Monterey
and Buena Vista. Yet, for the most part, they were the rud-
est and most ignorant of the frontier population; they knew
absolutely nothing of the country and its inhabitants; they
had already experienced much misfortune, and apprehended
more; they had seen nothing of mankind, and had never put
their own resources to the test.

"A full proportion of suspicion fell upon us. Being
strangers, we were looked upon as enemies. Having occasion
for a supply of lead and a few other necessary articles, we
used to go over to the emigrant camps to obtain them. After
some hesitation, some dubious glances, and fumbling of the
hands in the pockets, the terms would be agreed upon, the
price tendered, and the emigrant would go off to bring the
article in question. After waiting until our patience gave
out, we would go in search of him, and find him seated on the
tongue of his wagon.

" 'Well, stranger,' he would observe, as he saw us approach,
'I reckon I won't trade.'

"Some friend of his had followed him from the scene of
the bargain, and whispered in his ear that clearly we meant
to cheat him, and he had better have nothing to do with us.

"This timorous mood of the emigrants was doubly unfor-
tunate, as it exposed them to real danger. Assume, in the
presence of Indians, a bold bearing, self-confident yet vigi-
lant, and you will find them tolerably safe neighbors. But
your safety depends on the respect and fear you are able to
inspire. If you betray timidity or indecision, you convert

them from that moment into insidious and dangerous enemies. The Dakota saw clearly enough the perturbation of
the emigrants, and instantly availed themselves of it. They
became extremely insolent and exacting in their demands.
It has become an established custom with them to go to the
camp of every party, as it arrives in succession at the fort,
and demand a feast. Smoke's village had come with this express design, having made several days' journey with no
other object than that of enjoying a cup of coffee and two
or three biscuit. So the 'feast' was demanded, and the emigrants dared not refuse it.

"One evening, about sunset, the village was deserted. We
met old men, warriors, squaws, and children in gay attire,
trooping off to the encampment, with faces of anticipation;
and, arriving here, they seated themselves in a semi-circle.
Smoke occupied the centre, with his warriors on either hand;
the young men and boys came next, and the squaws and
children formed the horns of the crescent. The biscuit and
coffee were promptly despatched, the emigrants staring open-
mouthed at their savage guests. With each emigrant party
that arrived at Fort Laramie this scene was renewed; and
every day the Indians grew more rapacious and presump-
tuous. One evening they broke in pieces, out of mere wan-
tonness, the cups from which they had been feasted; and
this so exasperated the emigrants, that many of them seized
their rifles and could scarcely be restrained from firing on
the insolent mob of Indians. Before we left the country this
dangerous spirit on the part of the Dakota had mounted to
a yet higher pitch. They began openly to threaten the emigrants with destruction, and actually fired upon one or two
parties of whites. A military force and military law are ur-
gently called for in that perilous region; and unless troops
are speedily stationed at Fort Laramie, or elsewhere in the

neighborhood, both emigrants and other travellers will be exposed to most imminent risks." [1]

The meaning of such scenes was not lost on Jim Bridger. For years he had held, with other trappers, to the frontier gospel: *Hell's full of greenhorns!*

But now his mind was working, working fast—even under the rain of questions poured out by the disheartened emigrants. Patiently he answered them, though he could give them no encouragement. They needed help badly; their oxen had worn their hooves down to the quick, and could go no farther. There they were, hardly halfway to Oregon, with the mountains still ahead, encumbered with their womenfolks and children, with covered wagons full of unwieldy plunder —and *afoot!* They stood around, awkwardly waiting for Jim to tell them what to expect, what to do.

Jim warned them. They would find the whole country ahead swept bare of grass, and no buffalo along the Trail. And with the few worn-out teams they had, they could never get those heavy wagons over the mountains.

The emigrants, however, reckoned they might as well go on as go back. If there were no grass for their animals, if they could not take the wagons along, what of it? They offered to sell them—sell them at their value in the States, taking in exchange coffee and sugar at a dollar a pound or miserable broken-down horses, mere bags of bones, certain to die before they crossed the mountains. They sold all their cattle, some of them purebred Durham stock. All at once, business at Fort Laramie was booming.

Moreover, these emigrants had money—cash enough to make it worth White Head's time to turn right around and head back to the mountains as their guide. White Head was sure to run into the Sioux beyond Independence Rock, but he couldn't hold out at that price. Afterward Jim heard how the old coon talked the chiefs out of killing his party and got them all through safe to Fort Hall. Jim reckoned he himself could have done the same, if White Head had not got thar fust. . . .

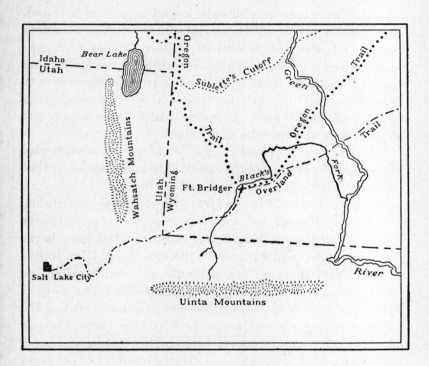

With his usual silent deliberation, Bridger sat and considered the plan that was forming in his mind. It was always his cautious custom to consider first every possible objection to any new enterprise; then, knowing the worst in advance, he could go ahead coolly, sure that he would not be caught off guard.

Why not build a fort to serve emigrants somewhere on the Trail to Oregon?

Nobody knew the country better than Jim Bridger, nobody could manage the cussed Injuns better, or fight them harder—if it came to that. No man was a better judge of horseflesh. As a trader, Jim was slick as a buffalo's nose. All these things he knew as well as he knew the palm of his hand.

But that was not all. He was one ahead of other mountain men; he was a skillful *blacksmith*, who could shoe a horse or an ox, repair a wagon or a gun. And if his fort should stand (as all forts did) on the bank of some river, he knew how to run a ferryboat to help folks across. Jim grinned, glowing with his wonderful idee. At last he had found a way to get ahead without leaving the mountains!

What's more, he could help a lot of people who needed help—and Old Gabe had the knack. He had been doing that all his life.

Of course he would have to live with the cussed emigrants, men who had never sot a beaver-trap, never seen Injuns sculped. But it was a heap better to put up with greenhorns for a few months in summer in the mountains than to live with them all the year round in the settlements. Jim saw how he could make a good living—maybe a fortune—just by working in the warm months—and still have most of the fall and spring and all winter to hunt and trap. He saw himself saved from disaster, back in the saddle again—a booshway with dollars in his possibles! A more excitable man would have found the prospect dazzling.

The question was, where was the best place for his fort?

Not on the parching, freezing Plains. He had seen that great buffalo pasture along the Platte turned into a lifeless desert by traffic on the Oregon Trail. He wanted some pleasanter place than that, he argued with himself—some place farther up the Trail. For it was clear that, the farther the emigrants were from the settlements, the more repair work there would be to do on their wagons, the more fresh stock and new outfits they would need. And the closer to the mountains they were, the more willing they would be to part with their heavy plunder for a song.

But all the time Jim was explaining to himself the advantages of a mountain fort, he knew in his bones just where he would build it. He could see the place now—that beautiful broad grassy bottom on Black's Fork of Green River, where fine fresh water rushed from the melting snows of the Uinta range—water alive with mountain trout, cold and clear, flowing in several channels, all of them lined thick with trees. *There* he would build Fort Bridger, there among his friends the Snakes (Shoshones), among the wild varmints, among his beloved mountains.

Jim Bridger made tracks quick—heading home to the mountains. There a few weeks' steady work with ax and adze, and his wonderful dream came true.

His fort consisted simply of an eight-foot stockade, with a corral adjoining on the north. Within that stockade stood four log cabins with flat dirt roofs. One of these housed Bridger's forge and carpenter's bench, another his store, the third his family and possibles, while the fourth was the home of his partner.

Jim persuaded his old friend Louis Vasquez to be his partner in his new venture and in December, 1843, sent a confident letter to Pierre Chouteau, Jr., the principal merchant in St. Louis:

"I have established a small fort, with a blacksmith shop and a supply of iron in the road of the emigrants on Black Fork of Green River, which promises fairly. In coming out here they are generally well supplied with money, but by the time they get here they are in need of all kind of supplies, horses, provisions, smith-work, etc. They bring ready cash from the states, and should I receive the goods ordered, will have considerable business in that way with them, and establish trade with the Indians in the neighborhood, who have a good number of beaver . . ." [2]

XV
MILK RIVER

Beaver!

It warn't human not to trap beaver. There war always one more river to explore. This time Jim hankered to lead a brigade to Milk River, out on the Plains north of the Missouri.

But Jim's responsible, paternal heart was concerned about his daughter. He aimed to give her a better raisin' than she could git at Fort Bridger.

Jim had found his venture in serving the tourist trade— for travel on the Trail was by no means all in one direction —very profitable. So, after a busy summer at Fort Bridger advising emigrants, shrinking tires, welding wagon-irons, repairing wagons warped and shrunk in the dry air of the parching Plains, dickering for broken-down wagons, horses, mules and cattle and for heavy plunder of all kinds, Jim sent his daughter Mary Ann, now going on nine years, off with a wagon train to the Whitman Mission School at Waiilatpui in Oregon, and got ready to head north. His old friend Dr. Whitman would give her the book l'arnin' that her father never had time for.

Jim was plumb tired of wagons, backwoodsmen, frightened women and children—tired of advising people who did not know how to do what he told them. It seemed to him, thinking it over that them thar greenhorns sot their foot in every trap along the Trail. If there war a rattlesnake within

a mile, they got bit. At night they left their saddles and
harness hanging on a wagon tongue where the wolves gnawed
the leather to scraps! They overloaded their wagons. They
let their stock stray. They lost themselves in sandstorms,
got drenched in heavy downpours, beaten and bruised by
hailstorms. If there war any mud or quicksand anywheres,
they war sartin sure to bog down; and in rocky ground they
smashed their wagon wheels plenty. At night frosts set their
teeth to chattering; by day hot winds burned the skin from
their red noses. They couldn't kill a blind buffalo if it stood
square in their trail, armed as they were with small-caliber
long rifles meant for deer and turkey. They got fever from
drinking water in buffalo wallows and dried-up cricks, and
mighty near all of 'em had the itch from living on nothing
but superfine flour and sowbelly. If they come out in the
spring, they grazed off all the grass at every camping place.
If they come late in the season, they generally burned it off.
It war a miracle that any of 'em lived to git thar—. And
when they died, there warn't no peace for 'em even in the
grave; before the wagons war out of sight, the cussed wolves
or Injuns dug 'em up again.

Jim had helped hundreds and hundreds of these feckless
farmers all summer long. It was no wonder that he hankered
for the beaver trail.

He had been on the move for more than twenty years, seldom camping in one spot for more than a few weeks at a
time. Restless as an Indian, like an Indian, he found sitting
still in one place bad for his health and spirits. So now he
got together what men he could find, and lit out, still dreaming of heavy packs of furs.

It warn't easy to find enough veteran trappers to make up
his brigade, and some of his men must have been raw recruits,

unused to hardship and Injun fighting. But Jim was so eager to trap again that he would let nothing stop him.

Our only account of what followed is that of Charles Larpenteur, a trader at Fort Union; he records Bridger's adventures in his usual acid style:

"Jim Bridger, being a great trapper, and having been told that there were many beaver on Milk river, thought of trying his luck in that direction. He left the mountains with a picked party of thirty men, all good trappers and Indian fighters. Nothing unusual transpired at Fort Union until about the month of November (1844) when Bridger and his men made their appearance, having come from Milk river with the intention of passing the winter with us. Mr. Laidlaw, who was in charge at the time, offered him all assistance he could afford, to make his winter quarters pleasant and comfortable, and so Bridger pitched his camp about half a mile from the fort. But he had been deceived by exaggerated reports of the quantity of beaver that could be had on Milk river, and his hunt had been a very poor one. The main substance of Bridger's conversation was his brave men, his fast horses, and his fights with Blackfeet, till we were induced to believe that, with such a party to defend us, there would be no danger for us in case of an attack by Sioux. At that time such affairs became quite frequent, and the Sioux generally came in large parties. Bridger soon had an opportunity to display the bravery of his men, whom he had cracked up so highly. A few days before Christmas (1844) a large war party made a raid on the band of horses belonging to the fort, running off six of them, and wounding one of the guard in the leg with buckshot. The alarm was immediately given, and the braves were mounted to pursue the Sioux. Bridger's clerk, who had been left in camp, came running into the fort out of breath, scared to death. 'Get up all the men you can! The Sioux are in camp—they are butchering us!' Mr. Denig and I, with a few men, all we could get, took our guns, and ran with all our might to render what assistance we could. Finding that this was a case in which we had to be cautious, we went along under the steep bank of the river till we thought ourselves about opposite the camp, where we stopped to listen for the cries of the reported butchering. Hearing nothing, we cautiously raised our heads over the bank, to see some of the performance. Neither seeing nor hearing anything, we came to the conclusion the murderous work had been done, and determined to go to the camp, expecting to find people cut to pieces and scalped. To our great surprise we saw nothing—not a sign that any Indians had been near the camp. Now assured that Bridger's brave clerk had lied, we returned to the fort laughing at his fright.

"During our absence on this dangerous sortie, Mr. Laidlaw was left alone—that is, without a clerk. I had, in my hurry, taken the key of the store with me, and pressing demands were made for ammunition. Mr. Laidlaw, who was a fiery, quick-tempered old Scotchman, smashed in the window of the retail store. Seeing this, on our entrance, we could not imagine what could have been the matter. No word had been received from Bridger's army, but we expected them to return with the recaptured horses and with scalps flying. But soon, to our great disappointment, came the report that a man had been killed; that a mare belonging to Mr. Ellingsworth, the Opposition bookkeeper, had been shot through the hip, and that the Indians were daring the whites to fight. The Opposition, who had seen Bridger's men turn out to fight, had concluded to join them. Mr. Ellingsworth had bought this fine American mare of Mr. Laidlaw, who had brought her here in the fall. An old half-breed Creek was also well mounted, and they both very soon came up with Bridger's party, who had halted at the foot of the hills. When Ellingsworth and the old man approached they saw the cause of the halt; the Sioux were on a hill, making signs for them to come on and fight. By this time their party had been re-enforced and Bridger's men, not accustomed to deal with such a large force, declined the invitation. The old half-breed, who was clear grit, put the whip to his horse, telling the balance to come on; but only Ellingsworth followed. The Sioux, who understood this kind of warfare, and expected the whites to accept the challenge, had left concealed in a ravine a small body of their party, ready to let fly in case the enemy attempted to come on. As the old Indian went by at full speed with Ellingsworth, the Indians fired a volley, which dropped the former dead off his horse and wounded Ellingsworth's mare in the hip; but did not come so near killing her that Ellingsworth could not make his escape. The Indians, seeing this, commenced to yell, and renewed their defiance. But the brave party concluded to turn back, somewhat ashamed of themselves. Bridger was extremely mortified, and said he could not account for the cowardice of his men on this occasion. At the funeral of Gardepie—that being the name of the old man—these words were pronounced: 'This burial is caused by the cowardice of Bridger's party.' This expression, it was thought, would result in a fight with the Opposition; but the discontentment disappeared without any disturbance. In the meantime the Sioux went away, having killed one man, wounded another's mare, and taken six head of horses. Bridger became very much dissatisfied with his men, who dispersed in all directions, and he returned to the mountains." [1]

Disgusted, Jim turned his attention to Fort Bridger, which soon kept him busy enough. It was not only "an oasis in the desert" for all travelers, the haven of all the swarming emigrants who needed repairs, supplies, and fresh livestock, but also the trading post for all the tribes around, the rendezvous for wandering Mountain Men, and a great information bureau for all and sundry. Everyone who passed, camped there; and whatever else he wanted, wanted Jim Bridger's advice as to trails and travel.

Now giving advice is a thankless job. Those who take it and prosper, never give credit. Those who reject it are scornful. While those who accept it and come to grief through their own ineptness are generally loud in bitter accusation. Jim and his colleagues did their best—but many of those who asked their advice were too green to profit by it.

In 1846 the Donner party halted at Fort Bridger for three days to decide upon the best route to California. There a new route was talked of known as the Hastings' Cut-Off, named after Lansford W. Hastings, who promoted it. This trail, skirting Salt Lake on the south, struck back into the old Fort Hall route on Humboldt River. Hastings declared his route was hundreds of miles shorter than the old road. To Vasquez and Bridger, this seemed the better route—not only for the saving in distance but because it brought more emigrants to Fort Bridger.

There is no proof that either of them saw the Donner party or advised them to go that way. But the Donner party decided to do it. And everyone knows how they were trapped by the deep snows on the Sierra Nevada and how they resorted to cannibalism in order to survive. . . .

When the Mormons came along next summer, they met Jim heading for Fort Laramie. Brigham Young camped on the Little Sandy to confer with him.

All that Brigham had to go by were the maps prepared by Colonel John C. Frémont—and divine guidance. Old

Jim had not heard about the divine guidance, and said he was "ashamed of the maps of Frémont, who knew nothing about the country, only the plain travelled road, and that he (Bridger) could correct all the maps published of the western world." [2]

Jim praised the Great Basin as a place for settlement. "It's my paradise," he declared; then with typical generosity added, "But you kin settle in it along with me." Still, Jim warned them, the frosts up thar mought be too heavy to raise corn. [3]

Jim spent the best part of a day trying to help the Mormons, warned them against the Utes, and advised at great length on the geography, climate, and resources of the whole country west to the Pacific Ocean.

But Jim's account took in so much territory that it left the Saints—unused to thinking in terms of anything bigger than a county—all at sea.

This long interview was recorded by several persons who attended. When it was over, Brigham invited Bridger to supper. He evidently wanted a private talk with Jim.

Naturally no record was made of their conversation at supper. But one or two things are clear. This meeting was the beginning of the rivalry of two strong men—a rivalry which brought heavy loss and near-disaster to them both. Strife was inevitable.

Bridger had everything Brigham needed. Brigham needed everything Bridger had. Both men were independent as hogs on ice. Neither was likely to give in—or give out.

To Bridger, Salt Lake Valley was "my Paradise"; to Brigham, it was "my Promised Land." Bridger was willing to share the Basin with the Mormons; but Brigham could not share his realm with a "gentile." It must have irked Brigham the way Old Jim ignored his sacred mission and his faith, treating the Saints like any other greenhorn emigrants. Brigham had a hard row to hoe, trying to keep up the morale of his poverty-stricken followers during the hard years ahead; he could not relish Bridger's frank discount of his promises.

Probably that night the two men talked about the prospect for growing corn in the Basin. Food for his people was Brigham's gravest problem then. That day (as we know from the Mormons' own records) Jim had told them that the Indians grew corn south of Utah Lake. But Jim could not honestly assure Brigham that he could raise enough corn in the Basin to feed his people. Maybe Brigham tried to ride Jim's opinion down. It would be like him, and like Bridger to stand up to him.

At any rate, when they all parted next morning, Bridger told the group of Mormon leaders that "it would not be prudent to bring a great population to the Basin until" it was "ascertained whether grain would grow or not." [4]

One thing is clear. Bridger did not go along to guide Brigham to Salt Lake. No doubt he would have gone, *if* he had been invited.

Afterwards Brigham declared that Bridger offered him one thousand dollars for a bushel of corn raised in the Basin.[5]

This story of Bridger's offer has many variants: Sometimes the Saints made it $100, sometimes $1,000—sometimes for an ear of corn, sometimes for a wagonload. But there is no record that any of those impoverished settlers ever tried to collect the forfeit from Old Jim.[6]

XVI
THE OVERLAND TRAIL

WHILE Brigham's caravans trailed away toward Salt Lake, Bridger stayed on at his trading post. That winter of 1847 he had graver matters than the Mormon migration to engage his mind.

Visitors were few when heavy snows piled up about the stockade, and the tipis of the friendly Snakes pitched among the dark boles of the cottonwoods along the Black Fork stood glazed with sleet like white steeples rising from the snowy earth.

One cold afternoon Bridger's dogs began to bark. Through the loophole he saw three dark figures, horsemen, covered with hoar frost, plodding toward the fort. Before he could get into his buffalo coat, Jim heard a slow pounding on the heavy gate. When he opened it, there stood his old friend Joe Meek.

Bridger was always happy when an old compañero of the beaver trail turned up, but for Meek he had a particular affection. Both had a ready wit and a keen sense of humor; they had been through many a hard scrape together. Both were good family men, and they had sent their daughters to school together at the Waiilatpui Mission in Oregon in charge of Dr. Marcus Whitman.

Bridger grasped Joe's cold mitten. "Hiya, old hoss. Come in and take a horn."

Meek held Jim's hand hard but made no reply. He stamped the snow from his moccasins and ducked to get through the tall door. The other men went off to put up the horses. Jim closed the door.

Still Meek said nothing. He did not pull off his blanket

coat or capoté, but stood motionless there, covered with hoar frost, pale as a snowman—or a ghost. He would not sit down. Jim knew now that something was wrong.

Meek brought bad news. The Injuns had up and murdered Dr. Whitman and his wife in their own house—and Meek's own daughter, Helen. Joe himself had found and buried the three bodies. The government in Oregon had picked him to head back to the states asking Uncle Sam to help.

Jim threw one arm around Joe's shoulder. His quick sympathy was mingled with cruel anxiety for his own child. Meek answered his unspoken question. "We don't know what became of Mary Ann, Jim. Them red devils carried her away."

The two bereaved fathers gripped hands and faced each other in choking silence. . . .

When the other men came in, Old Gabe made them welcome, served them a good dinner of hot meat, and put them to bed on the floor of his snug cabin. Jim himself did not sleep much that night. Next morning he loaded two pack mules with supplies for the party, gave them fresh mounts, and sent them on their way. Jim knowed he would never see Mary Ann again in this world.

As a result of that tragedy, Bridger rode back to Missouri the next summer to provide a safe home for his family. It was clear that the mountains were no place for civilized women and children. So Jim bought a farm outside Kansas City near Little Santa Fe.

But Jim could not stay in the settlements, and neither could his Ute Indian wife. Next summer the two of them were back at Fort Bridger. There, while his partner Vasquez kept the store, trading or selling horses, mules, buffalo robes, deerskins, clay pipes, tobacco, whisky, buckskin clothing and supplies of all sorts, Old Gabe looked after the forge or advised travelers, charting the trails on his cabin door with a piece of charcoal from the kitchen fire, making everyone welcome.

Unlike his Mexican partner, Bridger took no stock in *fofurraw.* But Mrs. Vasquez, a white woman from the settlements, had brought chairs out from the States. Bridger goodhumoredly allowed his guests to set on them if they took the notion.

That summer emigrants came rolling in from the southeast in steadily increasing numbers. Already there was danger that their stock would graze off Jim's pasture around the fort. He had to put up signs warning them off, pointing to other grazing grounds in the neighborhood.

"While his trading post flourished at Fort Bridger he was supposed to have a large amount of money in his possession. Some desperadoes entered his house one night for the purpose of robbing him. Bridger, awakening from his sleep, quickly said, 'What are you lookin' for?' One of the desperadoes answered, 'We are lookin' for your money.' Bridger replied, 'Wait jest a minute an' I'll git up and help you.' This disconcerted the robbers, and knowing their man they concluded not to wait until he 'got up,' but quickly departed." [1]

Jim was younger, more active, and hardier than his fat partner Vasquez, so he was the traveling partner for the firm, and frequently away on the Trail. Often Jim was at South Pass, advising emigrants bound for California not to follow Sublette's cut-off to Fort Hall—but to come via Fort Bridger (where he could serve them) and Salt Lake.

One such traveler tells us what he saw of Bridger's family and fort about the middle of June, 1849. Says he:

Mrs. Bridger, "a stolid, fleshy, round-headed woman, not

oppressed with lines of beauty. Her hair was intensely black and straight, and so cut that it hung in a thick mass upon her broad shoulders. In a corner of Mrs. Bridger's room was a churn filled with buttermilk, and dipping from it with a ladle, Mrs. Vasquez filled and refilled our cups, which we drank until completely satisfied.

"It chanced that we were enabled to repay the kindness shown by this lady without the least sacrifice on our part—a fact to be regretted. In the course of conversation, when speaking of the comforts of which she was deprived by living so far from the haunts of civilization, Mrs. Bridger mentioned the loss of a skillet lid, and her inability thus far to replace it. It was curious that it should be so, but such was the fact that we were the owners of the identical article coveted. Our skillet had been fractured and thrown away, but with that peculiar inclination which many possess of clinging to articles that had become wholly useless, we had treasured that skillet lid, and now in the briefest possible time, even before one could say 'Jack Robinson,' it was transferred to Mrs. Bridger's kitchen. Fifty skillet lids would not have been worth the smile which greeted us when making our presentation speech, and it was plain that it was altogether useless to attempt to get out of debt. As we turned to leave, a still further burden was placed upon us when we were given a roll of freshly churned butter of a rich golden yellow, and glistening, as it were, with drops of dew." [2]

That day Bridger's wife was happy over her new skillet lid. Three weeks later she died in childbed, leaving to him a baby girl whom he called Virginia.

Twice now death had struck at his family. There was no wet nurse handy, no baby food to be had for love or money for the new child. But Jim was bound not to lose his new daughter. When his cow went dry, Jim rode out with his rifle and brought in a buffalo's udder day after day and so kept his youngest always fat and sassy.

On August 11, that same summer, Captain Howard Stansbury, Corps of Topographical Engineers, U. S. Army, and his party came to the fort. Major Bridger entertained the officers "with great kindness and hospitality," and while their wagons were being repaired in his blacksmith shop, described the two emigrant roads from Fort Bridger to the Humboldt River: "the old road traversing the Bear and Portneuf Rivers and passing thence southwestward to the Humboldt, and the new route by way of Echo and Weber Canyons and the north end of Great Salt Lake to a junction with the main California road on the Humboldt River below the Point of Rocks. . . . The one was too far north and the other too far south; and evidently inspired by descriptions of the country given by Bridger, Captain Stansbury sought a more direct route between the two." [3]

So Jim piloted the Captain across Bear River, up and along the divide and down from Cache Valley to Ogden's Hole and Salt Lake. Then Bridger, his mission completed, went home.

There he stayed—except for a jaunt in the following spring with Kit Carson and others to Jackson's Hole and Yellowstone Lake, the Falls of the Yellowstone, Madison River, the Fire Hole River, and the Fire Holes of the Lower Geyser Basin. The tales of these trappers about the wonders they had seen only made people in the settlements laugh. "Old Jim Bridger's lies," they said.

In September Captain Stansbury offered Jim another job as guide.

"Major Bridger, although at a considerable sacrifice of his own interest, with great spirit, offered his services as guide, he being well acquainted with the ground over which it was my desire to pass. The offer was most cheerfully accepted."

Stansbury told Bridger just what he wanted. Said he, "Major Bridger, I want you to find a more direct route for wagons from Fort Bridger to the South Platte."

Bridger stared, but had the grace not to laugh in the officer's face. *Find* it! Without leaving his seat, in five minutes' time, Jim told the Captain where that wagon road must run, scratching a map with the stem of his clay dudeen on the earthen floor: From Fort Bridger east over Green River, up Bitter Creek, across the North Platte and Laramie River in the Laramie Plains to the south end of the Black Hills, then down Lodge Pole Creek to its mouth.

Having thus described the proposed route, Bridger led Stansbury over it. That trail was to be the route of the Overland Stage, the Pony Express, the Union Pacific Railroad.

Lieutenant J. W. Gunnison waxed enthusiastic about Jim. Bridger, in his opinion, was the greatest guide alive. Bridger had, he reports, "traversed the region from the headwaters of the Missouri to the (Rio Grande) Del Norte, and along the Gila to the Gulf, and thence throughout Oregon and the interior California. . . . With a buffalo skin and a piece of charcoal, he will map out any portion of this immense region, and delineate mountains, streams, and the circular valleys called 'holes,' with wonderful accuracy; at least we may so speak of that portion we traversed after his descriptions were given."

Bridger left the Captain at Fort Laramie. From Laramie Jim rode back to Fort Bridger and married a Snake woman. . . .

Lieutenant Gunnison delighted in Old Jim's accounts of the cliff dwellings.

But Bridger's accurate accounts of Yellowstone Park proved most exciting of all. Gunnison told everybody the wonderful news long before he had got his book published.

That fall, when Bridger went to Missouri, a newspaper editor interviewed him. But an incredulous friend cautioned the editor against taking any stock in "trappers' tales." So the editor killed Bridger's story—and the public went on laughing at Old Jim as their favorite yarn-spinner—"the biggest liar in North America!"

XVII

THE TREATY AT
LARAMIE

ALL over the Plains that summer of 1851 people were talking about the great peace treaty to be held in the autumn. Father Pierre Jean de Smet traveled among the tribes, inviting them to attend, and few of the chiefs who knew the Black Robe could refuse any request of his. To this day old Indians say he was one white man who "talked sense and told the truth."

It was high time for a treaty. The Oregon Trail following up the Platte through the buffalo country had frightened the game away. And, when a hundred thousand forty-niners came swarming over that trail, heading for California gold-fields, the Indians became thoroughly alarmed, suspicious, and resentful. Buffalo would not cross that broad beaten "medicine road" which had cut the Plains in two. After 1850 there were two herds instead of one: the Buffalo North and the Buffalo South. The coming of the white man had turned that great pasture along the Platte into a barren desert.

Neither the passing white man nor the starving Indian saw anything to admire in the other. The whites passed through too quickly to discover how false their notion of the

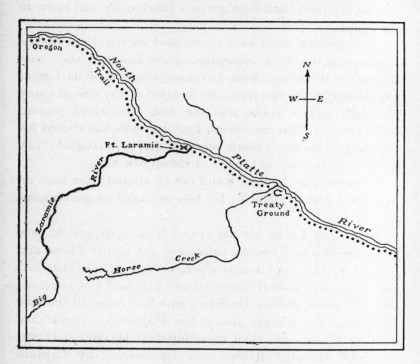

Plains Indian was—the notion which they had brought from the Dark and Bloody Ground, the notion that every Indian was a treacherous thief and murderer, thirsting for the blood of every stranger and delighting in torture of the helpless.

The Indian hunter, on the other hand, whose most necessary virtues were courage, generosity, and fortitude, could only despise the caution, thrift, and sharp practice of the

Yankees as the meanest vices; each being in his eyes simply a species of cowardice.

Because of this dislike and misunderstanding on both sides, there was constant friction and increasing distrust. But the Plains Indian had no newspapers to state his case, and so, by 1851, had been given a thoroughly bad name in the States.

Two military posts were established on the Trail up the Platte—one built in Nebraska, Fort Kearny; the other bought in Wyoming, Fort Laramie. Because of its former importance in the fur trade, its location at the hub of many radiating Indian trails, and the ease with which wagons could reach it from the States, Fort Laramie was chosen for the treaty ground. Troops began to arrive in August; they established themselves nearby at Camp Macklin.

Of course Jim Bridger could not be spared from such an important treaty council. He was on hand as government interpreter.

There Jim found his old friend Tom Fitzpatrick, now Government agent for the Indians of the Upper Platte and Arkansas; and the Commissioner, Colonel D. D. Mitchell; the fur traders Robert Campbell and Edmund F. Chouteau; and, of course, Father De Smet, who had come all the way down from his mission among the Flatheads. The scanty military forces—less than three hundred Dragoons, Infantry, and Mounted Rifles—were commanded by Captain R. H. Chilton. The Press was well represented.

Eight principal tribes had been invited, and came riding into camp by the thousands: Sioux, Cheyennes, Arapahos, Crows, Assiniboines, Mandans, Hidatsa, and Rees. Many famous chiefs attended, as well as younger men who were to be even more famous chiefs in time to come—Sitting Bull and Red Cloud of the Sioux.

The Shoshones, or Snakes, with whom Bridger traded, lived a long way from Laramie, and had not been asked to be a party to the treaty. Washakie, their chief, a man of Bridger's age, was Jim's close friend—and worthy of that friendship. Only the summer before Bridger had married a Shoshone woman. So his influence with the tribe was great, and the Snakes were thoroughly loyal to the United States. A treaty of peace with them was hardly necessary.

But Chief Washakie, as a true friend of the whites, had reason to feel slighted when not invited to come down to smoke at Laramie. The Snakes, being allies of the white men, certainly had a stake in any peace settlement made with their common enemies. At any rate, he decided to attend, and organized a party of several hundred warriors to ride with him and sit in on the grand council. It would be just as well to be there, in case the Commissioner should be tempted to give some other tribe part of the Snake hunting grounds.

It took courage to ride so far from home through hostile country and into a camp where enemies outnumbered them ten to one. But the Snakes were not easily daunted. White Bull, the Sioux chief, and nephew of Sitting Bull, who has warred with most of the tribes on the Northern Plains, told me that—of them all—the Snakes were the bravest and the toughest fighters.

Washakie and his party set out for the Platte. When a short way east of South Pass, a Cheyenne war party jumped them, and scalped two warriors before the Snakes could run them off. . . .

At Fort Laramie one morning Bridger informed Colonel Mitchell that the Snakes were approaching. The Colonel, anticipating Washakie's coming, had already exacted promises from the Sioux and Cheyenne chiefs that there would be no trouble. But now he wondered anxiously whether they would be able to control their young men. He ordered Bridger to escort the Snakes into camp. Jim prepared to meet them.

At high noon the Snakes topped a ridge from which they could see the great encampment. Already their dust had been seen; the whole camp turned out to watch them.

Washakie rode a little way ahead, followed by his warriors, all in their finest regalia, sitting their war horses proudly. A compact ruck of pack-horses, traveaux, women and children, well guarded, brought up the rear. Bridger watched them with pride in his wife's people.

Suddenly *Boots and Saddles* broke the silence. A handful of Dragoons rode out, ready for action—just in case. Still at a slow walk, the Snakes came on. All watched in silence.

Then Bridger heard a shrill, heartbroken wail—the lament of some Sioux or Cheyenne woman whose son or brother had been killed by the Snakes. Another woman joined in—and another—thin wails rising high in the stillness, stirring hatred and revenge in the hearts of their menfolks standing by, every man with arms in his hands. Jim watched the crowding Sioux among the tents; it would be a miracle if none of them lost his head to *that* tune.

It happened as he had expected. A Sioux warrior leaped into the saddle, and, quirting his pony, charged on the dead run towards the Snakes, bow and arrows ready in his hand.

Jim understood perfectly what was up. The Snakes had killed the Sioux's father, and now the son was out for revenge. More'n likely the hothead expected all the Sioux and Cheyennes to charge on the Snakes as soon as the first shot was fired. He himself might be killed; but, with thousands looking on, he could not fail to win undying glory. The chance to display his courage before all those people had been too much for him. Away he went, quirting his pony across the dusty plain.

The troops sat idle, their commander not knowing what to do. They were far too few to cope with those thousands of seasoned warriors; moreover, they could not afford to take sides. They were there to guard the Commissioner.

The Snakes halted as one man, and as one man yelled defiance at the Sioux. They sat their horses firmly, without a sign of wavering, silent, ready for anything. Even the women and children were quiet and self-possessed. All were self-reliant, and none more so than their chief.

Washakie kicked his war horse forward, and raised his rifle, awaiting the attack. Let the Sioux shoot first; Washakie had come in peace.

His confidence and steadiness must have impressed the lone Sioux. It certainly impressed everybody else—including Jim. Washakie could handle that Sioux.

Then a Frenchman, one of the interpreters, mounted quickly and took after the lone warrior. Slowly his horse gained on the Sioux pony. Just before the Sioux was near enough to use his bow effectively, the Frenchman caught up with him, reached out, dragged him off his pony, threw him flat in the dust. The Sioux tried to find his feet again, but the Frenchman jumped down, quickly struck the weapons from his hand, then stood over him with his gun. . . .

There was a long palaver, but not one in a hundred of the Sioux had a gun. So at length they led their discomfited troublemaker back to camp. The white men breathed more freely.

Bridger rode up to the officer commanding the troops and asked where he wanted the Snakes to camp. The Lieutenant in charge detailed Corporal Percival G. Lowe to show Major Bridger.

The Corporal was obviously thrilled at this opportunity to work with the famous scout; he asked if Jim had any objections to his remaining with him while the Snakes made camp.

" 'No, young man, these are the finest Injuns on earth; stay with me and I'll show 'um to you.' Soon the column was in motion, and they went into camp in their own peculiar way. Every prominent point was dotted by a sentinel, quietly wrapped in his blanket, gun ready for use.

"Bridger said: 'Well, you seen that fool Sioux make the run, didn't you?'

" 'Yes sir.'

" 'Well, ——,' referring to the brave interpreter, whom he knew well, 'saved that fellow from hell; my chief would 'er killed him quick, and then the fool Sioux would 'er got their backs up, and there wouldn't have been room to camp 'round here for dead Sioux. You dragoons acted nice, but you wouldn't have had no show if the fight had commenced—no making peace then. And I tell you another thing: the Sioux ain't goin' to try it again. They see how the Snakes are armed. I got them guns for 'um, and they are good ones. It'll be a proud day for the Snakes if any of these prairie tribes pitch into 'um, and they are not a bit afraid. Uncle Sam told 'um to come down here and they'd be safe, but they ain't takin' his word for it altogether. They'll never be caught napping, and they're prepared to travel anywhere. Awful brave fellows, these Snakes; got the nerve; honest, too; can take their word for anything; trust 'em anywhere; they live all about me, and I know all of them.' " [1]

The great encampment now settled down to a kind of armed truce, while it waited for the ox-trains bringing presents and provisions for the council. The wagons had been delayed, and since there was no longer any game on "the hungry Platte," it looked as if everybody would starve—and that at the very time when Indian honor required an unending series of feasts to entertain the chiefs and warriors of other bands. Father De Smet describes what followed:

"Notwithstanding the scarcity of provisions felt in the camp before the wagons came, the feasts were numerous and well attended. No epoch in Indian annals, probably, shows a greater massacre of the canine race. Among the Indians the flesh of the dog is the most honorable and esteemed of all viands, especially in the absence of buffalo and other animals. On the present occasion it was a last resource. The carnage then may be conceived. I was invited to several of these banquets; a great chief, in particular, wished to give me a special mark of his friendship and respect for me. He had filled his great kettle with little fat dogs, skins and all. He presented me, on a wooden platter, the fattest, well boiled. I found the meat really delicate, and I can vouch that it is preferable to suckling-pig, which it nearly resembles in taste." [2]

Jim Bridger and Tom Fitzpatrick, the most important old-timers among the whites, were kept busy all day long going from one dog-feast to another, as long as the pups held out. They could not refuse such hospitality, any more than Father De Smet, since by Indian etiquette a guest who did not eat everything set before him was guilty of insulting his host!

Jim was glad to take refuge in the camp of Washakie's tribesmen; for the Snakes would not eat dog meat, though they had mighty little else to eat until the wagons came. Even the ponies were hungry, having grazed down the surrounding prairies to the very grass roots. They had to move camp.

So they all trailed down the North Platte thirty-six miles

to the mouth of Horse Creek, which came in from the southwest, across from another stream coming in from the opposite direction. There the camps were so placed that Horse Creek and the military were between the Snakes and the Sioux. Bridger and Fitzpatrick had convinced the Colonel that only a bold front and a firm hand would enable him to control the unstable tribesmen.

Before the council could begin, it was first necessary that the Snakes and the Cheyennes should settle the matter of the two scalps taken a few days earlier near South Pass. Father De Smet recorded the negotiations:

"On this day the principal braves of the Cheyenne nation and forty warriors of the Shoshones were assembled. Several orations were delivered as preliminaries of peace.

"Then followed a feast, of which all partook. It consisted simply of corn, crushed and thoroughly boiled. . . . The feast over, the Cheyennes brought suitable presents of tobacco, blankets, knives, pieces of red and blue cloth, and deposited them in the center of the circle. The two scalps were also exposed, and then returned to the brothers of the two wretched victims, who were seated at the head of the circle, between the two chiefs of their nation. The brothers were solemnly assured that the 'scalp dance' did not take place. They wore, however, a very somber air, and on accepting the scalps were deeply affected. However, they embraced the murderers, received the donations, and distributed the major portion of them to their companions. After this, the usual signs of peace and amity, presents and reciprocal adoptions of children, were interchanged; their orators employed all their eloquence to strengthen the good feeling which appeared to reign in the assembly, and to render it lasting. The next night the Cheyennes visited the lodges of the Shoshones, who were encamped beside my little tent. Songs and dances were prolonged till daylight." [3]

But the Cheyennes evidently felt that this was a pretty one-sided arrangement. Some of them had suffered cruel losses at the hands of raiding Snakes, and even while the council was assembling, these staged a demonstration of their own.

"A Cheyenne squaw, leading a horse, with a boy, about ten or twelve years of age, mounted upon him, made her way into the entrance of the council arbor, and commenced her chant. The interruption was sudden, and for a few minutes not understood, but soon stopped by the Cheyenne chiefs. The purpose was this. Some years previously, one of the Shoshones, a Snake chief, who was then in the Council, had killed her husband, leaving this boy, then an infant, fatherless. She now came to present the boy and horse to the Shoshones, by which, according to their customs, the boy becomes the adopted son of the Shoshones, and entitled to all the rights and privileges of that tribe. The Snake chief had no right, by their customs, to refuse receiving the gift, and upon its reception became bound to treat the boy in every respect as his own child." [4]

When the excitement caused by this dramatic interruption had been allayed, Colonel Mitchell set about organizing the council as a constituent assembly. And from that moment, Bridger, as principal interpreter, had his hands full. He found himself in the midst of a heated discussion as to the precedence and seating of eight different Indian nations. The boastful Sioux, far more numerous than the others, declared themselves entitled to the place of honor. The haughty Cheyennes, whose deeds of valor had made them famous, were not prepared to yield to any nation. Other tribes, to save face, also made bids for the first place. Finally the worried Commissioner settled the matter arbitrarily.

Immediately a new difficulty arose—all the various bands and tribes within each nation began to wrangle as to their relative importance; each, with many voices and at great length, presenting its credentials to consideration and first rank. The harassed Commissioner finally had to settle this dispute in the same arbitrary manner.

But this only brought on an even more ticklish problem. Within each tribe or band every individual chief and brave insistently claimed precedence, each one eager to obtain official validation of his alleged priority. It would have taken all winter to hear their stories. The warlike exploits of all these men were many and various. A man who had been wounded in battle might claim that his daring had been greater than that of a mere horse thief; while the horse thief claimed he was certainly superior to the next fellow who had only captured a weapon. It was impossible to weigh the merits of these contenders. At last the Commissioner, at his wit's end, had again to intervene and seat the men arbitrarily.

During all the time spent in this futile argument, Jim Bridger was on his feet, listening attentively, translating carefully, often supplementing his talk by the fluid gestures of the sign language. That was exhausting work. It was a relief when the cussed Injuns settled down and lighted the pipe.

But even that did not end Bridger's difficulties, for the council had not yet even begun.

The points covered by the treaty were few, but highly controversial. First of all the white men desired *peace*, and the Indians professed themselves willing enough to have peace—*if* they could get it without losing their livelihood. As one of them put it: "*War is indispensable*. Of course we lose a few men every year, but so do our enemies. If we smoke with them, they will crowd into our hunting grounds, and we shall starve. Anyhow, I don't believe that our old enemies will keep the peace, if we make it. They cannot be trusted, and then *we* shall be blamed for fighting."

However, the old men—with the promised backing of the United States—were willing to try this novel experiment.

The second thing the white men wanted was permission to build *roads* and *forts* in Indian hunting grounds. That, every redskin felt, was asking a heap. So far all the trouble on the Plains between whites and Indians had come from that Great Medicine Road, the Oregon Trail. In fact, that was why they were holding this very treaty council. Yet now, instead of closing that troublesome trail, the government wanted to open others. There would only be more starvation, more strife. It seemed that the Grandfather at Washington was making peace with one hand and war with the other. But finally the chiefs gave in.

They agreed too that it was all very well for the government to pay *damages* to Indians for depredations white men committed; but who was to catch the criminals? And on the other hand, how could an Indian chief confidently promise to turn over to the white men an offending member of his own tribe for punishment? That was unheard of.

However, they all hoped this last problem would never arise; they gave way on that point too. But before they could do so, all the long-winded chiefs and swelling orators had to be heard from; Bridger listened and talked and translated and paraphrased and explained all day and every day until his tongue hung out.

Boundaries of the tribal lands had then to be agreed upon, with the purpose of keeping each tribe within its own hunting grounds—no matter where the game might wander! Inasmuch as the Indians had never grasped the notion that they would be expected to stay within their own boundaries, this matter was settled without much debate.

But when Colonel Mitchell, anxious to establish some authority with which the United States could deal, proposed that each nation elect *one head chief*, the Indians' imagination staggered.

Among them no chief had any real authority other than his personal prestige and the temporary backing of some warrior society. The Sioux alone were scattered over a territory as large as Texas; their nation comprised seven grand divisions, each of which comprised seven tribes, each of which comprised seven or more—usually many more—bands, making a grand total of nearly four hundred separate political units, all with their own ambitious and jealous leaders, all independent, nomadic, and self-supporting. No chief could punish, imprison, or tax his people. In fact, there was no government at all, except while a tribal hunt or ceremony was going on.

A chief was, in truth, hardly more than a spokesman for the warrior societies. Apart from that, his function was to prevent quarrels—usually by bribing troublemakers to keep the peace—and to see that nobody starved. To claim any real power over his jealous tribesmen was simply to invite assassination.

And so the Sioux spokesman finally declared: "We have decided differently from you, Father, about this chief for the nation. We want a chief for each band, and if you will make one or two chiefs for each band, it will be much better for you and for the whites. Then we will make soldiers (police) of our young men, and we will make them good to the whites and to other Indians. But, Father, *we cannot make one chief*."

But the distracted Commissioner, unable to see the solid good sense of these remarks, up and made a chief for *all* the Sioux—a man named Stirring Bear. Stirring Bear was thunderstruck. Yet he bravely accepted his appointment, though he declared it a sentence of death—as in fact it soon proved to be. He was a warrior; he could not refuse so hazardous an office without disgrace.

And so the Commissioner had his way. The Sioux held their first election, signed the treaty, received their presents, and promptly hit the trail to their hunting grounds. The chiefs rode off wearing pants for the first time—the uniforms of generals, colonels, captains, and lieutenants—with broad silver medals hung round their necks, and in their pockets fancy papers certifying to their good character.

As Washakie had feared, the treaty gave part of the Snake country to the Crows—the Big Horn Country clear up to the Wind River Range!

What Jim Bridger thought of these fantastic arrangements was never recorded.[5] But he was probably in agreement with his friend Washakie, who—most politely—made the correct comment on the treaty council: "Grandfather, I have come a great distance to see you and hear you. I threw my family too, away, to come and listen, and I am glad and my people are glad that we have come. Our hearts are full of your words. *We will talk them over again.*"[6]

Jim had good reason to be proud of his Shoshones. They had made no bombastic boasts or arrogant threats, no futile complaints, and no false promises. They could take care of themselves, if left alone. All through the weeks spent at the grand council, the Snakes had held church every Sunday, and listened with close attention to the preacher they had brought along. He taught them practical Christianity. Of him Bridger said, "I don't know nothing about religion as I used to hear it in the States; but me and the Snakes don't have no trouble in believing what *he* says, and I tell you he just leads the Snakes about right." [7]

When the council was over and the Indians gone, Bridger packed up his possibles and saddled his horse. It was time to hit the trail. He had taken a liking to Corporal Lowe, and when they parted, shook the young man's hand, looked at him keenly, and gave him good advice: "Young man, don't stay in the army no longer than your time's out, but come right up to Bridger. Thar's more money in the mountains than in all the rest of the world—gold till you can't rest, and I know where some of it is. Now be sure to come to me. Good bye." [8]

On the trail from Laramie, Bridger had time to think of his own problems again. It irked him that the Mormons, who talked so much about being friends with the Lamanites (as they called the redskins), were so resentful because he had sold weapons to the friendly Snakes. Looked as if the Saints only liked Injuns who were unfriendly to Uncle Sam.

XVIII
THE SAINTS
RAID FORT BRIDGER

THERE is generally a *cause* for every action a man performs, a cause by no means always identical with the *reason* for that action which the man offers to himself—and to others. Confucius gives us the practical though somewhat cynical suggestion that a wise man acts first, and speaks afterward according to his actions.

These principles of universal psychology may help us better to understand what lay behind the quarrel between Jim Bridger and Brigham Young, the Mormon leader. One thing is clear. Brigham soon took a strong dislike to Bridger, and apparently made up his mind to rid the country of him.

At first, when the Mormons needed Jim's advice and help, they were friendly enough. Later they were hostile.

Some would have it that all the trouble between these two men originated in a woman's spite. These persons would have it that, after Bridger's Ute wife died in childbirth, July 4, 1849, Jim married a Mormon woman, that they fell out and parted, and that her spiteful, whispering tongue was the source of all the evil rumors about Bridger current among the Saints.

This story hardly fits Bridger's known circumstances, tastes, and habits. He had as much sense as any Mountain Man alive—and hardly any Mountain Man alive was fool enough to wed a *fofurraw* white gal from the settlements. Pale as a ghost, thin as a rail, and green as grass, a white gal was no good in camp or on the trail. Moreover, Mountain Men had lived so long among the pesky redskins that their idea of female beauty war an Injun idee, and you can lay to that. Bridger sincerely respected his Injun women, treated them as wives, and adored his halfbreed children. And in those days, even if he had wanted to wed a white gal—would she have had him?

One thing is sure. If Jim did marry a Mormon, she was an all-fired heap of spunk to have stirred up all that trouble between Jim and Brigham.

The reasons given by historians for their quarrel is that Brigham believed Bridger was inciting the redskins to attack the Mormon settlements, and that Jim spied on the Mormons and reported their doings to Washington. As early as 1849 Brigham wrote, "I believe that Old Bridger is death on us."

That is the *reason* usually given. But there were also *causes* why Brigham should dislike Bridger:

First, when Brigham led his Saints to the Promised Land of Salt Lake Valley, he found Bridger there before him, already familiar with every nook and corner of the region, and—in effect—in possession. Bridger called that country "My paradise." And Bridger was a "gentile."

Moreover, the two men faced in different directions. Both were naturally paternal and protective, but in return for their services to others, each had been conditioned to expect a different reward. Brigham demanded power, authority; Bridger was satisfied with money and goodwill. The severe discipline imposed by life in the mountains had made Jim perfectly independent, with no craving to assume responsibility for any others, although he was willing enough to help them help themselves. Brigham offered his followers an attractive Utopia. But Bridger knew well enough that the price of Utopia is always a man's liberty and that the salesmen of Utopias demand immediate payment, though they can only promise delivery at some future date. So far, Bridger had never heard of a Utopia that had been delivered.

Old Jim had acquired the Indian's impatience of prayers which were not strong enough to bring a satisfactory answer, and it looked to him as if the Mormons would have to pray almighty hard to make corn grow at that altitude. Jim had all an Indian's tolerance, and he naturally expected others to show a like tolerance for him. If Jim was to live with Brigham, it would have to be on absolutely equal and independent terms. Jim Bridger did not know how to play second fiddle to any man.

Second, Brigham professed great friendship and love for the Indians, whom the Mormons called Lamanites, and believed were descended from the Lost Tribes of Israel. Here again, Bridger was before him, had cornered the Indian trade, made friends with the chiefs, armed the warriors, and married into the tribes. They all trusted the Blanket Chief absolutely.

Third, Brigham had a liking and need for military power, and held Danites, militia, and "destroying angels" at his command. Here again Bridger, who had armed the whole tribe of Snakes with modern rifles, had all the best of it. Brigham's greenhorns were no match for Injuns, and no Injuns in that region could match Bridger's Snakes.

Fourth, the Mormons were desperately poor, and Brigham badly needed a monopoly of the trade with emigrants on the Oregon and Salt Lake Trails. Here again Bridger was ahead of him—Fort Bridger sat astride the main trail to Brigham's capital and supplied all the wants of emigrants, on Brigham's very doorstep. In fact, Louis Vasquez and Jim Bridger even had a store in Salt Lake City, or Deseret—as the Mormons called it. Of course Jim let his portly Mexican partner run the store: no city life for Jim Bridger.

Fifth, Brigham had led his people to the Promised Land, declaring that he would make the desert blossom like the rose. But as yet—what with drouth and crickets—the country would not even bud. Bridger had warned the Mormons about that climate, and so far he was in a position to say "I told you so."

Sixth, the Mountain Man's endless generosity, his lavish hospitality, his Indian prodigality were in too painful contrast with the Spartan thrift and privations of the Saints. Brigham wanted his people to make ends meet, but always feared the effects of wealth. And these Mountain Men! Vasquez flaunted his prosperity in fine raiment and a coach and

four. Old Gabe lived simply, but gave away the half of all
he gained. What an example to Brigham's impoverished
Saints!

Seventh, Brigham had come to Utah to be the big buck of
that lick, and here again Bridger was before him—famous
from Mexico to the British Possessions, from the Missouri to
the Pacific. Brigham was a great man among the Mormons;
Bridger was a great man everywhere.

Eighth, Brigham and the Mormons had chosen the country around Independence, Missouri, as the site for their
Temple. The Missourians had run them out—and Bridger
was a Missourian and had, to boot, a farm not far from Independence on what might well have been Mormon land.

Finally, Old Gabe had done many favors to Mormons.
Nobody could be around Bridger long and not share in his
beneficence. But the Mormons in those days, feeling themselves at once outcasts and a chosen people, wished passionately to be self-sufficient. Brigham must have found it hard
to forgive Bridger's favors.

When you consider all these *causes* why Brigham should
hate Bridger, you hardly need to look further for *reasons*.

Jim shook his head. Looked like Brigham thought thar
warn't room enough for him and Bridger both in the mountains. Brigham war spilin' for a fight, like a buffalo bull in
flytime, faunchin' and pawin' up the dirt, swingin' his horns
—and bellerin' like all git out.

Jim was ready to be friends.

But when Bridger was pleasant and brought good news,
Brigham declared Jim was lying; when Bridger tried to
warn the pushcart prophet that the Utes were plotting
trouble, Brigham accused Jim of fomenting it.

The facts, as we have them, show that Bridger, on the contrary, was all for peace and order—since his living depended

on trails kept open for emigrant travel. Jim was intimate with Army officers sent out, and with Chief Washakie of the Snakes, who were always at peace with the Mormons. Business was good. Jim had no time for fighting.

Yet many a Mormon said and believed that Bridger was inciting the redskins to drive the Saints out of Salt Lake Valley. The Saints had been driven out of the States by superior force and the pressure of public opinion. But now, believing as they did, they were *not* going to be driven any farther—certainly not by *one man*.

Shaking the dust of the United States from their weary feet, the Saints had settled in Utah in 1847 while Utah still belonged to Mexico. The next year, to their manifest disgust, the first cession after the Mexican War handed them right back to Uncle Sam.

Considering how persecuted the Saints had been in the States, and how impoverished they were at first in their Promised Land, it is hardly surprising that some of them resented Bridger's prosperity on their doorstep and his influence over Mountain Men and Indians. All trails led to Fort Bridger—it was the social center of the mountains, a rendezvous and refuge for all.

Moreover, in 1849, the Mormons were unhappy under the territorial officers sent out from Washington, and greatly alarmed at the coming of Captain Howard Stansbury and Lieutenant J. W. Gunnison to make surveys. And when the Captain officially recommended that the United States government make a military post and Indian agency of Fort Bridger with Old Jim in charge, the Saints jumped a mile high. So, when—early in 1851—Brigham Young was appointed Governor of the Territory and acting Indian Agent, they thought the time was ripe.

The new Secretary of the Territory, Mr. B. G. Ferris,

was not a Mormon. He passed Fort Bridger on his way to the Mormon capital in October, 1852. His wife gives us our last picture of Old Jim in the mountain home he loved so well:

"On the evening of the 19th we encamped at Fort Bridger —a long, low, strongly-constructed log building, surrounded by a high wall of logs, stuck endwise in the ground. Bridger came out and invited us in, and introduced us to his Indian wife, and showed us his half-breed children—keen, bright-eyed little things. Everything was rude and primitive. This man strongly attracted my attention; there was more than civility about him—there was native politeness. He is the oldest trapper in the Rocky Mountains; his language is very graphic and descriptive, and he is evidently a man of great shrewdness. He alarmed us in regard to our prospects of getting through; said the season had arrived when a heavy snow might be looked for any day; urged us to stay with him all winter; showed us where we could lodge, guarded against the cold with plenty of buffalo skins; and assured us that he could make the benefit of our society and the assistance of Mr. Ferris, in his business, more than compensate for the expenses of living. This was a delicate way of offering the hospitalities of his establishment without remuneration.

"His wife was simplicity itself. She exhibited some curious pieces of Indian embroidery, the work of her own hands, with as much pleased hilarity as a child; and gave me a quantity of raisins and sauce berries—altogether, it was a very pleasant interview. He told us, if we were determined to go, to make as little delay as possible; and made a very acceptable addition to our larder, in the shape of fresh potatoes and other vegetables." [1]

Of course Vasquez, sitting snug in Brigham's capital, was

in place to keep his partner, Bridger, fully informed of what tricks the Mormons were up to.

Their first move against Bridger was an attempt to take over the Green River ferries, which had been owned and operated by Mountain Men for many a season past. But the Mountain Men unlimbered their guns, stood off the covetous Saints, and that season collected as usual some $300,000 from emigrants crossing in their boats.

Indignantly, the Mormons filed suit! [2] That was a big laugh around all the campfires in the mountains!

Ever since traders first came to the mountains, they had been swapping guns, powder, lead, and flints to the Indians with which to hunt buffalo and kill each other. But now all at once the defeated would-be ferrymen, trailing home to Salt Lake, made affidavit that James Bridger was trading powder and lead to the redskins—*to kill Mormons!* The sheriff was ordered to seize Bridger's goods, arrest their owner, and bring him a prisoner to Utah.

The Mormon capital was all agog at this daring expedition to take Bridger and his fort. At the time Old Jim was there alone with his family. But the bold sheriff was undaunted. Quickly he chose his stalwart deputies and rode out to catch Bridger—with a posse of one hundred and fifty men!

"The [Mormon] city was in a high state of excitement for several weeks, and in constant expectation of the arrival of the captive." [3]

Bridger, of course, knew what was up, and was not at home when the posse arrived at his fort. His poker-faced Snake wife had no idea where Jim might be. After due time the sheriff shrewdly surmised that Bridger was hiding in the mountains and that, sooner or later, he must return to the fort for supplies.

So, when the sheriff and his men had drunk up all Bridger's whisky, driven off all his livestock, and carried off in his wagons everything loose around the place, they quietly withdrew—to lie in wait until the old scout should come home again.

Old Jim had not been dodging Injuns for thirty year to put his foot now in a trap set by such a parcel of greenhorns. He might have laughed, if he had not been so all-fired mad.

After a long and fruitless wait, the disgruntled posse attacked and killed the ferrymen on Green River, looted their quarters, lifted their stock, and set out for home.

The members of that posse were strong, silent men—after that.

One lady in Salt Lake City reports, "What was his [Jim's] fate, or that of his family, none but the few 'Danites' who were engaged in that mission can tell; and for some reason the same men who had spoken freely to me of other crimes, were silent upon this point." [4]

As soon as the posse had pulled out, Bridger came down from his hideout, and in November hired a government surveyor to make a survey of the lands around the fort—some 3800 acres—on which he intended to file.

That winter a party of Saints were sent to move into Fort Bridger, with orders to marry the daughters of Indian chiefs in the neighborhood, and so gain control of the tribes.

Led by one of the Twelve Apostles, they came to drive the Mountain Men out of all that region. Twelve Mountain Men met and drove *them*.

The scared Saints moved away and spent a shivering winter camping in the snow. Meanwhile Bridger went to Missouri, and on March 9, 1854, filed his claim with the General Land Office, Washington, D. C.

Thirty years later the Mormons claimed that Brigham

had bought Fort Bridger from Old Jim in 1853—presumably at the time the posse was out looking for him. Jim Bridger's memory was one of the best—but he could never recall that deal. . . .

We have Bridger's own account of what happened that summer, recorded by his friend, Captain Marcy:

"Here he erected an establishment which he called Fort Bridger, . . . and here he was for several years prosecuting a profitable traffic both with the Indians and with California emigrants. At length, however, his prosperity excited the cupidity of the Mormons, and they intimated to him that his presence in such close proximity to their settlements was not agreeable, and advised him to pull up stakes and leave forthwith; and upon his questioning the legality or justice of this arbitrary summons, they came to his place with a force of 'avenging angels' and forced him to make his escape to the woods in order to save his life. He remained secreted for several days, and through the assistance of his Indian wife was enabled to elude the search of the Danites and make his way to Fort Laramie, leaving all his cattle and other property in possession of the Mormons." [5]

Bridger's letter to his Senator, G. B. Butler, gives the story in his own words:

"I was robbed and threatened with death by the Mormons, by the direction of Brigham Young, of all my merchandise, livestock, in fact everything I possessed, amounting to more than $100,000 worth, the buildings in the fort partially destroyed by fire, and I barely escaped with my life." [6]

4

GUIDE

XIX
SIR GEORGE GORE

JIM BRIDGER was not the man to sit at home indefinitely. Late in 1854 he turned up at Fort Laramie. There he found himself in the middle of a bunch of furriners.

These strangers formed the retinue of Sir George Gore, a sportsman from Sligo, Ireland. Well able to pay for what he wanted, Sir George had brought along several scientific friends and a considerable staff to help him hunt bear and buffalo along the Yellowstone. Already he had made an expedition into the Black Hills and the Rockies. Henry Chatillon and his brother had been acting as guides—the Henry Chatillon who had been guide to Francis Parkman when he was gathering material for his book *The Oregon Trail*.[1] Parkman had high praise for Henry, but Bridger's qualifications put Henry's in the shade.

In a small community like that at Fort Laramie, Bridger and Sir George were bound to meet. Sir George looked forward to the meeting, and Jim had not forgotten his pleasant contact with the hospitable Sir William Drummond Stuart.

Jim found Sir George, if possible, more affable and generous than Sir William, and of course the Irish sportsman was delighted to shake the hand of that mighty hunter and

scout, Major James Bridger. He set his heart on getting
Bridger to act as his guide for the coming year, and having
an income of some $200,000 a year was not the man to hag-
gle. He liked to do things in the grand manner—as was
proved by his elaborate preparations for the hunt.

Apparently the two men hit it off from the start. Jim
liked the lively, vital Irishman; he was a good horseman, a
crack shot, and as openhanded as an Indian. Sir George, on
the other hand, was eager to learn what Bridger could teach
him about the habits of game animals, Indian customs, and
living in the wilds. Moreover, Sir George had sufficient liter-
ary taste to appreciate the color and pith of the trapper
slang in which Jim habitually expressed himself. Sir George
was bubbling over with enthusiasm, sure that, with Bridger
as guide, the expedition would not only provide exhilarating
sport but improve his health.

Jim was no respecter of persons, and the Irishman's title
meant nothing to him. Jim liked the man himself, and they
got on together like a couple of thieves.

That fall of '54 was not the season to venture out upon
the freezing Plains, and Sir George planned to remain at
the fort until spring. Bridger agreed to stay with him if the
pay for his services could begin at once.

During the winter he became acquainted with the members
of the Irishman's entourage, which he found consisted of some
fifty men—"comprising secretaries, stewards, cooks, flymak-
ers, dog tenders, hunters, servants,"—besides a string of saddle horses and hounds galore.

Sir George found life at Fort Laramie very interesting,
and Jim was kept busy explaining the meaning of what went
on. Indians came to trade; trappers dropped in for a ca-
rouse; and in the long winter evenings or when cold and
snow kept the pair indoors, Sir George regularly pumped

Bridger about his adventures. By the time the first thunder bellowed in the spring, the two men were fast friends.

When the snow was gone, the outfit prepared to put out on the trail to the Yellowstone: "forty men, supplied with 112 horses—some very fine ones—12 yoke of cattle, 14 dogs, 6 wagons, and 21 carts.[2]

Jim guided the outfit up the Platte to Casper Creek, then headed north to the headwaters of Powder River. As summer advanced, the party moved slowly down the Powder to its mouth, hunting as they went. Leaving the Powder, they moved up the Yellowstone to the mouth of Tongue River. There, on the Tongue, they forted for the winter a few miles above the mouth.

Sir George, of course, was equipped with a perfect arsenal of guns of different calibers adapted to hunting every kind of game. Most of these were by the famous makers of that day: Joe Manton, Purdy, Westley Richards. Bridger had to admit that his booshway was fixed to make game come— from a chipmunk up to Old Ephraim himself. As time went on Sir George collected wagon-loads of trophies to show to his friends at home.

Bridger, like most hunters in the West, including Indians, had always been accustomed to get up while it was still dark and to do his hunting early in the morning. He had a hard time getting used to Sir George's lazy ways. For the Irishman slept until ten or eleven in the morning. On rising he bathed, ate a leisurely breakfast, and then went out alone or with one or two companions for the day's hunt. Often he stayed out until ten o'clock at night. But he seldom returned to camp without some trophies.

Bridger, like the Indians, hunted for meat or pelts. He never killed game for which he had no use. Hunting for horned heads was like going after sculps.

But Sir George, making the most of his one opportunity to hunt in the West, slaughtered the enormous aggregate of forty grizzly bears, 2500 buffalo, and uncounted elk, deer, antelope, and other "small" game. He collected trophies enough to stock half a dozen museums. The Indians who visited his camp showed resentment at this slaughter.

But whenever anyone criticized Sir George, he found Jim Bridger on his trail. Bridger "always commended him as a bold, dashing, and successful sportsman, a social champion, and an agreeable gentleman." Captain R. B. Marcy, who knew Bridger and met Sir George, bears witness to this; and he gives an amusing account of what went on when the day's hunt was over:

"His dinner was then ordered, to partake of which he generally extended an invitation to my friend Bridger, and after the repast was concluded, and a few glasses of wine had been drunk, he was in the habit of reading from some book, and eliciting from Bridger his comments thereon. His favorite author was Shakespeare, which Bridger 'reckon'd was a leetle too highfalutin' for him'; moreover, he remarked that he 'rayther calculated that thar big Dutchman, Mr. *Full-stuff*, was a leetle bit too fond of lager beer,' and suggested that probably it might have been better for the old man if he had imbibed the same amount of alcohol in the more condensed medium of good old Bourbon whisky.

"Bridger seemed deeply interested in the adventures of Baron Munchausen, but admitted after the reading was finished that 'he be dogond ef he swallered every thing that thar *Baren* Mountchawson said, and he thout he was a durn'd liar.' Yet, upon further reflection, he acknowledged that some of his own experiences among the Blackfeet would be equally marvelous '*ef writ down in a book.*'

"One evening Sir George entertained his auditor by read-

ing to him Sir Walter Scott's account of the battle of Waterloo, and afterward asked him if he did not regard that as the
most sanguinary battle he had ever heard of. To which
Bridger replied, "Wall, now, Mr. Gore, that thar must 'a bin
a considdible of a skrimmage, dogon my skin ef it mustn't;
them Britishers must 'a fit better thar than they did down to
Horleans, whar Old Hickry gin um the forkedest sort o'
chain-lightnin' that prehaps you ever did see in all yer born
days!' And upon Sir George's expressing a little incredulity
in regard to the estimate Bridger placed upon his battle, the
latter added, 'You can jist go yer pile on it, Mr. Gore—*you
can*, as sure as yer born.' " [3]

Sir George, of course, had no mind to stay in the fort
which he had built, along with the greenhorns who served
him. There was good grazing at the mouth of the Tongue,
and there he and Jim and a few others camped all winter
with the horses and hounds, where they could live outdoors
and find game more easily than around the fort. One member
of the party died during the winter; otherwise the expedition
was a complete success.

In the spring of 1856, as soon as the grass was high enough
to provide forage for the stock, Sir George reluctantly left
his happy hunting grounds and moved up Tongue River to
Wolf's Tooth Creek. There he crossed over by the headwaters of the Rosebud to Wolf Mountain, looking for a big
camp of Crow Indians. In their camp Sir George feasted in
the tipis of the chiefs and filled his memory with pictures of
Plains Indian life. Apparently he liked the Indians well
enough, but was disgusted by the squaw men in the camp.

Returning to Tongue River, the party built and launched
two flatboats. Sending the wagons overland, Sir George and
Bridger floated down the Yellowstone to its mouth and Fort
Union.

Fort Union was then the largest trading post in the West. It belonged to the American Fur Company. Major Culbertson was in charge. Culbertson made Sir George welcome, and the Irishman ordered two Mackinaws built in which to go down to St. Louis. He also bargained with the Major, trying to sell the livestock and wagons for which he had no longer any use. But when the Mackinaws were finished and the time came for settlement, there was some disagreement over the terms of the sale. Sir George thought Culbertson was trying to skin him.

Though recklessly openhanded when he thought himself well treated, Sir George was wrathy as a bear when he believed someone was trying to get the best of him. He lost his temper and refused to go through with the deal.

As the fur company was the only possible bidder, Culbertson may have thought that Sir George had no choice. But the Irishman soon showed that he would not be imposed upon. He put all his wagons and all supplies no longer needed in a great pile right in front of the gateway of the fort and set it all on fire.

To make sure nobody interfered, he posted armed guards around the conflagration.

When the goods were reduced to ashes, Sir George remembered that in those ashes were the iron parts of the wagons—and iron was valuable so far from civilization. Determined that no man of the fur company should profit by so much as a single bolt, Sir George ordered all the irons raked from the ashes and then thrown into the Missouri River. Unwilling to shoot his horses and cattle, he gave them to his retainers and to Indians about the fort, disdainfully left the two Mackinaws Culbertson had built for him at their moorings, stowed his precious trophies in the flatboats he himself had built at Tongue River, and floated away, down to Fort Berthold.

An Indian chief named Crow's Breast hospitably turned
over his roomy earth-lodge to Sir George and the few remaining members of his retinue. And in this earth-lodge Sir
George camped for the winter. At Berthold he found two
rival traders established, who were continually at odds over
the small trade of the Village Indians. Sir George amused
himself by taking an active part in this feud. Finding that
one trader had raised the price on beef cattle to $50 a head,

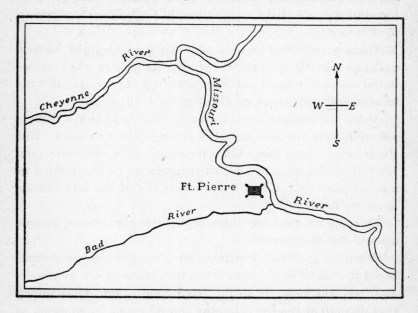

Sir George went over to the other, who was asking only $30,
and bought up ten times the number of steers he needed—
just to beat the price down.

Once Sir George was established at Berthold, Bridger's
services were no longer needed. Reluctantly the two men
parted. They were both friendly souls, but both tough fighters when wronged. Jim got into a dugout canoe and pad-
dled down the Missouri to Kansas City and his family. The

expedition had been a junket for Bridger. He reached home with his possible sack full of dollars.

Jim went on to Washington, D. C., to give his opinion on the Mormons and to learn the administration's attitude towards the Saints. While he was in Washington, a Senator from Missouri introduced Jim to the President. Jim must have gone home in a cheerful frame of mind. He was sure that the United States Government was at last going to do something about the cussed Mormons.

On his return Jim met Captain Marcy at Fort Laramie. Marcy reports: "As may be imagined, he did not entertain the most friendly feeling for the '*Latter Day Saints*,' and he would not probably have gone very far out of his way to have *saved* their *sculps*, as he termed the savages' battle trophies."

Wagh!

XX

THE MARCH SOUTH

To JIM BRIDGER it seemed that the longer Brigham Young and his Saints went on living under the government of the United States, the less they appeared to like it. They so resented the presence and conduct of the territorial officials sent out from Washington that before long most people in the States became convinced that all Mormons were seditious. President Buchanan ordered troops to Utah.

Bridger grinned. It was about time.*

When the Mormon War caught up with Jim, he happened to be at Fort Laramie, where he was promptly employed as a guide for the Army of Utah, July 16, 1857, at five dollars

---

* Captain Marcy describes Jim Bridger at this time as "about sixty years of age, tall, thin, wiry, with a complexion well bronzed by toil and exposure, with an independent, generous, and open cast of countenance indicative of brave and noble impulses."

a day. Besides his wages, Jim knew he would receive a toll
for every government wagon that crossed the North Platte
on Bridger's Ferry. Bridger bought and improved this ferry
with the purpose of putting out of business a Mormon ferry
nearby—and done it, too.

It was a funny war, Jim thought. And in truth the Mormon War was a fit subject for a comic opera, as wordy as it
was bloodless. The Army, moving towards Utah, professed
to be "kindly and peaceful," its officers merely scolded the
Mormons, and its soldiers had orders to fire only in self defense. On the other hand, the vacillating Mormon guerrillas
alternately burned government wagon trains and their own
fortifications—including Fort Bridger.

At a safe distance from all this carnage, a Mormon bishop
ranted, "The whole world cannot prevail against the Saints,"
while another spiritual leader boasted that he had "wives
enough to whip the States." [1]

Brigham Young—taking example from the Czar of Napoleon's day—pledged his people to a scorched earth policy and
prepared them to retreat, if necessary, all the way to Mexico.

Meanwhile, Bridger was getting the Army wagon trains
steadily up the trail and over South Pass. There winter
caught them, and as the Mormons had run off many of their
beef cattle and burned some of their wagons, the troops were
hungry and ill-housed. It looked as if the war would collapse
of sheer bad management.

Then Bridger pitched in. He had a talk with the commander of the Army, proposed a plan for better winter quarters for the men, and, on November 18, was successful in
leasing his claim and the charred ruins of Fort Bridger to
Uncle Sam for $600 a year, also agreeing that the govern-
ment might buy the lands at any time for $10,000.

So General Albert Sidney Johnston got a bargain, and

Jim Bridger put his lands where Brigham could not touch them.

That winter Jim had plenty on his hands, with a valley full of greenhorns in uniform. But he was so used to wintering in the mountains that he soon made life there almost as easy for them as it was for him. When "snow boats" sailed like balloons from the snow peaks, Jim would know a storm was coming, and hurried his officers and men into camp in good time. He taught them all to live in the snow and like it.

All winter long the Mormons gloated and boasted.

But when the spring thaw began, their warlike oratory dwindled to a whisper. Bridger had prevented Brigham's guerrillas from putting the troops at his mercy. They had come through the winter in good shape and were ready to march. Brigham promptly disbanded his militia and called for help from friends in the States.

Volunteer peace-makers hurried out from the States. Conferences and concessions followed, and then—after all the big talk—the Mormons knuckled under.

President Buchanan sent Brigham a *pardon*. Brigham did not refuse it, though he professed not to know what it was for—unless for the little matter of appropriating Uncle Sam's cattle and burning his wagon trains—and loudly proclaimed his rebellious followers to be "a loyal and law-abiding people."

The Mormons agreed to receive and obey the laws and officers of the United States.

Then—as Bridger saw it—Brigham, having saved his skin, set quickly about saving his face.

He ordered all the Saints in northern Utah to move out ahead of the troops—apparently on their way to Mexico! It was just about time for the farmers to put in their crops, but they let their crops go and obeyed orders. The trails were crowded with refugees and their nondescript baggage. Brigham cleared the country, he said, to prevent any show of resistance to the troops which might lead to trouble. And as a final grand gesture—still following the example of the Czar when Napoleon entered Moscow—Brigham ordered Salt Lake City evacuated.

Professing to fear that the troops would sack the city, the Mormons piled straw in their houses and left sentinels on guard, ready to set it in flames.

By that time Captain Marcy had obtained new saddle horses from New Mexico. The troops mounted these, and General Johnston led them into Brigham's capital. Jim Bridger rode as his guide.

That was a strange march—of an American army through the streets of a city of Americans—albeit not Americans by their own free choice. The scene was an unusual one on this continent, one of the most extraordinary of our history.

"All day long, from dawn till after sunset, the troops and trains poured through the city, the utter silence of the streets being broken only by the music of the military bands, the monotonous tramp of the regiments, and the rattle of the baggage wagons. . . . The only visible groups of spectators were on the corners near Brigham Young's residence, and consisted almost entirely of Gentile civilians. The stillness was so profound that, during the intervals between the passage of the columns, the monotonous gurgle of City Creek struck on every ear. . . . The troops crossed the Jordan (River) and encamped two miles from the city, on a dusty meadow by the river bank."[2]

Jim Bridger must have enjoyed that quiet ride through the broad echoing streets of Brigham's town. Old Brigham had run him out of his stronghold, looted his fort. Now Jim had leased that fort to Uncle Sam right under Brigham's nose—and had helped run Brigham out of his own strong-hold.

So now hyar he war, Jim Bridger, riding alongside the General at the head of Uncle Sam's boys, with a heart as big as thunder, whar nary a Mormon dared to show his nose.

Old Brigham had aimed to run Jim clean out of the mountains. And now, whar war Brigham?

Who did he think this country belonged to, anyhow? Jim reckoned maybeso this would l'arn him.

As soon as General Johnston could round up the runaway Saints and send them packing to their homes, Bridger knew that his work as guide was ended. He put in for his discharge in July, 1858, got it, and then lit out for his farm at Little Santa Fe, the only home he had left.

When he reached it he found, to his great joy, a new son, William, just six months old. But Jim also found, to his great sorrow, a new-made grave, where in his absence the child's mother had been laid to rest.

His loss was aggravated by his idleness. For the second time in his life, his profession was wiped out. Jim hardly knew where to turn to maintain his growing family.

It was a relief to Bridger when, on the recommendation of Pierre Chouteau, Captain W. F. Raynolds, Corps of Engineers, U.S. Army, engaged him as guide. Their mission was the exploration of the Yellowstone River and its tributaries, together with regions adjacent to the east and west. Bridger found the expedition well equipped, and staffed with enthusiastic and likeable officers. Of course there was no "exploration" on such a trip for Bridger; he had been over all that ground often enough. For him, it was a mountain junket—with all expenses paid and wages to boot. It was just the vacation he needed.

They set out from St. Louis on a steamboat at the end of

May, 1859, picked up their military escort at Fort Randall, and made sure that the Sioux were peaceful before they pushed on into Indian country. By the end of July, Jim had led them to the Little Powder River. They went on to the Tongue, explored the Big Horn and its mighty canyon, held pow-wows with Crows at Fort Sarpy, and, early in September, were on Soap Creek.

There they had their first mule stolen by an Indian horse thief.

Bridger had plenty of time to hunt along the way, and killed one of the largest elk he had ever seen. The head and horns had to be cut off so that they could put the carcass into the cart. What was left looked bigger than any mule in the herd. Buffalo, elk, deer and antelope, and bear all fell before Bridger's rifle. Meanwhile Jim was making firm friends of Lt. H. E. Maynadier, Dr. Ferdinand Vandeveer Hayden, Mr. Snowden, and other gentlemen in the party. By the middle of November he got them all settled in snug winter quarters at the Indian Agency of the Upper Platte.

It was an interesting mission for the officers. The Sioux tried to bluff them, traders sold their men more liquor than the men could carry, they saw the Pony Express gallop past, and listened eagerly to Bridger's detailed accounts of Colter's Hell.

Bridger's stories of that wondrous region so excited Raynolds that he determined to see those marvels for himself. Bridger was delighted. Now at last he saw his chance to get official backing for his accounts of the Hot Springs, the geysers, the Lake, and the Fire Hole River. Whenever he had told what he saw there, the press and the public had combined to laugh at him and refer contemptuously to "Old Jim Bridger's lies." Jim had retaliated—Indian-fashion—by spinning yarns and telling whoppers—which, however much he enjoyed it, was not the best way to convince the nation that he had been telling the truth about Yellowstone Park. The unbelief of the public as to his great discoveries was a mighty sore point with Jim. Now he had a chance to *show* the doubters. He was just as eager as Raynolds to take the party through.

But luck was against Jim. He found the snow so deep that, in all honesty, he was forced to advise the Captain to give it up. They pushed on to Three Forks by a route to the west of those natural marvels. Jim Bridger was still rated as the nation's biggest liar by the incredulous public. It was a bitter disappointment.

But though the public might jeer, this expedition convinced most intelligent Army officers that Bridger was a scout and explorer of the first rank. The map Raynolds made of all that region was used in Indian campaigns for years after, and it was manifest to anyone who studied it that Bridger had supplied most of the information charted on that big white paper, since the Captain's route showed that he had not visited half the places on his map. Bridger supplied the detail.

What is more, Raynolds filled his journal with praise of Bridger, praise of his knowledge of the country, his reliability and his competence as guide. In fact, Raynolds defends Jim for the only mistake he made on the whole expedition. When they were disappointed in their plan to visit the wonders of the Park, Bridger led them around it by way of Jackson's Hole and Pierre's Hole towards what he took to be Henry's Fork. As it turned out, the stream soon revealed itself as Spring Fork. Raynolds reports, "these little errors in matters of detail on his (Jim's) part are not remarkable, as it is fifteen years since he last visited this region, and they

fade into insignificance when compared with his accurate
general knowledge of the country."

Raynolds' map became the standard map of that region,
and so remained for many years after; at last Bridger's
topographical knowledge of the mountains had been set down
in black and white, to remain a permanent record of his
achievements as an explorer.

That map, and Raynolds' report on his expedition, soon
brought Jim another call for his services.

XXI
TALL TALES

It was now almost forty years since Jim Bridger went up
the Missouri under Ashley and Henry. When a stranger
asked him how long he had been on the frontier, it was his
habit to reply solemnly, "See yon hill? When I fust saw the
mountains, that was only a hole in the ground."

Kit Carson, owing to the publicity given his exploits in
the reports of Frémont's expeditions, had long been rated by
the public as the greatest scout on the Plains. But by 1860
so many officers and other men of standing had known
Bridger and seen his proficiency that Jim was coming into
his own. By many he was given the rating of being "the
best guide and interpreter in the Indian country." The
palm for prudence was generally given to him, though Kit
had a well deserved reputation for greater dash and hard
fighting. No doubt Bridger had made many a hostile Injun
come, though there are few authentic accounts of his killing
one. Kit, on the other hand, is known to have killed well
over a score of men. The two scouts were individuals, each
with his own peculiar merits.

Bridger's qualifications were many. His motto was "When

in Injun country, do as the Injuns do—and do it better."
He prided himself that he could outdo them sarpints at anything. He had lived with Indians and under the same conditions for so long that he thought and acted very often in
the same manner. His mind and habits were geared to
frontier life.

Jim had a marked linguistic gift and, wandering over the
West as he did for so long, had picked up Spanish and frontier French, besides nearly a dozen Indian tongues, including
those of the Snake, Bannock, Crow, Flathead, Nez Percé,
Ute, and Pend Oreille, with a smattering of others. He was
so adept in the use of the sign language that he habitually
accompanied his remarks with slight unconscious corrobora-
tive gestures. He was a crack shot and an expert trapper—
none better—while his courage and good judgment were
acknowledged by all who knew him.

Jim excelled also at trailing. He could read and recognize
sign made by any critter on four legs or on two, readily de-
termining the sex, age, gait, and often the purpose of any
animal whose trail he picked up. He could at once identify
the tribe of any Indian whose moccasin tracks crossed his
trail, and was so familiar with his own horse and those of his
companions that he could usually recognize the tracks of
any horse in the caballada. He could estimate accurately by
the warmth of the ashes of a dead campfire how long it had
been since those who built it had departed. If a track were
in sand, he could tell by the amount of sand that had crum-
bled into it how long before it had been made. In grass he
could tell whether or not the tracks had been made before
or after dewfall, before or after a shower. Even at night,
by dismounting and feeling the ground with his hands, he
could usually make out the trail.

In following a trail he rode or ran a little to one side of

it, so as not to obliterate the tracks in case he had to go back and verify his observations. He generally looked several yards ahead rather than straight down, since in that way he could see several tracks—instead of only one, which he might miss. This enabled him to follow at a good rate of speed. If he lost a trail, he had only to circle the last visible track until he picked it up again. But his main resources in trailing were his long experience, his imagination, and his great knowledge of the habits of Indians and animals, which enabled him to guess what they were up to and which way they were likely to go. Whenever he had to peer over a hilltop, he would cover his dark hair with a white cloth, invisible against the sky behind him. He knew all the tricks for covering tracks and could unravel the most tangled trail.

All Mountain Men shared these qualities, but Jim had one qualification which made him superior to most guides in the west. He had a phenomenal *memory,* and once he had seen a landmark, could remember and describe it accurately years afterward.

Many travelers, keen on their hunting, or in a hurry on the march, looked only forward or to left and right. But Jim had trained himself to look backward every little while, so that he saw the country he was traversing from both sides. Jim reckoned he might want to come back that way sometime, and so he made it a point to notice and remember all landmarks, front and rear.

His habitual caution became increasingly useful, now that he was piloting greenhorns through Injun country. Some thought him overcautious at times; but the recklessness and inexperience of his companions required such caution to keep the balance even.

In the summer of '61 he acted as guide for an engineer, Captain E. L. Berthoud. Berthoud reports that "when

Bridger was consulted as to facts, he was truth itself, but when he wished to tell stories, he was most skillful."

Jim's own experience and perhaps some knack picked up from his surveyor father often enabled him to correct estimates of the engineers he guided. Once they asked him which of two passes was the lower. Jim immediately pointed to one which looked to the others much higher. Seeing that they doubted him, Jim challenged: "Put your clocks on 'em and see." The aneroid barometer soon showed that Jim was right.

Berthoud was in the service of Russell and Holladay of the Overland Stage Company, who were seeking a more direct route from Denver to Salt Lake City. Bridger led him through Berthoud's Pass to Provo, Utah, down the west slope to White River, Green River, and up the basin of the Duchesne River. This was a much shorter route than the old one. Today the Pike's Peak Ocean to Ocean and Victory highways follow much the same route.

In 1862 Bridger put his children in the care of friends in a home he had bought in Westport. In the spring, while resting on his farm at Little Santa Fe nearby, he was offered work by the Government as guide to a party of officials on their way to Utah. President Lincoln had named two judges to the Supreme Court of Utah Territory, and Jim was chosen to pilot them through from St. Joseph, Missouri, to Salt Lake. He was offered good wages and presented with a brand new muzzle-loading rifle—at that time held to be the best military arm of its kind. It carried an ounce ball.

William S. Brackett, a member of this party, describes Bridger as he was at that time: "In person Bridger was tall and spare, but erect, active and energetic. His hair was brown and long and covered his head abundantly even in old age. His eyes were gray and keen; his habitual expression was mild, and his manners kind and agreeable. He was, like most old mountaineers, very generous and hospitable, and was respected and trusted by white men and Indians alike. He always treated Indians with justice, and had their confidence to a high degree. His wife was an Indian woman of the Shoshone tribe." [1]

The gentlemen in the party often questioned Jim about his explorations. He described to them the wonders of Yellowstone Park. But he soon was made to feel their disbelief. Hearing whispers about "Old Jim Bridger's lies," he got his dander up and decided, like any Indian, that if they would not believe the truth, he would give them *real* lies—generally making his questioner the butt of the joke.

He told these unbelievers of the peetrified forests in Yellowstone, of peetrified trees agrowin' with peetrified birds on them singin' peetrified songs.

A cussed medicine man of the Crows had once thrown a curse on a mountain thar, and ever since you could see grass, sage brush, prairie hens, elk, bear, and antelope all turned to stone just as they war that minute. The mountain streams and the waterfalls and mist over them were frozen into stone. Even the sun and moon shone with peetrified light.

One day, Jim said, he sighted a bull elk, drew a careful bead on the critter, and pulled the trigger. The elk did not even raise his head from the grass to show that he had heard the rifle crack. Jim crawled up as near as he dared and fired again. Still the elk grazed undisturbed. A third and fourth shot did no better. Jim was close now. He grabbed his rifle by the barrel, raised it like a club, and charged the elk. Suddenly he was brought up short, and found he had crashed into a mountain of clear glass. Through it he could still see that elk quietly grazing.

"Stranger still, the mountain was not only of pure glass,

but was a perfect telescopic lens, and, whereas, the elk seemed but a few hundred yards off, it was in reality twenty-five miles away." [2]

When some engineer wanted to know the elevation above sea level where he stood, Jim advised him to bore down until salt water was reached and then measure the distance. [3]

On Great Salt Lake, so Colonel Inman [4] says, Jim declared that in the winter of 1830 it snowed for seventy days. All buffalo caught in the storm died, but their bodies were preserved in the snow.

"When spring came, all I had to do," declared he, "was to tumble 'em into Salt Lake and I had pickled buffalo enough for myself and the whole Ute nation for years." . . .

The trip to Utah was not uneventful. Brackett has left an account of what happened:

"The last Sunday in June, 1862, was a bright and peaceful day. Our men were cleaning up their arms, saddles and equipments. Quite a number of our best shots had gone off into the hills hunting. There was no thought of Indians, for no Indians had been seen by us for many days. Late in the afternoon as the men were starting the fires to cook supper, we saw a strange white man riding toward our camp in hot haste. Down the valley he swiftly came, until he was stopped by one of our outpost guards who rode forward to meet him. After a short parley his tired horse came galloping to our camp.

" 'Indians! Indians!' he shouted as he threw himself off his horse and came up to our commanding officer. The man reported that his camp, five miles back to the eastward, on the ground we passed over the day before, had been attacked and that two men were killed. A few questions were asked him by Bridger, and then the bugles rang out 'boots and saddles.'

"Twenty picked men, under a sergeant, were ordered to
proceed at once to the scene of the tragedy. Several others
were permitted to accompany the force, one of our federal
judges and myself among the number. James Bridger was
ordered to go along also, and to carefully observe all Indian
signs and make report to our commander. Our train was
known to all emigrants along the road as 'the government
train" because we had United States troops to escort the
federal judges and their families. Hence, in case of attack
or alarm from Indians, the emigrants often came to our
camp.

"We learned from the strange man as we rode along that
his wagon train of twelve or fifteen wagons had been straggling along the trail in single line, and that when the rear
wagon was far behind and out of sight, a war party of Indians had suddenly swooped down upon it, had killed both
men and run off with the team of horses. . . .

"After a hard gallop of some five miles we came up with
the emigrants in camp. Their wagons were parked in a circle with their horses and fires inside, and armed men marched
about on guard. . . .

". . . I was riding with Bridger over a long hill when we
came upon the wagon that had been attacked, and the horribly mutilated bodies of the two men. About a hundred yards
from the wagon on the trail we came first to the body of an
old man. At the instant of attack he had probably jumped
out and run toward the other far off wagons. He was shot
through the back and his head was fairly chopped to pieces
with tomahawks, and the ax taken from the wagon lay beside
him, covered with blood. His body was filled with arrows,
and he was scalped and horribly mutilated. . . .

"Bridger calmly dismounted, knelt on the ground and
closely examined the foot prints around the body. Then he

pulled three arrows from the old man's corpse and closely examined them.

" 'Arapahoes and Cheyennes,' he said, as he followed the blood creases on the arrows with critical eyes.

"Leaving the first body, he went up to the wagon and found pieces of harness cut with knives scattered about. The Indians had got the harness off the horses by cutting nearly every strap. At one side lay the body of a young man who had been an invalid and was going to California for his health. Firmly clutched in his bloody right hand was a Colt's revolver with four chambers empty. The Indians had vainly cut this hand many times trying to get the pistol, but the grip of death held it firmly. Three bullets had pierced his body, and he was also scalped and mutilated. A dozen arrows bristled horribly upward from his prostrate corpse. With fiendish malignity the savages had cut off his ears, nose, and the fingers of his left hand, and laid them on his body. Both eyes were obliterated and other dreadful brutalities had been enacted which are simply unspeakable.

"As soon as Bridger saw the pistol he walked around the wagon in a circle, carefully examining the grass and sage brush. Suddenly he stooped and seized a piece of sage brush and broke it off. On it was a speck of blood. Widening his search he soon found more blood and came back saying:

" 'The boy has peppered one of the scamps, anyway!' All around on the ground the Indians had scattered rice, flour, coffee and sugar in their hasty plundering of the wagons. Of course, they carried off both horses. . . .

"Wrapping the poor mutilated bodies in blankets we laid them in the wagon they had often slept in during life. They were afterward given decent burial by their friends of the emigrant train. Under Bridger's guidance our command then hunted for the trail of the Indians. Bridger said they were about twenty in number, and were doubtless, by this time, far on the other side of the Sweetwater on their scampering ponies, safe from capture or successful pursuit. A picked force of fifteen cavalrymen was afterwards sent on the trail of the savages, but failed to overtake them during their pursuit of five or six days." [5]

At Salt Lake City Brigham Young called in person upon the two federal judges and their party at the principal hotel. Brigham arranged to have the party escorted through Echo Canyon by his Mormon troopers, whom Brackett describes as "fine riders . . . all well mounted and armed . . . more efficient in the pursuit and punishment of hostile Indians than either regular troops or eastern volunteers." Brigham probably thought a display of his military power would do his unwelcome visitors good.

Just how Bridger felt on this visit to the stronghold of his enemies, who had stripped him of his fort, we can only guess. Probably he thought of Brigham with curses—not loud but deep—and was glad to head back to the Plains.

At Fort Laramie Jim was soon engaged as guide for a small military party on a trip to Fort Halleck and back. At one time Jim had feared that he would be stranded in the settlements. But now his reputation was so great that every time he headed home to Missouri, somebody stopped him and hired him to go to the mountains again.

Jim was a born topographer and his preference for the mountains was inspired by reasons very like those of the Scotch railway engineer who, on being taken to England, exclaimed, "Mon, mon, you canna build railways in this country. Where are the hills to run your tunnels through?" Certainly, if it was exploring and mapping that Jim enjoyed, he was in clover in Wyoming; that was a pathfinder's paradise.

In the party heading for Fort Halleck was Lt. Col. William O. Collins and his son Lt. Caspar W. Collins, for whom the town of Casper, Wyoming, was named after his death at Platte Bridge in '65. Young Collins then proved a gallant officer; in a skirmish with the Cheyennes, he met his death charging a large party of warriors with an arrow sticking in his forehead.

Bridger's party consisted of the two officers already mentioned and Lieutenant O. S. Glenn, a sergeant, two privates, a wagon master, a teamster, and a cook. Though they encountered sleet and rain, the trip was a junket enlivened by much hunting of elk, deer, and grizzlies, a delightful march through the Black Hills, and a dog feast at the camp of a squawman. The close companionship on the trip enabled these officers to appreciate Bridger's qualifications and character, and on October 1, 1863, at Fort Laramie, Lieutenant Glenn employed Bridger as guide and interpreter with wages at $5.00 a day.[6] Jim continued in this service until April 30, 1864.[7]

During this period Bridger acted as guide for Captain J. Lee Humfreville on a scout through the Bayou Salade or South Park of Colorado. With them rode a squawman with an Arapaho wife and some of her kinsmen.

Now Humfreville had a flair for romantic—not to say sensational—yarns, but apparently based his stories upon actual experience. According to him, on this occasion they encountered a large party of hostiles and took their stand on the slope of a hill, where they were under fire from enemies hidden in the brush and tall grass. The Captain hesitated to divide his party to dislodge the snipers. But Bridger soon grew restless and challenged an Arapaho warrior to go into the brush with him and fight hand-to-hand with the hostiles.

The Arapaho language is very difficult, and the white men

who mastered it can be counted on the fingers of one hand. So, when the cussed Injun refused, Bridger "abused him soundly by means of the sign language." Finally the Arapaho, stung into action by the shame of Bridger's taunts, grasped Jim by the hand, and the two ran forward together —straight into the brush. There was the crash of a six-shooter. Soon after, Bridger came running back, "holding in his hand the scalp of a warrior covered with warm blood." The Arapaho did not return.

Captain Humfreville then tried to send an Arapaho to set the grass on fire. He would not budge. But "Bridger ridiculed them so unmercifully that the whole party accompanied him, and the grass was fired."

The fire quickly burned out the snipers, and they scattered in every direction, then mounted and returned to the fight. From the hillside Bridger's party could now see every move the Indians made. Jim picked off one, and some of the troopers also emptied saddles. And as evening came on, the hostiles pulled out. This is one of the few accounts we have of Bridger killing an enemy.

During that winter Humfreville shared his quarters at Fort Laramie with Bridger. The backgrounds of the men were so different that each found the habits of the other trying, to say the least. For forty years Bridger had lived in a world where clocks were unknown, and, like his Injun in-laws, thought it ridiculous to regulate his life by such a mechanism. He ate when he was hungry and drank when he was dry and went to bed when he felt sleepy—sometimes in the middle of the afternoon. This would get him up shortly after midnight, when he would make a fire, roast some meat for his breakfast, and eat it; afterwards, like as not, singing Injun songs, using a tin pan for his tom-tom.

Captain Humfreville found this very disturbing to his

military routine, and slyly decided to keep Jim up somehow until bedtime—by reading to him. They began with *Hiawatha*. Jim, the Captain reports, "would sit bent over, his long legs crossed, his gaunt hands and arms clasping his knees, and listen attentively, until a passage was reached where Longfellow portrayed an imaginary Indian, when Bridger, after a period of uneasy wriggling on his seat, arose very wrathy and swearing that the whole story was a lie, that he would listen to no more of it, and that 'no such Injun ever lived.' " Jim closed his ears to "such infernal lies." Humfreville had to turn to reading Shakespeare. But Richard III was too much for Jim: he swore he "would not listen any more to the talk of any man who was mean enough to kill his mother."

Of course Fort Laramie, so haunted by Indians, was alive with lice; and Bridger had his share. He challenged the Captain to rid him of them. Humfreville turned Jim's shirt and leggins inside out, poured a train of gunpowder along the seams, touched it off, burned the vermin—but also ruined the buckskins. Angrily Jim declared, "I'm agoin' to kill you for that," and threw a real scare into the Captain. Poor Jim had to go around for several days clad only in a buffalo robe and a cloud of indignation.

But for all his fun at Bridger's expense, Humfreville had the highest respect for him. ". . . 'old Jim Bridger,' was the most efficient guide, mountaineer, plainsman, trapper, and Indian fighter that ever flourished in the Far West. He knew more of that country and all things within its borders than any one who ever lived. . . . having trapped from the mouth to the source of nearly all its rivers and streams. Although Bridger had little or no education, he could, with a piece of charcoal or a stick, scratch on the ground or any smooth surface a map of the whole western country that was much more correct than those made at that time by skilled topographical engineers, with all their scientific instruments. I have seen Bridger look at a printed map, and point out its defects at sight." [8]

In the spring of '64, Bridger ran his great race with John M. Bozeman, who had laid out the Bozeman Trail on which Fort Laramie and Fort Phil Kearney were afterwards built.

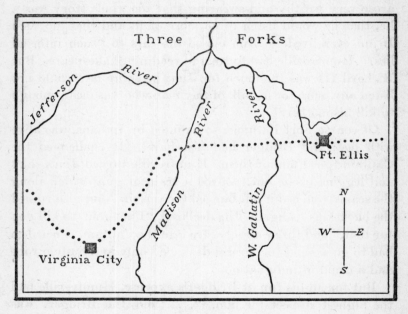

Bozeman's route crossed the Powder above Pumpkin Buttes and kept along the eastern edge of the Big Horn Mountains to Montana. Bridger thought Bozeman's trail too much exposed to the hostiles.

Bozeman had already brought wagons over his trail, but no wagon had ever passed over Bridger's proposed route west of the Big Horns.

Bozeman, confident that his trail was the best, let Jim

have a few days' start, and, going through Bozeman Pass into the Gallatin Valley, followed the route pointed out by Sacajawea to Captains Lewis and Clark, while Bridger reached the valley by following the creek now bearing his name. Both wagon trains arrived at Virginia City about the same time.

Having got his gold-seekers through safely, Bridger headed south and reached Fort Laramie about midsummer. There again he was hired as guide for a thirteen-day scout against hostile Sioux. By midwinter he was back on his farm at Little Santa Fe.

All these expeditions ended as usual in leaving him high and dry at home in the settlements. But though he had lost his fort, he had more lasting monuments in the mountains: Bridger Creek, Bridger Peak, Bridger Pass, the Bridger Mountains, Bridger Crossing, Bridger's Ferry, Bridger Lake, Bridger Flat, Bridger's Road, and the Bridger Trail. At times Jim feared he faced a bleak future, as the miners and farmers swarmed in and settled all over the mountains. But he need not have alarmed himself.

The disappearance of wild game had enraged the hungry Indians. War was breaking out all over the West, and the Army found the services of Jim Bridger indispensable.

CHIEF OF SCOUTS

XXII

THE POWDER RIVER EXPEDITION

JIM BRIDGER's stay at home did not last long. In January, 1865, General Grenville M. Dodge, then commanding the Department of the Missouri, summoned him to act as Chief of Scouts and principal guide for the Powder River Expedition. He arrived at Fort Laramie in the spring, and after riding out on a wild goose chase under Colonel Thomas Moonlight, Jim settled down in the cool, breezy portal of the Fort to wait for General Connor and listen to the news and gossip of the trail. Jim was considerably bothered by what he heard.

With one hand Uncle Sam was trying to make a treaty with the Sioux, and with the other sending three columns into the Powder River country under General Patrick E. Connor to deal the Sioux "a hard blow." One of Connor's columns, under Colonel Nelson Cole, was heading northwest from the Lower Platte. The other, under Colonel Samuel Walker, was preparing to start from Fort Laramie. Connor told Jim that the three columns were to meet on the Yellowstone at the mouth of Tongue River.

Jim didn't see how you could make peace and war with the

Sioux at the same time, and he knew how those Injuns hated invaders of their best hunting grounds. Any peace made thataway would mighty soon turn to war anyhow. Might as well get on with the war. It was a heap easier to make war on the Sioux than to make a peace with them that would stick.

The Army paid Jim ten dollars a day and supplied him with rations, a horse, weapons, ammunition, and a staff of scouts: Nick Janice, Jim Daugherty, Mitch Bouyer, John Reshaw, Antoine Le Due, and Bordeaux. With Jim to guide and advise him, and with all these younger men to do the scouting, it looked like the General had about all the help he needed. But Connor was never content. He also brought along Captain Frank North and his battalion of Pawnee scouts. The Pawnees were terrible scrappers, and hated the guts of the Sioux. *Wagh!*

But, as if this were not enough, Connor also had Captain Nash's company of so-called "Omaha" scouts—mostly Winnebagos, recently brought out to the Plains from the woodlands of Minnesota. Seemed like the General was taking *all* the scouts thar war with his own outfit, leaving Cole and Walker to get along the best they could—with maps! Jim Bridger had his own opinion as to the reliability of military maps.

Connor had a reputation as a fighter dating back to the Mexican War. He was not very big, but he was red-headed, a hot-headed Irishman with blood in his eye. He issued a general order: "You will not receive overtures of peace and submission from the Indians, but will attack and kill every male Indian over twelve years of age."

The General sure talked fire, and the more Jim saw of Connor's volunteers, the bigger the fire looked. Jim was now 61 years of age and might have known better than to go

traipsing around Sioux country with a cavayard of greenhorns. But General Dodge had asked him to go and to carry
that wild Irishman and his men through that tough country
and keep them from setting their feet in a trap.

"Old Jim Bridger," they called him. That riled Jim. He
reckoned he could ride as long and fight as hard as any two
men in the outfit.

Jim may have felt a little professional pique when Frank
North and his Pawnees turned up; but if so, he said nothing.
The Yellowstone River was a tolerable big crick, layin'
square across the General's trail. But if Connor thought he
needed all those scouts along to find it, that was his business,
and maybeso the Pawnees could kill some Sioux—which was
more than Jim expected of Connor's Volunteers. As for
finding hostiles, that would be no trick at all. The Sioux
and Cheyennes would see to that.

But if Connor and his men meant fight, most of Walker's
troops were sulky. Every day there were desertions, and
when, early in June, the time approached for Walker's six
hundred men and pack train to leave Laramie and strike out
east of the Black Hills, the men of his own regiment, the
Sixteenth Kansas Cavalry, began to mutter. The Civil War,
for which they had enlisted, was over. Their term of service
had nearly expired, and would expire long before the Powder River Expedition ended. The men grumbled, "We've
lost no red devils, and we don't aim to hunt for none. Let the
Regulars lick the Sioux; we did not enlist to fight Injuns."
When their orders were read out to Walker's men, they flatly
refused to march. They were poorly equipped for a campaign.

General Connor let no grass grow under his feet. He
ordered out his own command—infantry, cavalry, artillery
—formed them in line of battle and gave the mutineers five

minutes to fall in and obey orders. He was just about ready to fire when the Volunteers gave in.

Jim Bridger shook his head. He was not impressed by the cocky officers with their white paper collars and gold braid, and even less by their green, unwilling troopers. Some of the soldiers were armed only with pistols and sabres.

Connor's column left the fort at the end of July, crossing the Platte on rafts. His soldiers seemed to think the expedition was a junket. They ran their horses half to death chasing jack rabbits and buffalo. The officers, instead of marching with the troops to maintain discipline, rode recklessly off nearly every day to hunt elk or buffalo, sometimes lost themselves or were gone overnight. Before they had gone north far enough to get a clear view of the Big Horn Mountains to the left, the four blue columns of the Pumpkin Buttes ahead, and the Black Hills far to their right, the careless volunteers had already set the prairie afire, sending great billows of smoke up into the clear blue sky—an invitation to all Indians for fifty miles around. Bridger was disgusted.

He pushed on, leading the column as quickly as might be over the dry country from the Platte to Powder River, and by the middle of August had them safely encamped in the timber beside that rapid, muddy stream. Everywhere he found Injun sign, much of it fresh: small fires, still smoking; hundreds of circles of trampled grass, each around its center of pale ashes, where a tipi had stood; whole groves of trees badly girdled by gnawing ponies; and the still stinking carcasses of "good Indians" swinging high in burial trees.

While Jim and his scouts explored the country round, General Connor set about building a stockade on the broad level bench between the river and the bluffs. He seemed to forget his rendezvous at the mouth of Tongue River; he put the command to work cutting timber and building the new post, then called Camp Connor and afterward Fort Reno.

During all this time Jim's routine was much the same. Every morning he was up before the bugler. He had a quick cup of coffee and a few bites of jerked buffalo meat. Then, throwing a saddle on his horse, he would lead it over to the General's tent. After a brief conference with Connor, Jim mounted and rode quietly away about his scouting. On the march he rode all day far in advance, sending his subordinates out on flank and rear. Around sundown he would come riding back, make his report to the commanding officer, and then set about cooking his own supper, usually at the mess-fire of his scouts. When darkness settled down, Jim would slip off from camp a little ways and roll up in his blankets for the night. He made friends with one or two officers, but during the day he was seldom with the troops and much too busy to be sociable. He had his hands full to get that herd of greenhorns through hostile country, to find good camping places for them where there was plenty of grass, wood and water, and to keep them from losing their scalps.

So far things had gone better than Jim expected, but he wondered what might happen when they ran into a big bunch of Injuns.

He had not long to wait. Scouts came riding back to report an Indian trail. The trail showed a war party traveling fast; forty head of horses, nearly half of them shod and therefore certainly stolen from the whites, some of them loose horses. There were about twenty-five warriors. The trail showed traces of one pole-drag or travois, probably carrying a wounded man, and from the direction taken, probably a party of Cheyennes. Jim was relieved when Connor ordered Captain North's Pawnees to lead the pursuit. They knew how to fight Injuns.

The Pawnees followed the trail on a lope until sundown, and on into the dusk until it was too dark to see. Then two of the Pawnees dismounted and kept on, following the trail when in doubt by feeling the ground with their hands and observing the lay of the land. At daybreak the two saw the Cheyennes' smoke across the river! They ran back to report. The main body of scouts came up with the Cheyennes just as they were pulling out of camp.

"The Pawnees were riding in column of twos, and from this the hostile Indians supposed that they were white troops. They stopped to fight, dismounted and spread out in line of battle on the side of a small hill. The Pawnees rode steadily forward until they were within two hundred yards of the line of the enemy, when they began to shout their war cry and to slap their breasts. The discovery that these were Pawnees seemed to disconcert the enemy, who called to each other, '*Panani,*' and forthwith broke and ran." [1]

"The Pawnees, desirous of getting even with their old enemy, the Sioux, rode like mad devils, dropping their blankets behind them, and all useless paraphernalia, rushed into the fight half naked, whooping and yelling, shooting, howling. . . . Some twenty-four scalps were taken, some twenty-four horses captured, and quite an amount of other plunder, such as saddles, fancy horse trappings, and Indian fixtures generally. The Pawnees were on horseback twenty-four hours, and did not leave the trail until they overtook the enemy. There was a squaw with the party; she was killed and scalped with the rest." [2]

"At the beginning of the fight the animal attached to the travois became frightened and ran away and the wounded man on it rolled off, dragged himself to the edge of a nearby ravine and threw himself over the cut bank into it. He hoped to be overlooked and to escape. The Pawnees saw the act, and after killing the other Cheyennes returned for this man. The bank over which he had fallen was so high and steep that no one of the Pawnees was willing to clamber down after the man at the bottom, but a Pawnee sergeant with a sabre went around to the mouth of the ravine, followed it up and killed the wounded man. Among most Indian tribes there was seldom any taking of adult male prisoners. The loss of the Pawnees in the fight was only four horses." [3]

These hostiles had with them the scalps of several white men and clothing of white women and children. Of the stolen horses, four were government animals and one belonged to the Overland Stage Line.

"On their return to camp they exhibited the most savage signs of delight, and if they felt fatigued did not show it— rode with the bloody scalps tied to the end of sticks, whooping and yelling like so many devils. In the evening they had a war dance instead of retiring to rest, although they had been up more than thirty hours. . . . They formed a circle and danced around a fire, holding up the bloody scalps, brandishing their hatchets and exhibiting the spoils of the fight. They were perfectly frantic with this, their first grand victory over their hereditary foe. During the war dance they kept howling, 'Hoo yah, hoo yah, hoo yah,' accompanying their voices with music made by beating upon . . . a drum.

"These howling devils kept up the dance . . . until long after midnight, when finally the general, becoming thoroughly disgusted, insisted upon the officer of the day stopping the noise. After considerable talk, Capt. North, their commander, succeeded in quieting them, and the camp laid down to rest; but this war dance was kept up every night until the next fight, limited, however, to 10 o'clock P.M." [4]

Nearly every day thereafter there was an Indian scare or

a skirmish. They moved on to Crazy Woman's Fork, hunting buffalo, killing a monstrous grizzly. By good luck, nobody was hurt. They marched on through those delightful foothills of the Big Horns, across the clear rushing streams, and so arrived at a lake—a pretty sheet of water several miles long.

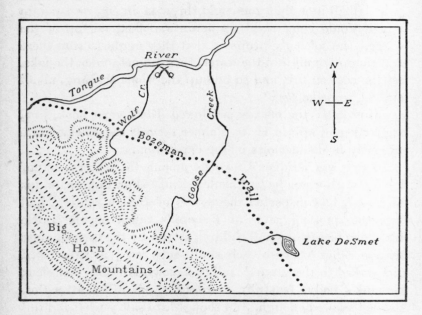

This, Jim Bridger told them, was Lake De Smet, named for Father Pierre-Jean De Smet, the Jesuit missionary to the Indians.

By this time Jim Bridger was beginning to be a little annoyed at the way he was regarded by the young officers with the command. Most of the soldiers respected him as a brave man and an expert, but some of the young fellows seemed to think him only a quaint character, full of queer ideas and silly supersitions. Jim could see they didn't believe half he told them. If that was the way they wanted it, he could tell them plenty.

So, when they reached that strange body of water hemmed in by big red bluffs, with its oil well flowing alongside, Old Jim, poker-faced, told them a pretty story. The bottom of the lake, he said, was a vein of pure coal. The water had so much alkali in it that you could throw in an egg or a potato and it would come right up again and float on top of the water. Jim solemnly proposed that they ought to stop there and pump the oil into the water, then tunnel under the lake, set the coal on fire, and so bile up the whole shebang, alkali and oil, to make *soap!*

Apparently the officers swallowed Jim's yarn hook, line, and sinker. Captain H. E. Palmer records the scheme quite seriously in his memoirs of the expedition.

Palmer was Bridger's favorite among the officers, one of the few with whom he had made friends. For Palmer, on his way west, had inspected the results of Indian raiding, had seen the smoking ruins of Eubank's ranch on the Little Blue; the bodies of small children swung by the heels against the log cabin to crush their skulls into red jelly; the hired girl staked to the ground, full of arrows, horribly mangled; Eubank's body, fearfully mutilated; and other atrocities. Palmer knowed enough, Jim thought, to savvy what fightin' Injuns amounted to: an eye for an eye, a tooth for a tooth, blood for blood. So Jim was hardly prepared for what followed.

One day after the command left the Piney, Jim and the Captain, riding in advance, reached the watershed between the Powder and the Tongue. The grand view there brought them up short. They reined up their horses together: Jim to look for Injuns; Palmer to admire the noble prospect. To their right—northeast—the Wolf Mountains; to the left the north end of the Big Horns; far ahead the blue outlines of the hills beyond the Yellowstone. Immediately below them lay the valley of Peno Creek.

All that morning Bridger had been explaining to his friend how to trail Injuns, how to distinguish moccasin tracks of one tribe from those of another. But now both sat silent. While the Captain admired the landscape through his field glasses, Bridger scanned the distant hills with the naked eye. What Jim saw was mighty interesting. He waited for the Captain to give some sign that he had also made the same discovery. It was a courtesy to the younger man.

But to his surprise, Jim saw that the Captain had discovered nothing. So, when Palmer lowered his glasses, Jim said, "Do you see those 'ere columns of smoke over yonder?"

"Where, Major?"

Jim pointed. "Over by that saddle," he explained.

The saddle looked as if it might be fifty miles away. The Captain eyed Jim, raised his glasses again, and took a long, long look. The distant hills were slightly hazy everywhere; but for the life of him, Palmer could see no smoke. By this time the Captain had discovered Bridger's sense of humor and learned that Jim liked to stretch the blanket and fool greenhorns when he had a chance. Fearing that Old Jim was having fun with him now, the Captain pretended that he could see the smoke. Said he, "We'd better get off our animals and let them feed until the General comes up." They dismounted.

When the General arrived, the Captain reported the smoke. Connor raised his glasses and searched the horizon. Then, with the self-assurance of a commanding officer, he declared that *no* columns of smoke were to be seen.

Somehow Jim managed to keep quiet. He just turned

away, mounted his horse, and rode off. The Captain persuaded the General to look again. Still Connor could see nothing. What he could not see, he would not believe. Then the Captain let the General in on Jim's "joke."

Now the General was not giving Old Jim an opportunity to claim that his scouts had led him to an Indian village that he would not attack. Connor sent Captain Frank North with some Pawnees to investigate. . . .

By the time Captain Palmer caught up with Bridger, Jim had got enough control of his indignation to use his tongue. For the first time on that expedition he began to grumble. Said he, "I'm plumb sick of these damn paper-collar soldiers telling *me* there are no columns of smoke!"

But the Captain was so pleasant that Bridger gradually relaxed, and, as they rode down to the creek, told him how it happened to be named after Peno, the trapper. Peno had been going up the creek looking for beaver, every little while climbing the steep bank to take a peek at the country around for safety's sake. Scouting along the bank he saw a bunch of buffalo close by. It was a tempting shot; Peno set his trigger and fired. But the bull he hit did not drop. Instead it whirled and charged. Peno, having no time to reload, hightailed it for the creek. The bank was twenty feet high. Just as he reached the brink, the bull's broad forehead caught him in the seat of the pants. Peno sailed up and over the bank head-foremost into the water, but was almost hoisted out of the creek when the heavy bull landed beside him with a mighty splash. Peno was unhurt and scrambled ashore. But the bull was so injured it could not follow. Peno got away. That was the story. . . .

Next day the feckless "Omaha" scouts incautiously attacked a grizzly. The animal killed one and mangled two others.

That quiet August evening Jim Bridger watched General Connor's column going into camp on Tongue River. The teamsters of his ninety creaking wagons had just rolled them into position to form a defensive corral, as Bridger had taught them to do. Already the wolves were beginning to sound off from the barren hills. Men of the various messes were busy gathering fuel and starting fires; pale woodsmoke drifted across the river, touched with color by the last rays of the setting sun.

Up the river Jim saw two horsemen coming. From the continual rise and fall of their right arms, he knew the riders were Injuns. They were not traveling very fast, but from the rate at which they quirted their ponies, he could see they were in a great hurry. Jim went over to the General's tent to report their coming and interpret their message. By the time the General came out, the foremost weary Pawnee scout jogged in, his swaying pony literally on its last legs.

Captain North had discovered an Indian village—just where Jim Bridger had reported his columns of smoke!

The Pawnee scout, using the graphic sign talk of the Plains tribes, gave Bridger his message: *Enemy camp— yonder—maybeso one sleep. Father* (Captain North) *say send all Pawnees and one war party pony soldiers.* He added *Cut off* to indicate that he had come to the end of his message. Bridger interpreted for the General.

Connor's eyes gleamed. "Only one day's march, eh? Ask him how big the hostile camp is."

Jim raised and wagged his open hand in the sign for the question, then put the tips of his two index fingers together to form an upright triangle. Then, with the index finger of his right hand, he quickly folded down one after another of the extended fingers of his left. Those gestures meant: *How many's the lodge?* For every lodge would count two warriors, and at this season probably three or more, since in summer young men slept out-of-doors and visiting warriors without women were sure to have come from the agencies to the buffalo country.

The scout signed back: *I know not.* Those congenital horse thieves, the Pawnees, had had eyes only for enemy horses, not enemy tents. Seeing Bridger's disappointment, the scout added, *Plenty pony.*

Bridger nodded. Yes, plenty pony—and plenty warrior too. Those columns of smoke he had seen so far away could never have come from a small camp of fifty tipis. Captain North had asked for only one company of cavalry. Jim advised the General to take every man he could spare. When the bugler sounded *Boots and Saddles,* every man not needed to guard the stock and wagons was soon mounted.

With Connor and Bridger in the lead, they headed up Tongue River, planning to strike the enemy camp at daybreak. Connor gave strict orders: No smoking; all talk must be in whispers; no horse must be allowed to whinny. As a final precaution he warned the bugler not to touch his instrument. By the time darkness had fallen, they were well on their way upstream.

But there was no trail to follow through the darkness. Men and horses stumbled on all night through brush, over fallen trees, making slow progress; when day broke, they were still nowhere near the enemy.

Still they kept on, marching under the high river-bank, half the time in the water. There was no halt for breakfast. Captain North came to meet them. Under his guidance they approached the village, still apparently undiscovered. Connor sent back whispered commands, warning his men to keep their horses on a tight rein and not allow a one of them to whinny.

At last the trail led up the steep bank to a level prairie of five or six acres fairly swarming with Indian ponies, with a big camp of several hundred tipis a half mile to the left. It was nine o'clock in the morning.

The command closed up. Connor rode his horse up the steep bank with his men at his heels. They wheeled left into line.

The moment the cavalry appeared, the Indian ponies set up a tremendous whinnying and thundered away toward the crowded tipis. There a thousand dogs began to bark, while hundreds of savages made the hills ring with their fearful warwhoops.

The troopers fired one volley from their carbines. Jim Bridger, seeing how the troops were outnumbered, knew that their only salvation lay in a bold charge straight into the hostile village. Connor signaled the bugler. *The Charge* rang out. Connor and his men were on their way.

At the moment of attack the Indians had been breaking camp. Many of the warriors had caught their horses, and already half the women and children were mounted and moving out along the trail. Jim recognized the redskins for Arapahos—Chief Black Bear's band. Connor rode hell-for-leather, leading his men pell-mell among the tipis. There in the dust and gunsmoke they fought hand-to-hand.

Indian arrows lanced the air. For a while it was every man for himself in the dust and confusion, but the soldiers' better arms and better discipline and the surprise of their coming finally gave them an advantage. Before long the hostiles had left their camp and were high-tailing it up Wolf Creek with General Connor hot on their trail. Just what Bridger was doing is not recorded, but evidently it was plenty: "During this engagement Bridger seemed always to be in the right place at the opportune time." [5]

After pursuing the Indians some ten miles, the General looked round to discover that only fourteen men were following him, the horses of the others having played out. Connor halted and was busy taking the names of the brave men with good horses who had stuck with him when the Arapahos, seeing him stop, came dashing back to surround his handful. Thereupon the General postponed his paperwork and beat a retreat, picking up the men who had dropped out as he went back, thus continually increasing his fire-power. Shortly after noon the entire command was back in the Arapaho camp.

There they pulled down some 250 big Indian lodges all filled with buffalo robes, blankets, furs, stacks of fat parfleches full of dried meat, and other Indian plunder. The General ordered all the lodge poles stacked in heaps, and on top of these all the loot. Afterward he set the stacks afire.

Connor had captured a score of Indian women and children—whom he soon released; and more than a thousand head of Indian ponies—which he tried to hold. That was difficult. For while their camp was burning, the hostiles kept coming back to attack the troops, taking cover in the trees around. Though they "did most of their fighting with arrows," they might have recovered all their ponies had it not been for the Pawnees. The Arapaho ponies were constantly trying to break away and run back to their masters.

Connor's dash up Wolf Creek, on top of the long night march, had stove up most of the cavalry horses. So, while the camp burned, the troopers kept busy trying to catch and saddle the ponies they had taken. For it was a long fifty miles back to the wagon corral on Tongue River.

Now Indian ponies did not like the smell of white men any better than cavalry horses liked the smell of Indians, and these ponies had been frightened by the gunfire, the yelling, the smell of gunpowder, and blood, and smoke, and the banging of the General's artillery. It was no wonder they dodged the rope and had to be choked down before they could be saddled. They fought like wildcats. For a good half hour the prairie was covered with pitching, rearing, crow-hopping, wind-milling buckers, all swallowing their heads, boiling over, craw-fishing, jackknifing, unwinding all their natural cussedness. The air was blue with troopers taking a dive—and blue with cursing too. It was not until Bridger and the Pawnees took a hand and taught the troopers to mount Injun-fashion, from the right, that the ponies were finally mastered. By that time every unwounded man in the command had been thrown at least once.

This impromptu rodeo on the battlefield became a legend in the Army and later inspired Frederic Remington to paint his well-known picture of the scene.

Outnumbered as they were, the soldiers could not destroy the hostiles. Ammunition was getting low, and it was clear that the command could not long remain on the battlefield. They had a number of wounded—and no ambulance. The General's aide, his bugler, his orderly had all been hit at his side. One officer and a sergeant had been shot, and one poor hospital steward had an arrow, which had entered his open mouth, lodged in the root of his tongue. There was no surgeon; to get the arrow out his friends thought it necessary to cut off his tongue! But, however badly hurt, the wounded had to ride.

Before three o'clock that afternoon the column moved out, continually harassed by hostiles charging and circling on their fleet ponies, giving wonderful exhibitions of horsemanship. One of the scouts—a Winnebago, naturally—was killed. By that time the troopers were so short of ammunition that only one man in ten had any left at all.

About dark the Arapahos left them.

The troops reached the wagon corral at two o'clock next morning, having been in the saddle—when not bucked off—for thirty-three hours, under fire for six or eight hours, without any rest, or any food except a few mouthfuls of buffalo jerky salvaged from the captured camp. The courage and stamina of Connor's Volunteers satisfied Jim Bridger. They had behaved like men.

Bridger naturally expected that he would be given credit for locating the Arapaho camp, since he had pointed out the columns of smoke which marked its site. He might reasonably have expected to be given credit for the victory also, since it was on his advice that Connor had taken enough men to attack the big camp successfully and so get safely away. Had the General followed Captain North's advice, there must have been a massacre.

But the Pawnees gave all the credit for Connor's decision to their tribal god. Connor's decision to take a strong force was to them but one more proof that their god was looking after their beloved Father, Captain North.

Jim, of course, did not care a hoot what the Pawnees thought. But when he realized that all the officers from the General down still believed that he had seen no columns of smoke and thought that he had *guessed* the location of the camp correctly just because he understood about where Indians would be camping in that country, Jim Bridger was fit to be tied.

He could not figure it out. These greenhorns would not believe *anything* he told them; they could not even *see* what he pointed out to them. Why on earth had they brought him along?

On the first of September, in the silence of early morning, a single cannon shot was heard. No two men could agree

from what direction the sound had come, and it was not repeated. But it served to remind the General of his rendezvous with Walker and Cole at the mouth of Tongue River.
He sent Captain North with some scouts and troops looking
for Colonel Cole.

Jim Bridger remained in camp. There the cannon shot
was soon followed by another portent.

All the way from Laramie thousands of big gray buffalo
wolves had surrounded the camp, making night hideous with
their infernal howling. Jim Bridger found their racket re-
assuring; where wolves were plenty, Injuns were generally
scarce. He slept soundly through their wild concert, for the
wolves had sung him to sleep nearly every night for forty
years.

But that night Jim heard a howl which brought him wide
awake and sitting up in his blankets with prickles running
up and down his spine.

It was the howl of a wolf that he heard, but it was *no ordinary howl*. The sound was weird and eerie—exactly like the
death wail of an Injun woman. Jim and his fellow scouts
stared at each other across the dying campfire with wide and
troubled eyes. They all recognized that sound—it was the
howling of a "medicine" wolf.[6]

Jim knew it for a sure sign of trouble. When you heard
that, there was only one thing to do—hit the trail pronto.
Jim awakened Connor and hastily advised the General to
break camp immediately.

General Connor, red-headed and victorious, was not going
to have anyone say that he had been frightened out of his
bed and his camp in the middle of the night by the howling
of any wolf, however "supernatural" it might be. If that
howl was like an Indian lament, it probably meant that the
Indians had been imitating the wolves. There would be noth-

ing queer about that; many Indian customs had been borrowed from animals. More than likely, he suggested, some
hostile Indian hiding in the hills was making that weird noise
to scare the Pawnees.

Bridger shook his head. "That's no Injun. You can tell
an Injun's wolf howl from a real wolf howl easy enough. A
real wolf howl don't have no echo." And if Injuns *had* imitated the howl of the medicine wolf when mourning for their
dead, Jim reckoned they had good reason for it; Injuns
warn't fools. Earnestly, Jim kept on, relating gruesome
incidents of past disasters which had followed on such warn-
ings from the wolves.

But the General had no ears for Jim's "absurd" proposals.
In fact, he did not know what the old scout was talking
about. Connor had not spent forty years on the lonely
Mountains and the teeming Plains, living in the open at all
seasons like the wary redskins—sensing what they sensed,
feeling what they felt. The delicate balance of wild nature
was unknown to him.

He was unaware of that sensitive living network covering
the earth in which any disturbance is felt and expressed in
some way by every creature touched by its widening circles
of influence. When the General rode over a ridge, the ensuing bird calls and animal movements which warned all creatures of his intrusion passed without notice from the General.
To Connor, a bird call was just a noise, not a communication of the bird's state of mind or a meaningful signal to all
who had the sense to understand it. Connor had not the
faintest notion why a wolf howled—or was silent. A coyote
on the prairie's rim, a yellow coyote was to him, and it was
nothing more.

Jim Bridger did not know where to begin l'arning such
ignorant babes in the woods. Jim knew how swiftly moc-

casin telegraph spread news among Injuns, and he reckoned that there was an animal telegraph as well. Only a fool would refuse to heed its messages.

Jim himself could smell hostile Injuns when they were anywheres around, and it stood to reason that a wolf—with its keen nose—roaming all over the country the way it did, could smell death or trouble coming a heap better and a long ways off. To Jim it seemed more'n likely that the men who fired that lone cannon shot were in trouble. A starving man, or a scared man, smells a heap different from a man who is fat and sassy. And a heap of scared, starving men together might make a stink a wolf could sniff miles away. And just the same, like as not, with every other kind of trouble or danger. One thing was sartin. When medicine wolves howl thataway, thar is only one thing to do—*pull out and make tracks.*

The paper-collar officers, new to Indian country, laughed at Jim's "superstitious" fears. Their attitude towards wild animals was the same as their attitude towards the enemy— "There they are, boys; give 'em hell!" They went grinning back to their comfortable beds, heedless of the coming woe.

Finding that the General would not budge, Bridger, Nick, and Rulo packed up their plunder and struck out on their own hook. The three made camp in the timber by themselves half a mile downriver. They knew that trouble was surely coming. If the General hankered to stick his clumsy foot in such a trap, 'twar'nt their funeral! *Wagh!* . . .

From that hour one disaster after another plagued the expedition, until it collapsed in total defeat and the disgrace of its commander. Suddenly the weather turned cold, with rain and snow and mud; bitter winds killed the stove-up horses on the picket lines. Captain North rode back from Powder River to report. He had found five or six hundred dead cavalry horses, evidently belonging to Cole's command. Many of them had been shot on the picket line. The sign showed that Cole, continually attacked by hundreds of Sioux and Cheyenne warriors, had no chance to let his animals graze and so had had to shoot them, and burn his saddles and equipment. Connor began to wonder what had happened to Walker's mutinous column.

After some days the Pawnees found Cole and Walker, and Connor, in desperation, ordered out his command to fight through to their relief, though by now his own mules were too weak to pull the provision wagons.

When found, Cole's men had long been living on mule meat. Walker's men were all barefoot and starving, having had no rations for more than two weeks. The beaten men looked more like ghosts or tramps than soldiers. They were "as completely disgusted and discouraged an outfit of men" as ever was seen. But with Bridger to guide them, they finally got back to Camp Connor.

There the final blow fell. The General received letters relieving him of his command. This dismissal had been caused by his harsh order to "kill every male Indian over twelve years of age."

Connor makes no mention of the medicine wolves; it was left to Captain Palmer to record that incident. But of his campaign Connor wrote, "Harm rather than good was done, and our troops were . . . driven from their country by the Indians."

Defeated and demoralized though the white troops might be, the Pawnee Scouts were fat and sassy. They had covered themselves with glory. All summer long they had been killing tribal enemies. They had collected nearly a hundred scalps and a big bunch of ponies—and all without the loss of a man! Most wonderful of all, the white men had actually *paid* them to do this! Now they could go home to their villages and dance all winter!

Old Gabe must also have felt some justifiable pride in his own work. Though Cole's and Walker's men had been licked, under his guidance Connor had burned the Arapaho camp. Moreover, Jim had brought the whole outfit safely back to Laramie.

That was something to be proud of, when you considered how those men were armed and led. There was no sense to it. All they had done was to rile the Injuns and make them sassier than ever. It looked like the Army had forgotten all about how the Sioux rubbed out Lieutenant Grattan and his whole command right here at Laramie not a dozen winters back. Jim reckoned thar would be some turrible massacrees before Uncle Sam tamed the Sioux.

While he waited at the fort for his discharge, Jim wondered what he could do about that.

XXIII
RED CLOUD'S DEFIANCE

THE Civil War was over, and the military establishment was being rapidly reduced. Following our usual stupid custom, Congress was cutting War Department budgets, stripping and crippling our armed forces everywhere. In the interest of this false economy, Western forts were under-manned, under-officered, and inadequately equipped. Scouts and guides serving the troops were now discharged at the close of each summer's campaign.

Bridger received his discharge on the last day of November, 1865, but did not leave Fort Laramie for some time after.

Jim suffered from rheumatism at times, and he had drunk

so much mountain water that now the goiter under his jaw
was larger than ever. The Indians had given him a new
name—"Big Throat." He must have felt tired after his
campaign.

But Bridger had a big idea in mind and, sometime in
December, set out from Laramie, heading east. He found

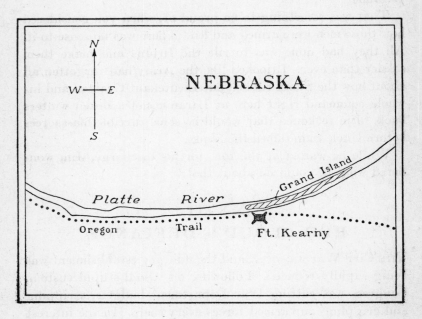

some young veterans of the late campaign already perched
upon the mail sacks stacked in the overcrowded ambulance.
Tossing his own pack aboard, he asked, "Where are you
boys going?" Jim hoped it was not far.

They told him they were going clear through to the Missouri River. That was bad news, he reflected, but at Julesburg he could catch the stage. Making the best of it, Jim
said, "So am I, and if we travel together, I reckon it is best

to be sociable." Jim's son, Felix Bridger, was a veteran of the Civil War.

For two days and a night Jim was jostled among his companions, their baggage, and the mail sacks; and when he reached Julesburg, learned that all space on east-bound Overland coaches had been taken for the next ten days.

However, Jim and his fellow travelers soon joined a train of empty wagons heading east for Fort Kearny. Filling the bed of one of these with hay, they spread their blankets and traveled on very comfortably together.

Shotwell,[1] one of the veterans, was much impressed by the reception Jim got the first time they stopped at one of the roadhouses to stretch their legs and get a bite to eat. The manager, vigorously shaking Bridger's hand, said "Come right in, Jim; the place is yours as long as you care to stay."

Bridger replied, "Here are two soldier boys traveling with me; I stay with them."

"It is all the same," replied the man, "Bridger and his friends included."

They all had the best dinner the place afforded, good places to sleep, breakfast next morning, lunch at the noon hour, and not a penny to pay. It was the same at every stop. Nobody on the Trail would let Jim Bridger pay for anything.

At this time Shotwell describes Jim as well-proportioned, slender, about six feet tall, "straight as an Indian, muscular and quick in movement, but not nervous or excitable; in weight probably 160 pounds; with an eye piercing as the eye of an eagle that seemed to flash fire when narrating an experience that had called out his reserve power. There was nothing in his costume or deportment to indicate the heroic spirit that dwelled within, simply a plain, unassuming man."

Jim entertained the boys with tales of his adventures and invited them to go on home with him.

The editor of the *Kearney Herald* was evidently a much more enterprising and intelligent man than most journalists of his day in the Missouri Valley; on January 6 he devoted almost the entire second page of his newspaper to the report of an interview with Bridger:

"PERSONNEL: Col. Bridger, the hero of Fort Bridger and Bridger's Pass, is sojourning at the Overland House in this City. The Col. is the oldest American settler of the Rocky Mountain Region. . . .

"He is perhaps sixty years old, fully six feet high, raw boned, blue eyes, auburn hair (now somewhat gray) is very active and communicative. He has guided numerous military expeditions against the Indians, and of these together with his own independent forays, he relates many interesting and thrilling incidents. . . .

"The Col. has no faith in mounted expeditions against Indians. He says what all frontiersmen know to be true, that the Indians' [ponies] can travel steadily for weeks together, and subsist upon cottonwood bark only, and their riders will build fires of the huge piles of Buffalo chips found where the herd wallows.

"He thinks that our mode of hunting savages with mounted men and wagon trains is simply absurd, since it results only in heavy loss of animals and unnecessary exposure of troops who are compelled to return for rations or halt for their train to overtake them, which gives the savages exultant triumph, leaving the warriors smoking their pipes, whose bowls are tomahawks and the helves thereof the stems.

"The Col. is now en route for Washington. He says he wants to tell the authorities how to manage the Indians; that if they will let him select a party of men, he will follow the

Indians on foot, week after week, faring as they do, and will eventually overtake and surprise their villages.

"He says that there is now a large party of Sioux encamped on the lakes just north of the forks of the Platte, that they are protected from the wind and have good water and grass.

"He is of the opinion that troops unacustomed to the frontiers are stampeded by the yell of the Indians when the enemy is in small force and might easily be managed by experienced 'Dodgers.' He thinks that the expedition, the 18th U. S. Infantry, now moving against the Sioux, is planned more sensibly than any before fitted up in this country, since their wagon train is to establish a temporary base from which pack mules will supply the troops." [2]

At Fort Kearny, Jim found his old friend Colonel H. E. Maynadier, who urged him to hurry back to work as guide for the expedition.

If Jim went immediately to Washington that winter, he must have made good time; for on January 25 he was enrolled as Chief Guide at Fort Kearny at a salary of $10 a day. This tour of duty lasted only until January 31, and it may be that Jim got a discharge so soon in order to spend the month of February in the east. He was again enrolled as guide by Maynadier on March 5, serving until mid-June, this time at only $5 per day.

Certain it is that he brought no authority back with him to organize his proposed company of Dodgers. If he suggested that to the military authorities, it is just possible that to Jim should go credit for the idea which led to the organization, in 1868, of the company of civilian scouts commanded by Major George A. Forsyth, of General Sheridan's staff. For the military were very slow to give a civilian scout any credit for anything, or any authority to do anything which an officer might do; and certainly the employment of a company of *civilian* scouts is not an idea likely to occur to the military mind. Everybody knows how the military belittled Buffalo Bill, and how his Congressional Medal of Honor was taken from him—after the poor old boy was dead, at that!

At any rate, Jim certainly visited Missouri, only to find how different his treatment was in the settlements from that he received on the frontier.

"While on a visit to St. Louis, one of his old mountaineer friends of the American Fur Company met him on the street, and greeting him, said: 'Jim, what are you doing here?' With an oath he answered, 'I'm trying to find my way out of these —— cañons'; adding, 'This is the meanest camp I ever struck in my life. I have met more'n a thousand men in the last hour, and nary one of 'em has asked me to come to his lodge and have something to eat.' " [3]

Colonel Henry B. Carrington was to command the expedition. Bridger reported to him.

Carrington had no experience of Indian fighting and, much impressed by the reports of Bridger's knowledge, skill, and judgment, relied heavily upon him and made Jim "the Colonel's confidential guide at all times." Though a civilian, Jim became in fact the most useful member of Carrington's staff.

The expedition moved out on May 19, but long before that date the War Department, still pinching pennies, had cut Jim's wages to $5 a day.

Colonel Carrington was a high-minded, idealistic officer, and though he had not served in the field during the Civil War, had a well-disciplined outfit, with 226 mule-teams besides ambulances, horsemen, and a band of 25 pieces. Some 260 persons were in his charge, including a number of officers' ladies, their children, and Negro servants. These had come along in the expectation that the expedition would be a peaceful junket, inasmuch as Commissioners were even then trying to negotiate a treaty with the Sioux at Fort Laramie. General Sherman himself had personally advised the ladies to accompany the expedition, "as very attractive in its objects and wholly peaceful!"

Carrington's orders were to open a wagon road around the Big Horn Mountains to Montana. These orders were in direct violation of the Treaty of 1865 made by Generals Harney and Sanborn; Carrington had written orders from General Sherman to "avoid a general Indian war if possible." But Jim Bridger, though quiet, aloof, and reserved, was emphatic enough on one point—that the Sioux and Cheyenne would *never* make peace, or keep it if they made it, or submit to having a road built and forts established in the middle of their best hunting grounds.

The Colonel faithfully enforced all regulations for the march which Bridger suggested, and his men, some of them veterans of the Civil War who wished to round out their experience with some Indian fighting, carried them out to the letter. His wagon train traveled in an orderly manner, always closed up, and formed a corral as soon as a camp ground was reached. Pickets and mounted guards watched all animals turned out to graze, and every effort was made to keep clear of Indians along the trail. At night guards were posted around the wagons. Everything was as well managed as though Bridger himself had been in command.

The expedition moved out each morning at daybreak and ended every day with guard mount and a band concert. They passed Elm Creek, Plum Creek, Fort McPherson, Julesburg and Fort Sedgwick, Pumpkin Creek, the crumbling dome of Court House Rock, Chimney Rock's tall column, Fortification Rock, Scott's Bluff, Fort Mitchell—on towards Fort Laramie. On the way up, they had trouble crossing the Platte. The water was high, and they had to rig a ferry with a flatboat brought from Denver. Then suddenly the river went down, and they had to ford it after all. Finally Bridger got them all across with only the loss of a few mules and spoiled supplies.

All the way the Trail was marked by "Mormon milestones"—the carcasses of dead oxen. After catching many fish in Cold Creek, they made camp four miles east of the fort. There two sergeants were drowned while swimming.

Shortly before sunset, a Brulé Sioux, Standing Elk, came in to have a talk. Bridger smoked with him. Standing Elk said, "A treaty is being talked over at Laramie with a great many Indians. Some of them belong in the country to which you are going; but the warriors of those bands have not come to the council, and will not. You will have to fight them. They will not sell their hunting grounds to the white men for a road."

At Fort Laramie they found Indians gathering for the treaty council, all ready to receive their presents.

Up to this time most treaties had been made with the chiefs and had often failed because the warrior societies, the real power in the tribe, had not signed them. But this time not even all the chiefs would sign. Man Afraid of his Horses and Red Cloud were particularly dissatisfied. The council was not over when Carrington brought his troops into Laramie. He endeavored to have his orders changed to permit him to await the conclusion of the treaty, but was peremptorily told to go ahead "immediately."

The United States Government was determined to keep open the roads to the goldfields in the West. The Civil War had bankrupted the country, and the precious metals were then "our sole reliance to liquidate the accruing interest of the national debt."

When the Sioux chiefs demanded where Carrington was going, the Colonel frankly told them: to occupy and establish posts in their hunting grounds.

This was too much for Red Cloud. Angrily he declared, "The Great Father sends us presents and wants a new road, but the White Chief goes with soldiers to steal that road before the Indian says yes or no." Another chief told Carrington frankly that within two moons his command "would not have a hoof left."

Messengers sent to invite some of the bands to council had come back badly beaten. It was now as clear to Carrington as to his Chief Guide that plenty of trouble lay ahead.

From headquarters at Omaha Colonel Philip St. George Cooke had written to Carrington, "There must be peace."

Shortly after—to save the nation five dollars a day—he directed Carrington to discharge Bridger!

XXIV
THE CHEYENNES'
WARNING

WAR DEPARTMENT records show Bridger discharged on June 15. But when the order reached Carrington, now fully aware how indispensable Bridger's services were to his command, the Colonel promptly endorsed the order "Impossible of Execution."

On June 16, Carrington raised Jim's pay to $10 a day.

Apparently the Colonel was too wise to say anything about the matter to Bridger; Old Gabe might have become indignant and abandoned the expedition forthwith. The Colonel kept him on the payroll as Chief Guide—actually his intelligence officer and ex-officio chief of staff—and prepared to head into the country of the hostile Sioux.

Carrington sent his wagons to the fort to get the one hundred thousand rounds of rifle ammunition for which he had requisitioned. Unfortunately, there was on hand less than one thousand rounds that could be used in his infantry rifles. But few seemed to care; it was assumed that the treaty would make a lasting peace.

The command left Fort Laramie June 17. Two days later they made camp in the canyon of the Platte. On his way from Fort Kearny Bridger had insisted that no one should stray from the wagons, and Carrington had warned everybody against wandering off to pick flowers, shoot prairie-dogs, or hunt. It had been a long march over the barren Plains, and now, naturally enough, officers and ladies wished to do a little sight-seeing. Several of them left camp to hunt for agates and listen to the multiplied echoes of their pistol shots.

Jim thought that canyon war a mighty unlikely place for greenhorns to go gallivanting. So, as the party started off, Bridger gave them warning: "Better not go fur. There is Injuns enough lying under wolf skins, or skulking on them cliffs, I warrant! They follow ye always. They've seen ye, every day, and when ye don't see any of 'em about, is just the time to look out for their devilment." But the confident young officers, veterans of the Civil War, called Jim's warning "quaint."

The command reached Bridger's Ferry next day. The squawman in charge was named Mills. Bridger found him considerably excited. Only the day before Indians had raided the Ferry Ranch and swept away most of his livestock. Profanely, Mills laid his loss at the door of the Sioux chief Red Cloud and his band of Bad Faces.

Bridger's Ferry was, naturally, a very efficient one, rigged with cables and pulleys to take advantage of the current of the stream; Jim got the command over the North Platte quickly, making a round trip every eleven minutes. Only the cattle had to swim.

Laramie Peak now lay behind them on the left; Pumpkin Buttes far ahead to the right. Passing along between them, the wagon train crossed the Dry Fork of Powder River and so came to Fort Reno. Fort Reno was the last place inhabited by white men short of Montana. But Bridger "had a head full of maps and trails and ideas, all of the utmost value to the objects of the expedition." So the ladies remained cheerful during the ten days Carrington halted at the fort.

Jim found three emigrant trains there awaiting permission to move. Few of the emigrants were armed; many were openly contemptuous of the Sioux. One of the wagon masters was particularly optimistic and loud-mouthed. "Shucks," he bragged, "I can't be scared worth a continental."

While he stood prating to Bridger and the Colonel in the sutler' store, a half-breed suddenly rushed in to give the alarm.

Everyone ran to the door to see. Sure enough! There went the sutler's horses and mules, running in a compact herd, Sioux raiders riding flank and rear, heading towards Pumpkin Buttes.

Carrington lost no time. Bugler Adolph Metzger blew *Boots and Saddles*, and away went Lieutenant Adair with 80 mounted men. Bridger and the Colonel looked on. They found it "excessively provoking to see the coolness of those Indians as they favored their ponies in bad places, and seemed to calculate exactly how long they could take things easy and when they must hurry."

It was some days before the lieutenant returned. He reported that he had chased the horse thieves nearly 70 miles, clear past the Buttes, but had failed to recover any of the stolen stock. He did bring in one broken-down Indian pack pony, laden with navy tobacco, brown sugar, a cavalry stable frock, calico dress patterns, and other things given a few days earlier to these very Indians at the Laramie peace treaty.

Meanwhile Carrington posted orders at Fort Reno instructing emigrants on the management of wagon trains, warning them to corral whenever they saw Indians.

Bridger laughed to think how little good those orders would do. He knew the tribesmen had not yet begun to fight. Indians could not organize quickly. What the Colonel had seen so far was only a smidgin to what would happen once the Sun Dances were over and the young men rode to war. And in fact before long every single wagon train passing over the Bozeman Trail was attacked, more than a thousand head of horses and mules captured, and nearly two hundred white men killed or wounded. The white men at Fort Reno called it "Red Cloud's War," but Jim knew that many another chief would lead his warriors to the attack . . .

Jim guided the command on to Crazy Woman's Fork. There he found two small pieces of a cracker box planted by the trail; something was written on the boards with a lead pencil. Jim took these scribblings to the Colonel, who read the message. It informed them that two wagon trains had been attacked thereabouts only a few days before. Both trains had lost livestock.

The command moved on, passing Lake De Smet one day before noon, and made camp on the Little Piney, where the Colonel proposed to build Fort Carrington.

Bridger, who knew all that country so well, told Carrington that Goose Creek or Tongue River just ahead offered much better sites with plenty of grass and timber and no big hills to overlook the post. Apparently the Colonel had set his heart on the Little Piney; but he could not openly disregard Bridger's opinion. He rode out himself to make reconnaissance of those valleys up the trail. Significantly, he left Bridger in camp.

The gold rush to Montana was very tempting to some of the raw recruits in the command. A few of them deserted. But they soon came hurrying back, reporting that the Sioux had sent them to tell the Colonel that he *must* take his soldiers out of that country.

On July 15, Carrington came back from his reconnaissance, still determined to build his fort on the Little Piney. He ordered work begun that very day.

A trader, French Pete, was encamped nearby.

Before sunset, ominously, one of French Pete's men came in bringing a warning from the Cheyennes that the Sioux meant business. Carrington promptly sent the fellow back to invite these still friendly Indians to a pow-wow.

"At twelve o'clock, June 16th, a few Indians appeared on the hills, and after showing a white flag and receiving assurance of welcome, about forty, including the squaws of chiefs and warriors, approached the camp and bivouacked on the level ground in front. Meanwhile, hospital tents had been arranged for this first interview with the inhabitants of Absaraka.

"A table covered with the national flag was placed across one tent, chairs were placed behind and at the ends for officers of the garrison, while other seats were placed in front for visitors.

"Trunks were opened, epaulettes and dress hats were overhauled, so that whatever a full dress and a little ceremony could do by way of reaching the peculiar taste of the Indian

for dignity and finery, was done. The band of the 18th
played without, as the principal chiefs were brought across
the parade-ground to the tents and introduced to their seats
by Mr. Adair. The Cheyennes came in full state, with their
best varieties of costume, ornament, and arms; though there
was occasionally a departure from even the Indian origin-
ality in apparel. One very tall warrior, with richly wrought
moccasins and a fancy breech-cloth, had no other covering
for his person than a large gay umbrella, which, as his pony
galloped briskly up, had far more of the grotesque and ludi-
crous in its associations than it had of the warlike and fearful.

"Some were bare to the waist, others had only the limbs
bare. Some wore elaborate necklaces of grizzly bears' claws,
shells, and continuous rings, bead-adorned moccasins, leggings, tobacco pouches, medicine bags, and knife scabbards,
as well as armlets, earrings, and medals.

"The large silver medals included, one each, of the admin-
istrations and bore the medallion heads and names of Jeffer-
son, Madison, and Jackson. These medals had belonged to
their fathers who had visited Washington, or had been the
trophies of the field or trade.

"Those who claimed pre-eminence among the band were
'Black Horse,' 'Red Arm,' 'Little Moon' (Two Moon),
'Pretty Bear,' 'The Rabbit that Jumps,' 'The Wolf that Lies
Down,' 'The Man that Stands alone on the Ground,' and
'Dull Knife.'

"As these were the Indians who had sent the message of
the 14th, or were in their company, the question of their
inclination and temper was one of no little interest to all.

"The formal assurance of the Laramie Peace Commission
before its adjournment, that satisfactory peace had been
made with the Ogillalla and Brulé Sioux, and that the Ara-

pahoes and Cheyennes had only to come in for their presents, inspired some hope that possibly the reception of this first band encountered, might result in substantial advantage beyond the mere range of the band itself.

"As the front of the canvas was open, the ladies gathered in the headquarters tent close by, parted its folds and enjoyed a dress-circle view of the whole performance. As pipes passed and the inevitable '*how*,' the rising up, and the shaking of hands were interludes between all solemn declarations, as well as the prelude to a new speech, or the approval of something good that had been said, the scene seemed just about as intelligible as a rapidly-acted pantomime would be to a perfect stranger to the stage.

"The red-sandstone pipe had its frequent replenishing before a single 'how' indicated that either visitor wished to make himself heard. The scene was peculiar.

"In front of them all, and to the left of the table, sitting on a low seat, with elbows on his knees and chin buried in his hands, sat the noted James Bridger, whose forty-four years upon the frontier had made him as keen and suspicious of Indians as any Indian himself could be of another. The old man, already somewhat bowed by age, after long residence among the Crows as a friend and favorite chief, and having incurred the bitter hatred of the Cheyennes and Sioux alike, knew full well that *his* scalp ('Big Throat's') would be the proudest trophy they could bear to their solemn feasts; and there he sat, or crouched, as watchful as though old times had come again, and he was once more to mingle in the fight, or renew the ordeal of his many hair-breadth escapes and spirited adventures. . . .

"Near Major Bridger stood Jack Stead, the interpreter. Born in England, early a runaway sailor boy, afterward a seaman upon the *Peacock* when it was wrecked near the mouth of Columbia River; then traversing the Rocky Mountains as one of the first messengers to report the Mormon preparations to resist the United States, and the renewal of Indian hostilities, the same year; with hair and eyes black as an Indian's, and a face nearly as tawny from hardship and exposure; a good shot, and skilled in woodcraft; with a Cheyenne wife, fond of big stories and much whisky; but a fair interpreter when mastered and held to duty; and watchful as Bridger himself to take care of his scalp,—Jack Stead was the first to break the silence and announce that Black Horse wanted to talk.

"Adjutant Phisterer, called by the Indians 'Roman, or Crooked Nose,' acted as recorder of the council, keeping full notes of the conference; and few were the diaries or letters home that did not embody the history of our first visit from Indians, and repeat some of their expressions of purpose or desire.

"Neither did the Indian advocate appear to disadvantage, as the exponent of his rights and wants. Erect and earnest, he cast off the buffalo robe that had been gathered about his shoulders and in his folded arms, and while it now hung loosely from his girdle, stepped halfway toward the table and began.

"With fire in his eye, and such spirit in his gesture as if he were striking a blow for his life or the life of his nation; with cadence changeful, now rising in tone, so as to sound far and wide over the garrison, and again sinking so as to seem as if he were communing with his own spirit rather than feeling for a response from the mind of another, the Cheyenne chief stood there to represent his people, to question the plans of the white chief, and solemnly advise him of the issue that was forced upon the red man. It was an occasion when all idea of the red man as the mere wild beast to be slaughtered, quickly vanished in a prompt sympathy with his condition, and no less inspired an earnest purpose, so far as possible, to harmonize the intrusion upon his grand hunting domain with his best possible well-being in the future.

"Other chiefs followed 'Black Horse,' in harangues of varied length and vigor; and all agreed that they preferred to accept protection and become the friends of the whites. They came to represent one hundred and seventy-six lodges, and had been hunting on Goose Creek and Tongue River, when they met Red Cloud; but said that one hundred and twenty-five of their young men were absent with 'Bob Tail,' having gone to the Arkansas on the war-path and hunt. They had quarreled with another band of Cheyennes, who lived near the Black Hills east of Powder River; and said there was a third band south of the Republican hostile to the whites. Two of the chiefs had with them Camanche wives whom they had married in excursions to the south.

"They gave the history of a portion of our march, and stated correctly, what Red Cloud had assured them, that half of the white soldiers were left back at Crazy Woman's Fork. They said that Red Cloud told them, the morning before the messenger was sent to the camp, that white soldiers from Laramie would be at Piney Fork before the sun was overhead in the heavens; that the white chief sent soldiers from Reno after Indians who stole horses and mules; but the white soldiers did not get them back.

"They also stated that the Sioux were having a sun-dance, insisting that the Cheyennes must make common cause with them and drive the white man back to Powder River; that some of Red Cloud's men had already gone back to interrupt travel on the road; that they had left their squaws in the village with thirty of their old men, and were afraid the Sioux would rob them in their absence if they should stay too long in the white man's camp; but that if they could have provisions, they would make a strong peace, and let a hundred of their young men, whose return would be in two days, go with the white soldiers against the Sioux.

"Before the council broke up, Brevet Major Haymond arrived with his four companies and went into camp northwest of the fort near the river crossing.

"The Indians became very restless as the afternoon progressed, and at last bade good by; receiving papers indicative of their good behavior, and entering into an agreement to leave the line of road and go upon or south of the upper plateau of the Big Horn Mountains. They afterward visited Fort Casper, behaving well, and no doubt observed their obligations as best they could.

"The presents given consisted of some second-hand clothing of the officers, twenty pounds of tobacco, a dinner of army rations, and enough flour, bacon, sugar and coffee to give them a meal in their village and convince the absent of their kind treatment. They left with apparently cordial good feeling, and the understanding that they were not to approach emigrant trains even to beg; but might go to Laramie, or other military posts when hungry, as long as they remained the friends of the whites." [1]

XXV

BLOODY JUNKET

THE SIOUX lost no time in making their threats good. At 5 o'clock next morning, July 17, a number of them crept stealthily up to the horseguards, jumped over the rookie picket, captured the wagon master's bell mare, and so ran away with a great herd of mules.

Major Haymond left orders for his mounted men to saddle and follow; he dashed off after the thieves with only his orderly. Afterward Bridger wondered what the two of them would have done if they had overtaken the Sioux before the rest of the command came up! The horse thieves of course, anticipating pursuit, ran the captured animals through their main party of several hundred warriors, so that Haymond and his men were ambushed on Peno Creek and surrounded. He managed to send a messenger to the post, and Carrington sent out two companies of infantry and fifty mounted men to his relief. Two men were killed, three wounded.

Haymond, falling back, had come upon the train of French Pete. Pete and his five men lay dead, scalped and mutilated, among their plundered wagons. Out of the nearby brush came his Sioux wife with five frightened children, begging to be taken to the fort. Because of their haste, the Indians had not killed Pete's animals, and Haymond was able to bring the wagons and the woman and children in.

Bridger got Mrs. Gazzeau's story in the sign language.[1] With some emotion, she signed that the Cheyennes, after leaving the post the day before, had come to Pete's camp and stayed until midnight smoking and trading. During the evening a party of Sioux chiefs came up from Tongue River to find out from Black Horse what the white men had said to the Cheyennes and whether the white chief was going back to Powder River as they had warned him to do. Black Horse replied, "The white chief will not go back; his soldiers will go forward."

The Sioux demanded, "What presents did the white chief give you?"

Black Horse replied, "We had all we wanted to eat. The white chief said he wanted all the Arapaho and Sioux and all the other Indians in this country to go to Fort Laramie and sign the treaty and get their presents."

Such talk from their old allies the Cheyennes enraged the Sioux. They jumped up, unstrung their bows, and beat Black Horse and the other Cheyennes over the back and face, yelling as if counting coup on enemies.[2]

Then the Sioux hit the trail.

After that demonstration, Black Horse warned French

Sioux arrow, sign of war and victory. Sign of broken gun indicates that the troops will be defeated

In case of Sioux warriors against other enemy tribes, this sign is on the buffalo skull. Straight arrow is sign of victory; broken arrow, defeat for enemy

Pete to go to the Cheyenne village and on to the mountains, but advised him to send a messenger to the white chief quick, or the Sioux would kill him. Instead Pete decided to come in to the post in the morning. He was on the road when the Sioux horse thieves passed and killed him and all his men. The woman said she and her children had run into the brush; the warriors had not followed her . . .

Major Haymond moved his camp to a point just below the fort.

Now that Carrington knew where his fort was to stand, he sent Captain Burrows to Fort Reno for provisions on the 19th. Bridger went along as guide, riding as usual out ahead of the wagons and their escort. Burrows planned to make camp on Clear Fork, but beside the trail Bridger found buffalo skulls with Injun signs marked on the broad white foreheads. These marks he interpreted to mean that a battle was to be fought that day on the Crazy Woman and that all hostiles who saw the marks should be on hand. Jim urged Burrows to make a forced march and rescue the wagon train.[3]

The marks on the skulls did not impress Burrows. He was skeptical of Jim's interpretation and inclined to laugh at him. He had no reason to think there was anybody on the Crazy Woman; but Bridger was so earnest that, to humor the old scout, the Captain pushed on. Bridger rode out ahead of the plodding infantry. When he looked over the ridge, he saw wagons corralled and men lying in a ravine at the foot of the slope. They were pointing their rifles at him. One shouted to him "Halt!"

Jim reined up.

"Who goes there?"

"A friend."

"What's your name?"

"Jim Bridger." They beckoned him on and he rode through the ravine and on up to the wagon corral.

Several hundred Indians, they told him, had been after them, but had pulled out when they saw the coming dust made by Burrows' command. One soldier had been killed.

Another train with only ten men as escort had been attacked by fifty Indians at the same place. Lieutenant Daniel, scouting ahead for a good campground, was killed, scalped, and cut to pieces. One of the Sioux had then put on the officer's clothing and danced back and forth within sight of the helpless people with the wagons—daring them to come out and fight. In this scrape the Army chaplain handled a rifle like the other men, trying to kill "as many of the varmints as possible."

This wagon train had been warned by Black Horse and his Cheyennes.

"I knew there was hell to pay here today at Crazy Woman," Jim said. "I could see it from the signs the Injuns made on the buffalo skulls. But cheer up, boys, Captain Burrows and two hundred soldiers are coming down the road thar about two miles away." He pointed to the dust rising in the distance.[4]

A few days later Bridger and the detachment were back at Fort Carrington. They brought along an order changing the name of the post to Fort Phil Kearney.

While the fort was building, Bridger, in addition to his duties as advisor and scout, found time to play with the children and entertain the ladies in the camp. The gold craze of the time amused him, and though gold color could be panned out in almost any of the streams around the fort, Jim was disgusted by the constant questioning of men who thought of nothing but the diggings and the fortunes to be made in them.

He told one group of eager listeners that out thar in the Yellowstone country thar war a mountain with a great big *diamond* on it. Any man lucky enough to git the right range could see it fifty mile away . . . One sucker offered Jim a new rifle and a good horse if he would tell him how to find that diamond.

Walking about in the fort, Jim was constantly on the alert, scanning the hills around, catching flashes from the signal mirrors of the Sioux, looking for snipers behind every stump or thicket, alert to the messages of the birds and animals in the neighborhood.

At night wolves hung about the slaughter yard of the quartermaster outside the stockade near the creek, fighting over the offal there, often dying from the poison put with the meat to kill them. Indians, seeing that the sentry, who wished the wolves to eat the poison, would not shoot them, donned wolf skins, crept up, and shot him from the banquette. Scarcely a day passed without one or more fights; at times it seemed that the post cemetery grew faster than the fort itself.

Already in July Carrington was demanding reinforcements, asking permission to hire Indian auxiliaries, though still confident that he could hold the fort and carry out his mission. A large portion of his command was constantly on the road escorting emigrants or carrying the weekly mail to Laramie. He was so understaffed that two officers alternated as officer of the day and in turn commanded detachments, while attacks by ever-increasing numbers continued day after day.

But the Colonel never faltered. Early in August he sent Colonel N. C. Kinney and two companies to the northwest to establish Fort C. F. Smith. The new fort was to have a strong garrison because a lot of miners nearby—lately Confederates—were eager to join the Sioux in fighting Carrington's bluecoats.

Just before Bridger and the troops arrived on the site selected, the Sioux had stampeded a hundred mules from a passing train of emigrants.

The new fort was established on the Big Horn 91 miles to the northwest. Colonel Carrington had orders to lay out a wagon road to that fort and on to Virginia City—a total distance of 365 miles. He sent Bridger to find the best and shortest route. Jim mapped out a road 20 miles shorter than the old trail, and he reported that 30 miles of that could be cut off as soon as it was safe to improve the road.

The Colonel was anxious to learn all he could of the numbers and plans of the hostiles. The best source of information was the friendly Crows whom Bridger had known so long. At that time, for a wonder, the Crows and the Sioux were at peace.

While at Fort C. F. Smith, he induced some Crows to come in and talk. They reported 500 lodges of Sioux on Tongue River, and the Cheyennes confirmed that.

Later Jim visited a camp of 600 Crows not far from Clark's Fork, where Chiefs White Mouth, Black Foot, and Rotten Tail declared they were for peace, but that some of their young men wished to join the Sioux so as to gain their favor and re-establish title to Crow lands which the Sioux and Cheyennes had recently overrun. The chiefs reported the Oglala and Minniconjou, Hunkpapa, Cheyenne, Arapaho, and Gros Ventres of the Prairie all united to attack the forts before snow flew. Piegans and Bloods were hostile too, but the Nez Percés, Flatheads, Blackfeet, Assiniboine, and Cree had so far refused to join the league against the white men.

Jim Beckwourth helped Bridger gain all this information. But Beckwourth's help did not amount to much. He claimed to be adopted by a Crow woman, and to have been made a chief in the tribe. But on one of his missions to the Crows, he suddenly died—Bridger heard by poison. What he had to report, if anything, Jim Bridger never learned.

But Bridger learned plenty from the Crows himself. By all accounts the hostiles were swarming to the big camps on Tongue River, on the Powder, the Big Horn—everywhere.

Rotten Tail told Big Throat that he and his party had been fully half a day riding through the hostile camps on Tongue River—that 1500 lodges were planning to attack Fort Phil Kearney.

This information, reliable as it was alarming, made Colonel Carrington work like two beavers to complete the fort.

Jim told the Colonel that the Crow chiefs had offered to send 250 warriors to help fight the Sioux. Jim urged him to accept; set an Injun to catch an Injun.

But Carrington had no authority to hire the Crows, no money to pay them—and no arms to equip them. He was so woefully short of ammunition for his own troops that he had to keep the facts secret; the Springfield rifles which most of the men carried were useless in the saddle. Yet the only response the Colonel could get from his superiors was the threat of a court-martial if he failed to get the mail through to Laramie every week. Apparently all they cared for was regular paperwork!

In answer to Carrington's appeal for more troops, they suggested that, if he had not enough to guard the whole road, he might abandon Fort C. F. Smith!

To top all this, they ordered the Colonel to discharge all his scouts—including Bridger!

Carrington could not get along without Bridger. The Colonel remonstrated with his superiors, and Bridger was not discharged.

On his return late in October to Fort Phil Kearney, Jim saw that things were rapidly moving to a showdown. Since late August the number of hostiles about the post was greatly increased. There had been constant attacks on wagon trains up and down the Trail, attacks on miners camped under the very walls of the fort. One man had been shot through a loophole, and hardly a day passed but someone lost his livestock or his hair. The wood train on its daily journey to cut timber at the Pinery seven miles away seldom returned without a brush with Indians, though the ninety wagons were guarded by as many as a hundred men from the little garrison.

On September 13, at nine o'clock, the Indians tried to stampede the horse herd. Captain Ten Eyck pursued the horse thieves until late at night. Private Donovan came back with an arrow stuck in his hip, but as soon as the surgeon had removed it, started out again. After riding fifteen miles the troops had to give up the chase. Those heavy cavalry horses could not keep pace with nimble Indian ponies in such rough country, and single-shot rifle and Navy Colt were no match for high-velocity arrow and rapid-fire bow.

At midnight that same day the haymakers on Goose Creek called for help. The messenger reported one man killed; that hay had been stacked over the five mowing machines and set ablaze; that the Sioux had stampeded a herd of buffalo through the valley, thus sweeping away more than two hundred cattle belonging to the post. Lieutenant Adair rushed fifty men to the aid of the haymakers, but found the Sioux too many for him. Still nothing Jim Bridger could say would make the people in the fort realize their danger.

One fine Sunday afternoon Ridgeway Glover, artist and correspondent for *Frank Leslie's Illustrated Weekly*, went for a stroll—unarmed. Monday morning Lieutenant William H. Bisbee found him only a few minutes' walk from the post, naked, "dead, scalped, and badly mutilated, lying face downward across the roadway." [5]

Only once, Bridger learned, had the troops scored any considerable victory. On September 23 Indians had suddenly dashed in and stampeded 24 head of cattle. By this time Carrington had learned that delay in pursuing Indians was fatal. Since they usually attacked about daybreak, he always had his horses saddled and bridled before that hour, ready to go. The moment the alarm was sounded, girths were tightened, bits were put into the animals' mouths, men mounted, and away they went. That day Captain Frederick H. Brown dashed out at the head of 25 soldiers and citizens and actually caught up with the savages—probably because the cattle they were driving could not run like ponies. There was a sharp fight at close quarters. Brown recovered the cattle and knocked over a good many Indians.

That was the story they told at the fort. Bridger nodded. The Crows had told him all about that scrape: that day, he said, the Sioux had lost 13 killed and many wounded.

Four days later Private Patrick Smith was scalped at the Pinery, shot with arrows, left for dead. Creeping through the thickets, he found the arrow shafts caught on the bushes, but he managed to break them off so that he could crawl the half mile to the blockhouse. He survived until the surgeon pulled an arrow from his breast.

All these harassing attacks, together with the victory of Captain Brown, roused a fury of impatience among officers and men for revenge and action in the open. But one and all kept doggedly on with their work, waiting for the day when the fort would be completed and the great garrison flag broken out on the new pole in the middle of the parade ground.

That was quite a ceremony. On October 31, after morning inspection, the whole command turned out in brand new uniforms. The band played hymns and sentimental music: *Old Hundred, Nearer My God To Thee, Annie Laurie, When the Swallows Homeward Fly.* Judge Kinney read "an appropriate poem of Miss Carmichael's chaste and spirited collection. Chaplain White offered a prayer, and principal musician Barnes, who with William Daley fashioned the flag-staff, presented to be read an original poem of his own, which at least did justice to his patriotic spirit." [6]

Following this, Colonel Carrington made a high-minded though somewhat flowery speech. He called attention to the losses and achievements of the command and to the fact that their pledge to "guarantee a safe passage for all who seek a home in the lands beyond" had been made good. He praised the men for their labor and faithful service in building what General W. B. Hazen had declared the best fort he had ever seen in this country. Then the Colonel declared a holiday.

The companies snapped to attention and presented arms, the flag went up, the cannon roared, the ladies waved their handkerchiefs, all to the long roll of the drum corps and the strains of *The Star-Spangled Banner*. The Sioux obliged with a demonstration in force and many mirror signals flashed from the great bare hills around.

That evening there was the usual levee at the Colonel's quarters with music and dancing. It was payday. Fort Phil Kearney celebrated.

Now for the winter campaign!

XXVI
FORT PHIL KEARNEY

ONCE Fort Phil Kearney was completed, Colonel Carrington found himself between the upper and the nether millstones, and Jim Bridger occupied much the same position.

On the one hand there was General Philip St. George Cooke, department commander at Omaha, who wished the Indians subdued without delay. During the construction of the post, while authorities in the East still had faith in the Fort Laramie treaty, pressure on Carrington for a campaign

had been light. For, since the disastrous defeat of Connor
and his colleagues the summer before, the War Department
was not too eager for another cavalry campaign in warm
weather. But now that winter was coming and the Sioux
were known to be hostile, General Cooke kept urging a "short
winter campaign." He wished Carrington to "surprise Red
Cloud in his winter camps" and advised him by telegram
that "two hundred or three hundred infantry, with much
suffering, perhaps might thus accomplish more than two
thousand troops in summer." The General reminded Carrington that he had "four companies of infantry and some
cavalry available for punishing a long arrear of outrages."

Jim Bridger laughed at the notion of those greenhorns
surprising the Sioux camp—a camp that extended some
twenty miles along Tongue River. By a mircle the troops
might surprise the Injuns camped on the first mile. After
that, warriors from the other nineteen miles of camp would
do the surprising.

On the other side, Carrington was under relentless pressure
from his subordinates—particularly the hotheaded younger
officers, proud veterans of the Civil War, who chafed under
confinement and inaction. They regarded the Colonel as a
mere garrison officer without experience in, or spirit for, the
field. They had come out from the States to *fight* Indians,
and the minute one of them arrived he would, unless checked,
ride off single-handed looking for Red Cloud's scalp!

The ringleader of these eager young men was Frederick
H. Brown, Quartermaster at Fort Phil Kearney, recently
commissioned Captain.

Considering his faithful service in the Civil War, Brown
felt that he had been passed over, not having been promoted
so rapidly as other officers of his regiment. He was keen to
distinguish himself. He could scarcely attend to his regular

duties because of his preoccupation with Indian fighting. He was always on the alert.

Following his lead were Lieutenants George W. Grummond and Horatio S. Bingham, who had held higher rank during the Civil War. And when in November Brevet Lieutenant-Colonel William J. Fetterman came to the fort, he too fell under the spell of the belligerent Quartermaster.

Fetterman had come to take command of the second battalion of the 18th Infantry, now being reorganized as the 27th Infantry, and so expected to take command of Fort Phil Kearney when Carrington should rejoin the first battalion of the 18th at Fort Reno. Fetterman had a reputation for courage and gentlemanly manners and was the senior officer under Carrington at the post.

In his ignorance of Indian warfare, Fetterman was quite contemptuous of the Sioux. He declared that he was "sure a single company of regulars could whip a thousand Indians" and that "a full regiment could whip the entire array of hostile tribes." He bragged, "With 80 men I could ride through the whole Sioux nation."

Colonel Carrington reports: "To this boast my Chief Guide, the veteran James Bridger, replied in my presence, 'Your men who fought down South are crazy! They don't know anything about fighting Injuns.' "

Anyone could see, Jim thought, that these young fellows from the East couldn't savvy what they were up against. They were mighty few, and most of their men were rookies. Their horses were not fit for that rough country. The soldiers could not ride. They were armed with cumbersome single-shot infantry rifles which they could not fire from the saddle. They were not familiar with the country or the climate. And they knew nothing whatever about the numbers, tactics, and strategy of their fierce and wily foes. It was a

rare thing that one of them could hit an Injun on horseback
—even when standing on the ground. Ammunition was too
scarce to allow much target practice.

On the other hand, the Sioux and Cheyennes were good
bowmen and spearmen, splendid horsemen, born scouts, experienced veterans since boyhood, men who never got drunk,
never deserted, and seldom attacked unless they had every
advantage. Moreover, the cussed Injuns outnumbered Carrington's greenhorns at least ten to one.

All this Bridger tried to make clear to the soldiers. He
had spent forty years outguessing and outfighting redskins,
and he had his hair yit. But Jim made little progress.

Though the officers came to respect the plain, farmer-look-
ing man, in his store clothes and low-crowned, soft felt hat,
for his sober habits and his shrewdness in estimating Indian
motives, they could see no real use for the old man hanging
about the fort. He never left the stockade unless ordered to
go, and apparently had adopted the Indian way of seeing
without being seen.

It was not a way that appealed to dashing young officers,
eager for adventure. "Scout! We don't need anybody to
scout for Indians here—they're always around!" That was
what they said. It amused them to watch Old Jim come out
of his tent, shade his eyes, scan the hills around, and say,
"When you don't see 'em, that's when they're full of devilment."

"Boys," Jim would say, "the trouble with you is you're
all spunk and no gumption."

It may be that, as Mark Twain believed, Americans of
those days had false notions about war. The romantic literature of their time and the genteel tradition made them attach
an altogether exaggerated importance to valor as a factor in
victory.

Jim Bridger had never read the novels of Sir Walter
Scott. He never thought of himself as a hero or talked about
his bravery. · He was a seasoned fighter. To him fighting was
simply a job to be done. Courage he took for granted; *judgment was the thing.* For forty years Old Gabe had been helping incompetent and reckless men out of trouble, and he knew
well enough that looking after his men was the first duty of
a chief or an officer. Riding out like a fool knight errant
seeking adventure or making a grandstand play to show off
one's courage for the ladies had mighty little to do with
soldiering.

When he tried to make these young hotheads understand
Injun warfare, they were very *kind* to him—very *polite.*
But among themselves "they counted the old man as behind
the times in modern artillery art."

Meanwhile Jim and the Colonel did what they could to
make the fort secure. The wood train wagons now moved
out in parallel columns, so that they could corral instantly,
swinging the two columns together front and rear, driving
the mules inside the circle of wagons, as each team moved up
beside the wagon ahead. They established a lookout on Pilot
Hill. The Colonel taught the pickets to use signal flags to
communicate with the post; Bridger taught the pickets to
ride or run Injun-fashion in a circle on the slope of the hill
to give warning when Indians came in sight. The Colonel
probably wished definite information which Indians could not
interpret; Jim Bridger wished the hostiles to know they had
been discovered. Everything done at Fort Phil Kearney
shows a curious combination of the ideas of Carrington and
Bridger.[1] They made a great team.

Their policy was "not to precipitate or undertake a general war while there was but a handful of men at the post."
The command at this time had less than fifty serviceable

horses: General Hazen, on his tour of inspection, had taken away twenty-six of Carrington's mounts and as many picked men to ride them as an escort.

When Fetterman and Brown asked the Colonel for fifty mounted men to go with fifty citizens to attack the Indian camps on Tongue River, Carrington showed them his morning report. It showed that had he permitted them to go, he would have had to give up sending the mail, call in his pickets, and would still have lacked eight horses of the desired fifty. Already it had been demonstrated that fifty men and an officer had not been able to protect the haymakers within a few miles of the post. Brown told the Colonel he saw that the raid on Tongue River was impossible, but declared, "I just feel that I could kill a dozen myself."

Thus foiled in the attempt to annihilate the cohorts of the Sioux at one blow, Fetterman cooked up a scheme to trick the enemy. One bright moonlight night he asked permission of the Colonel to hide men in the cottonwoods along the Big Piney. His plan was to leave some hobbled mules between that stream and the fort and so decoy the Indians to their death. Brown and Grummond warmly seconded Fetterman in his request.

The Colonel yielded. Bridger grinned.

The three officers and their men waited vainly by their baited trap. But nothing happened. For the Sioux were busy with a scheme of their own and, shortly after Fetterman had led his men back to barracks, stampeded a herd of Government animals on the *other* side of the post.

Ironically, the mail train that brought the news that "a satisfactory treaty with all the Indians of the Northwest has been made" was surrounded by Indians near Lake De Smet and had to be rescued by a detachment from the fort . . .

Ten years later all officers on the frontier were well aware of the splendid efficiency of Sioux and Cheyenne warriors. Then Custer praised their tactics and "individual daring," their "wonderful horsemanship," which he believed the best in the world, surpassing that of the Cossacks themselves. Then General Charles King called them "foemen far more to be dreaded than any European cavalry," Colonel Ford reported them "the finest skirmishers" he had ever seen, and one of Crook's staff officers declared them "the finest light cavalry in the world." Major Walsh of the Royal Northwest Mounted Police described the Sioux as "superior to the best English regiments." General Anson Mills reported "the Indians proved then and there that they were the best cavalry on earth . . . their like will never be seen again." General Frederick W. Benteen said the final word: "Good shots, good riders, the best fighters the sun ever shone on." . . .

In November, 1866, military men on the frontier had not the experience required to justify such opinions. But that experience was not long in coming:

On the morning of December 6, pickets on Pilot Hill signaled—as usual—that the wood train was surrounded and required relief. At the same time Indians were seen swarming upon Lodge Trail Ridge, flashing their mirror signals and watching with field glasses to see what the soldiers in the fort might do.

The commanding officer sent Colonel Fetterman with mounted infantry to relieve the wood train. With him rode Lieutenant Bingham at the head of the cavalry detachment. Carrington's instructions to Fetterman were to drive the Indians back over Lodge Trail Ridge. Meanwhile Carrington and Lieutenant Grummond with thirty mounted men would cross the Big Piney and attempt to intercept the Sioux in their retreat.

The catch in this program was that the Indians would not

retreat. Some two or three hundred of them engaged Colonel Fetterman hotly.

During this action Lieutenant Bingham, without consulting the senior officer, rode off to the west, followed by fifteen cavalrymen. Fortunately Lieutenant Wands, who had been delayed by transferring his saddle to another horse and had been unable to catch up with Carrington, joined Fetterman's party by mistake. Wands had a repeating Henry rifle, which enabled him to save the troops there, most of whom were armed only with revolvers.

While Wands and Fetterman were fighting off the overwhelming Sioux, Carrington and Grummond had been moving forward according to the original plan. Impulsively Lieutenant Grummond dashed off without orders and joined his friend Bingham. The two disappeared in short order.

Carrington found Bingham's detachment dismounted on one of the forks of Peno Creek.

A big bunch of Indians now developed on Colonel Carrington's front, while others appeared on his flanks. After turning the point of the hill, he found he had only seven men and a bugler with him. The Indians circled to draw his fire. An Indian shot down Private Maguire's horse and came running up to scalp him, but the little party halted and helped Maguire up behind one of his comrades. The Colonel ordered the recall. Corporal Baker came over the hill from the north to report that Lieutenant Bingham had gone beyond the second hill now screened by at least eighty Indians.

Shortly after, Fetterman brought his men to join Carrington, and the combined force moved to the rescue of Lieutenant Bingham.

They had advanced only a few rods when they heard a cry, "For God's sake come down quick." They saw Lieutenant Grummond and three troopers fleeing for their lives before a party of seven Indians, whose spearheads were close to their backs.

Carrington and Fetterman saved Grummond's party and pushed on. They found Lieutenant Bingham dead and Sergeant Bowers mortally wounded—his head split with a hatchet. Three dead Indians lay around Bowers—men whom he had killed with his revolver before going down.

Private Donovan, one of bravest men in the regiment, made his report. He said that one of the Indians had been unhorsed and was running off afoot, Lieutenants Grummond and Bingham had left their men, then surrounded by thirty Indians, to ride off after this lone warrior.

General Bisbee confirms Donovan's report: ". . . a stray Indian was seen not far distant from the troops. Lieutenants Grummond and Bingham, mounted, ran for him in hopes of a capture. The lone Indian meantime shouting and dodging their bullets and sabres. Soon more Indians appeared among the hills and ravines, making retreat the only course, whereupon a break was made for a hill where three soldiers were seen. No sooner had this point been reached than scores of redskins developed. No course remained but a dash for the main body in doing which Bingham was killed immediately. Sergeant Bowers, of my company, fell nearby, the two others wounded, Lieut. Grummond only escaping unharmed." [2]

Afterward Lieutenant Grummond, according to his fellow officer Bisbee, "very hotly asked the Colonel if he was a fool or a coward to allow his men to be cut to pieces without offering help."

But Fetterman, at any rate, confessed that he had learned a lesson: "that Indian warfare had become a hand-to-hand fight requiring the utmost caution."

Fetterman had nothing to reproach himself for—except ignorance. He had remained with his men, had performed his duty, and had suffered no loss. He was not an officer who would leave his command to chase a stray enemy. Had Bingham and Grummond exercised equal judgment, perhaps no lives need have been lost that day.

The day after the burial of the two men killed in this fight, the President of the United States, in his message to Congress, congratulated the country that the Indians were at peace! . . .

Fine crisp weather, inviting to action, followed day after day, and the impatience of men and officers increased. The constraint of constant confinement to the limits of the stockade became intolerable; officers began to wonder when—if ever—Colonel Carrington proposed to launch his winter campaign. Carrington proposed to postpone that until he received the reinforcements promised.

Continually the officers talked of action. Captain Brown was now particularly eager, since he had been relieved as Quartermaster and was awaiting orders to leave the post. And his eagerness for action was stimulated by the knowledge that Indians were now swarming about the fort, increasing their numbers day by day. Brown informed Carrington that he wished they would hurry up those reinforcements. Said he, "I am going to have one more good fight if I have to work night and day to finish my papers."

On the night of December 20 Brown called upon his friends wearing two revolvers and with his spurs fastened in the buttonholes of his coat and leggins wrapped—as he put it "ready day and night"—to tell everyone that he must have one scalp before he left for Laramie.

Realizing the desperate nature of battle with the Sioux and fearing torture if captured, he and Fetterman made it up together that each would always keep one shot for himself.

Torture! Suicide! Heroics! At all this Jim Bridger could only shake his head.

XXVII
AMBUSH

EARLY next morning, Bridger's rheumatism warned him that the weather would soon take a turn for the worse. Some snow had already fallen, and remained in places; there was ice on the Big Piney; but as yet there had been no bitter weather. Now, Jim felt in his bones, a blizzard was coming. It was high time; in another four days it would be Christmas.

That morning, soon after breakfast, the Colonel's orderly summoned Bridger to headquarters. The Officer of the Guard had just come in to report a delegation of Cheyenne warriors led by Chief Two Moon at the gate. After a word with Bridger, the commanding officer ordered the Cheyennes admitted and brought to headquarters.

Bridger knew well enough what the dark, sawed-off chief with the big mouth had come for—to spy out the fort and find out whether the cussed Injuns could hope to storm it, take it, burn it. So far, all the Cheyennes who had visited the post had been friendlies. But Jim was suspicious of Two Moon: the Cheyennes had been allies of the Sioux a long time, and the Sioux were mighty warlike.

Bridger knew only a few words of choking, hissing Cheyenne. He used the sign language, and with an air of perfect confidence emphatically told Two Moon that the fort was impregnable; that the Sioux were fools if they thought they could take it; that the soldiers' hearts were big; and that, if the Sioux tried an attack on the fort, they would be killed and driven off, and there would be a heap of crying in their villages.

Seeing Big Throat talk so big, Two Moon would not let him have all the best of it. He swelled up as big as a small man could, and his big mouth sneered his skepticism. For all Jim could tell, Two Moon shared the confidence of the Sioux hotheads. Jim advised Carrington to let the Cheyennes see everything. No use tellin' an Injun; *show* him.

Accordingly, the Cheyennes were conducted over the fort. They inspected the magazine, the blockhouses, the sentry walks along the stockade, the battery of mountain howitzers —"the guns that shoot twice"—parked on the parade ground.

Then Two Moon and his warriors stalked out, rode off into the hills, and rejoined the hostiles hiding in the coulees there. Two Moon told what he had seen, and repeated Big Throat's warning. The chiefs all knew Bridger; they respected his opinions: in council they had laid plans to lure the troops into the hills, out of range of the big guns, and so rub them out. Now they would do it.

Fort Phil Kearney was practically complete, and stocked with provisions and firewood to withstand a siege of many months. Soon there would be no need of cordwood or saw-logs from the Pinery. That morning the wood train rolled out on what Jim thought would be its last trip that winter.

About 11 o'clock, Jim heard the children playing on the parade ground yelling, "Indians." Stepping from his quarters, he saw the flags wig-wagging frantically on Pilot Hill, where one of the pickets rode his horse in a circle—the signal for "Many Indians." At headquarters, Jim learned the flags warned that the wood train had corralled south of the Sullivant Hills, not three miles from the post.

Such an attack on the wood train was so frequent that it was almost routine—but a routine that never became commonplace or dull to the tiny garrison and their womenfolk in the fort. Immediately, Carrington ordered out a detail to relieve the train. Bridger stood by, watching.

The Colonel knew that most of his officers would be eager to go. Every one of them well knew the Colonel's conviction "that in Indian warfare there must be perfect coolness, steadiness, and judgment. . . . They (the Indians) cannot be whipped or punished by some little dashes after a handful, nor by mere resistance of offensive movements. They must be subjected and made to respect the whites."

The Colonel must have felt, too, that Fetterman still cherished some resentment because of Carrington's refusal to authorize his expedition to Tongue River. If so, the Colonel must have experienced a certain anxiety when Fetterman left off walking back and forth before his quarters and came over to ask that—as senior officer—he be allowed to command the detail.

Jim watched the Colonel. Carrington seemed to hesitate.

However, Carrington agreed. Fetterman hurried off to complete his preparations.

Just then Lieutenant Grummond, whose house stood next-door to the Colonel's, came out, and eagerly urged that he be permitted to take a detachment of cavalry. Again Carrington assented. All told, the cavalry—armed with new carbines—and the infantry—still packing their old muzzle-loading muskets—numbered 78 officers and men. By the time the detail was formed, two civilians—Wheatley and Fisher—came up, bringing their repeating Henry rifles. Both were rated good shots; the officers were glad to have them.

Lieutenant Wands, acting adjutant, relayed Carrington's commands to Fetterman: "Support the wood train, relieve it, and report to me. Do not engage or pursue the Indians at its expense. Under no circumstances pursue over the ridge Lodge Trail Ridge as per map in your possession."

Afterward, still fearing that Fetterman or Grummond might be tempted to rashness, Carrington crossed the parade ground and from a sentry platform halted the mounted party and repeated his orders: "Under no circumstances must you cross Lodge Trail Ridge." [1]

As the detail left the post, Captain Brown, rarin' to go, joined it without orders on his own hook. He was not going to be cheated of his last chance at the Sioux.

Already Jim could see a lone Injun on Lodge Trail Ridge, and several others below the fort at the road crossing. But the howitzers soon dropped a few case shot spang among them, knocked one off his horse, and flushed about thirty more out of the brush. They all broke for the hills and coulees to the north.

Bridger watched Fetterman go. He did not take the west road towards the Pinery—the road where the wood train was corralled. Instead he headed off to the northwest across Big Piney towards Lodge Trail Ridge. Jim reckoned Fetterman aimed to head off the Injuns coming from the north to attack the train, or maybeso to jump the Injuns already thar from behind. Anyhow, he was soon out of sight of the post.

By that time Carrington had discovered that no surgeon had gone with the detail. Immediately he ordered Dr. Hines to go, with the Colonel's own orderly, join the wood train, and report to Colonel Fetterman. The surgeon hurried on his way.

Meanwhile the picket on Pilot Hill astonished Bridger: it signalled, *The wood train has broken corral and is moving to the Pinery.*

Not long after, Dr. Hines returned to report that the wood train, unmolested, was on its way—that Fetterman's command was somewhere on the Ridge to the northward out of sight—but that so many Indians were visible ahead that it was impossible to join him. The doctor could not get through.

It was now almost noon.

Suddenly Jim heard a shot in the distance. Then several. Then a volley.

Jim reckoned the cavalry had made contact with the enemy, fired at them, and was waiting for the infantry to close up.

After some time there was a second volley—a third—a fourth. Each time the sound seemed farther.

Carrington hastily climbed up to the lookout tower above his headquarters, could see nothing, and ordered out a relief detail. Within ten or twelve minutes Bridger saw Captain Ten Eyck, Lieutenant Matson, Dr. Hines, and Dr. Ould rush through the gates on the run—with infantry, cavalry, wagons and ambulances—crash through the ice of the Big Piney, and head up the Virginia City Road to the high ground north of Lodge Trail Ridge.

At once the whole fort was busy as an anthill. Non-coms were breaking out and issuing extra ammunition, prisoners were brought from the guardhouse to sentry duty on the banquette, couriers galloped away to bring back the wood train and its guard. Hardly more than a hundred men were left to hold the fort.

Bridger could see one lone Injun on top of Lodge Trail Ridge. He vanished. There was nothing to see. All Jim could do was to listen.

For nearly half an hour the firing continued, steadily increasing in intensity. Suddenly there was a lull.

Then Jim heard:

A quick volley—

Another—
The rattle of file-firing—
A few scattered shots—
Dead silence. . . .

Aching silence that never ended—silence to freeze the blood.

Suddenly, Old Jim, his eyes glued on the hills to the north beyond the Big Piney, watching for a sign of Ten Eyck's men, began to shiver. His teeth chattered. His eyes watered to the sharpening wind, and the tears froze before they could fall. The weather had turned bitter cold. That blizzard was coming—one day too late. Or, maybeso, just in time.

Jim saw a horseman lunging down the slope across the creek—a messenger from Ten Eyck. When he got in, Jim was at headquarters to hear his message read: *Peno valley full of Indians; several hundred on the road below and westward, yelling and challenging me to come down to battle; but nothing can be seen of Fetterman.*

Colonel Carrington sent the courier back, informing Ten Eyck that forty well-armed men with 3,000 rounds were on their way to join him. He ordered the Captain to *unite with Fetterman, fire slowly, and keep men in hand.* But Jim knew from the Colonel's stricken face that he understood.

The long, bitter afternoon dragged on. The frost grew so sharp that it would bite a man's ears just while he was crossing the parade ground. But nobody thought of the cold.

Where was Fetterman?

A few believed, many hoped, all feared, some despaired. Old Gabe comforted the women and children as best he could.

Darkness fell on the desolate fort.

Finally Jim heard the rattle of thimbles, the crackle and

crunch of snow under hoof and tire, as Ten Eyck's detail rolled slowly through the double gates. In the wagons lay forty-nine naked, frozen, horribly mutilated bodies. Others still lay on the bleak icy slopes of Massacre Hill. Ten Eyck reported that in less than 40 minutes the Sioux and Cheyennes had destroyed the whole command.[2]

XXVIII
MASSACRE

The shock of this disaster filled everyone in Fort Phil Kearney with horror, grief, and alarm. The ladies and their children were shaken, and one of the Negro servants went temporarily insane.

Jim Bridger's influence was a steadying one. Mrs. Carrington records: "To us women, Bridger was always a patient listener, a kind advisor, sympathetic as if we were children looking at him as one of our safest champions in hours of danger."

The confidence of men and officers was shaken as well by that disaster on Massacre Hill, and quite as much by the doubt in their hearts whether they could defend the post if the Indians followed up their victory and stormed it. Their total strength, soldier and civilian, was now only 398 men. The supply of ammunition was so low that there was not in the fort a single full cartridge box—20 rounds—for each enlisted man.

No one slept that night.

Next morning at officers' meeting, Bridger and the Colonel discovered "a universal disinclination, generally expressed, to venture a search for the remaining dead." It was argued that a large draft upon the men in the fort for such

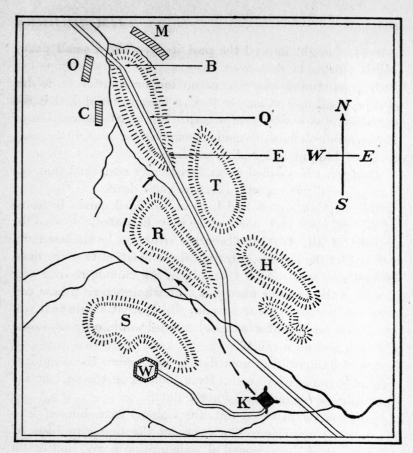

FORT PHIL KEARNEY BATTLEFIELD

K   Fort Phil Kearney

W   Wood Train in Defensive
Corral

S   Sullivant Hills

R   Lodge Trail Ridge

H   High Table Land

C   Cheyennes

O   Oglala

M   Minniconjou

B   Where the **Trap was**
Sprung

Q   Where the Infantry Fell

E   Massacre Hill, where the
Cavalry Died

T   Hilltop from which Captain Ten Eyck's Com-
mand Viewed the Field of
Battle

– – – – →   Route of Colonel
Fetterman

a mission might imperil the post itself, while a small party might quickly be destroyed.

Bridger found the officers no longer indifferent to his opinions; all now seemed to feel, as Carrington did, that the old scout was a very useful man. The swift destruction of Fetterman's command made them realize how little they knew of Indians and Indian warfare.

Bridger, when called upon, laconically remarked that Injuns generally managed to recover *their* dead.

Colonel Carrington had been called hard names by some of his officers. But now, while they hesitated, he was the bravest of all. In that desperate situation he declared: "I will not let the Indians entertain the conviction that our dead cannot and will not be rescued. If we cannot recover our dead, as the Indians always do, at whatever risk, how can you send out details for any purpose? That single fact will give them an idea of weakness here and would only stimulate them to risk an assault."

Colonel Carrington immediately announced the organization of a party of 80 men. Every soldier in the post fit for duty eagerly volunteered for the detail.

Before they marched out, the Colonel went himself into the powder magazine. There he cut the Boorman fuses of spherical case shot, opened all ammunition boxes, and laid a train of powder which would blow up everything at the touch of a single match. In the magazine he placed water, crackers, and other supplies, and gave secret instructions that in case the savages attacked in overwhelming numbers during his absence that day, the women and children were to be placed in the magazine; and in the event of a last desperate struggle, the Officer of the Day was to set off the ammunition and blow them all up together rather than have any of them captured alive. . . .

Naturally, Jim Bridger accompanied the expedition.

As they advanced, they left picket guards on each hilltop, each guard in sight of two others, so that close communication with the fort could be maintained at all times. Thus, if an attack were made on the post, the party could speedily return; or if attacked, could summon reinforcements from the fort.

It was savagely cold. Not an Indian could be seen anywhere, nor could Jim discover any fresh Injun sign.

The battlefield lay beyond Lodge Trail Ridge, where the road to Virginia City followed down a high narrow ridge running a little west of north, roughly parallel to Peno Creek. This ridge dropped away to the north for some two miles in a series of sags and humps to a flat in the forks of Peno Creek. Here and there along the road a few large rocks or boulders lay in groups. This narrow ridge fell away steeply from the road on both sides to the bottoms far below.

When Bridger and the others reached the top of the ridge where the road began to descend, he found the ground littered with arrows, pointing every which-way, showing that the attack had come from all sides. Fetterman had marched down the road following the Indian decoys until hundreds of Sioux and Cheyennes hidden on either side the ridge had rushed in to destroy him.

At the top of the ridge nearest the fort on a space scarcely 40 feet wide, they found most of the bodies of the cavalrymen lying among a group of large boulders, where they had evidently taken cover after letting their horses go. Nearby lay Colonel Fetterman and Captain Brown, each with a bullet hole surrounded by powder marks in his temple. Dead cavalry horses all lay with their heads toward the fort. Even the small dog, which had accompanied the command, lay there—its little body pierced with arrows.

As Bridger and his comrades moved down the slope along the road towards the flat, they found the bodies of infantry-men. Lieutenant Grummond lay about a mile beyond Fet-terman. At the farthest end of the ridge, some two miles from the top, lay the most distant bodies. Down there between two rocks they found Wheatley and Fisher, the two civilians, each with a little pile of empty cartridge shells beside him to show how steadily he had used his 16-shot repeating rifle. The damage the two citizens had done was proved by the treatment of their mangled bodies. Wheatley's bristled with more than a hundred feathered shafts.

All the poor naked bodies were so pitifully crushed and hacked and slashed to pieces that every man who saw them sickened. Horror and rage ensued. Only six of the dead showed bullet wounds. All others had been killed with ar-rows, knives, spears, or clubs.

Bridger had seen a good many dead men in his time, and not a few hacked to pieces by savages—but nothing on this scale.

Because the Indians had thriftily removed the clothing from the dead bodies before defacing them, Carrington was convinced that his soldiers had been taken alive and tortured to death.

Such a notion could never have occurred to Jim Bridger. He knew the Plains Injuns better than that, knew that the mutilation was caused by the resentment of the Indians at their own losses, by the excitement and jubilation after months of futile skirmishing. The abundance of arrows ly-ing about also must have counted. Arrows were expensive and hard to make, and a warrior might hesitate to waste his own on a dead body. But where arrows could be picked up everywhere, a Sioux could let himself go and still keep his quiver filled.

In any case, there could have been no torture, for there had been no time for it. Captain Ten Eyck had arrived on the battlefield too soon.

One body he found lying unmarred under a buffalo robe— that of Bugler Adolph Metzger.[1]

Carrington's men were busy all that afternoon assembling the thirty-two dismembered bodies on the field and depositing them in the wagons. They heard the sunset gun before they could head back to the fort.

As they approached in the darkness, their hearts were cheered by a white light shining clear as a star high over the post, and knew it for a lantern at the masthead—proof that no Indians had come near.

The little hospital at Fort Phil Kearney was much too small to lay out all those dead. Many of the bodies had to be placed in tents, cabins, and spare rooms. Identification was so difficult in some cases that nearly every man in the post was called in to inspect the dead. Many offered their own new uniforms to clothe dead comrades for burial. Meanwhile the ladies comforted Mrs. Grummond and combined their resources and efforts to make her mourning garments for the funeral.

But the burial could not take place at once. It was twenty degrees below zero. The ground was frozen hard as iron, the frost so bitter that gravediggers could work only in fifteen-minute relays. They kept at it steadily day after day to complete the burial pits by the morning after Christmas.

All this while the fort resounded to the whine of saws and the pounding of hammers as coffins were put together. Finally, in a pit fifty feet long and seven feet deep, seventy-six soldiers and two civilians were laid to rest. Fetterman,

Brown, and Grummond were buried together in a common grave nearby.

Meanwhile the blizzard closed down in a blinding smother of fine, freezing flakes, blotting out the day. But John "Portugee" Phillips, a miner in the employ of the quartermaster, volunteered to carry news of the disaster to Fort Laramie—236 miles—through that bitter storm. He planned to ride by night and stay hidden by day, his saddle bags filled only with grain for his horse and a handful of hardtack for himself. Bridger and the little garrison waited anxiously for the reinforcements promised long before.

All this while the whole fort was on the alert. At night there were lights in all quarters. Every man remained at his post. Non-commissioned officers were stationed in every building, and neither officers nor men ever undressed.

And now the snow began to fall heavily, drifting deep about the post so that in places a man could walk over the stockade. This caused fresh alarm—lest the Indians should come running over the drifts into the fort. And so men kept shoveling snow day after day to keep the stockade clear.

The danger, the grief, the suspense, the bitter cold, were bad enough. But Carrington and his officers also felt in their bones that this disaster would, very likely, result in a court-martial for them all. Someone would be the goat. Jim Bridger reckoned maybeso he mought be discharged agin.

After days of waiting, the picket on Pilot Hill began to signal. Then the sentry before headquarters heard the bugle and the long roll of drums. Jim looked out and saw a dark body of troops coming over the snow to the fort. The garrison was saved.

People at the fort made a great hero of Portugee Phillips because of the danger he ran of attack by hostiles on his long cold ride to Laramie. Bridger fully appreciated the cruel hardship of such a terrible ride, but as for Injuns—well, hardly. Not in that blizzard. Injuns wouldn't be out hunting scalps in such weather. They had too much sense.

Some of the men in the fort credited to the cold weather the failure of the Indians to attack the fort after Fetterman was killed. That might have counted, no doubt. But Jim, knowing Indian ways, reckoned that after such a massacree the Sioux would want to go home quick and hold a victory dance whar the squaws could see.

The weather grew steadily colder until the mercury froze in the bulb of the thermometer. Towards the end of January, in the very worst of it, Carrington received orders to take his battalion to Fort Casper. It was thirty-eight degrees below zero. Teams could make only about six miles a day through the deep snow.

Luckily, Jim Bridger was considered too "old and infirm" for such a march. He was left at the fort.

Afterwards Jim heard of the terrible hardships Carrington's men had to endure because of this stupid order from headquarters. Every man in the command was frostbitten, several lost fingers; two had to have their legs amputated and died from the operation. The officers' ladies got through by keeping the sheet-iron stoves in their covered wagons red-hot with burning pine knots. Yet no sooner had Carrington reached Fort Casper than he was ordered to Fort McPherson. . . .

Forty-four years before, when Leavenworth bungled the attack on the Ree villages, Jim Bridger had formed his opinion of the military mind. Nothing that had occurred since that time had caused him to change it. Yet, of all the officers Bridger had worked with, Carrington had been most willing to listen to men who knew the country and the cussed Injuns.

Jim went around the rest of his days defending the Colonel
when anyone blamed him—as many did.

Bridger remained on duty at Fort Phil Kearney and was
still there when the commissioners were sent out to investigate the disaster. Jim had his own sources of information
among friendly Indians and learned all about the fight from
the Crows and Cheyennes. He learned that it was a great
mix-up, that the soldiers fought hard to the end, and that
several Injuns were killed by arrows fired through or across
the command by warriors on the other side. One of the
stories he heard was of the bravery of the bugler, who had
knocked down several Indians, beating them over the head
with his battered copper instrument. Jim heard that only
fourteen or fifteen Sioux had been killed and three or four
Cheyennes. Others might have died of their wounds later.
Crazy Horse had led the Oglala; Black Shield the Minniconjou Sioux. Red Cloud was not present. . . .

We catch only glimpses of Bridger during the following
year:

"F. G. Burnett, who was in the employ of the sutler who
maintained establishments at Forts Reno, Phil Kearney, and
C. F. Smith, was on duty at those posts in the summer of
1867." He says:

" 'Jim Bridger was a remarkable old man and had a wonderful memory. He seemed never to forget a trail that he
had ever traveled, or the distance between streams or water-
ing places, whether good water or bad, and also whether
there was wood, and if there was good feed for the stock.
So we always knew what sort of a camp the one ahead would
be, and what kind of country we would have to travel in
order to reach it.

" 'His eyesight was failing when I knew him, so that he
could not shoot very good, and he would always swear at us

if we got a shot at an Indian and missed him, remarking that he never missed one when he was our age. He was devoid of fear and rarely talked of his exploits, and history has lost many a thrilling adventure by his indifference to publicity. He was a great friend of Chief Washakie of the Shoshones. They were about the same age, and had many hair-raising experiences together. If he was cornered and asked to talk, he would tell the most outlandish yarns and then chuckle to himself and wonder if his questioner had gotten what he wanted.' " [2]

In the summer of 1867, while Bridger was still at Fort Phil Kearney, there was another famous fight nearby, when Captain James Powell and First Lieutenant John C. Jennes with thirty men defended a wagon-box corral one hot August day against about a thousand Sioux and Cheyennes led by Crazy Horse, High Hump (High-Back-Bone), Thunder Hawk, and Ice. The fight lasted for more than three hours.

That day the troops were armed with new repeating rifles and maintained such a volume of fire that the Indians were unable to carry off all their dead. The fight was a draw—six men being killed on each side, and as many Indians wounded. It was broken off when a relief party marched out from the fort and the howitzer began to boom.

It is certain that Jim Bridger had no part in the Wagon Box Fight, though he may have gone out with the relief party. But now, old and ailing as he was and not employed to fight, he may have remained at the fort throughout the whole affair.

In the fall he went down to Fort Laramie for a much needed rest. John Hunton, resident trader at Fort Laramie for many years, bunked in the same room with Bridger. Hunton writes:

"Here he remained, occupying the room with us most of the time, until about the middle of April, 1868.

"He made two or three trips to Cheyenne and Fort D. A. Russell, during the time he was here, but I do not think he was absent at any time to exceed ten days. He seemed to prefer to be around here, and to be alone, or with some one or two persons who did not annoy him by constant questions. Sometimes he seemed to like to talk, and always made a good listener when the subject of conversation interested or pleased him. When it did not, he always curled his upper lip with a sneer and left the audience. He told me many times he did not like to sacrifice his feelings, intelligence or personal pleasure, 'when it was such an easy matter to walk away from a damn fool talking.' I have more than once seen him walk away from a group of army officers in the officers' club room (where he was always a welcome guest) because some officer would comment on something or somebody when Bridger would think the comment was made in ignorance or malice." . . .[3]

By the following spring the commission sent to investigate the Fetterman affair had discovered what Bridger could have told them—that the building of forts in Sioux hunting grounds by the troops was in violation of the existing treaty. Anyway, troops were needed to protect the new transcontinental railroad then building across the country. Accordingly Uncle Sam ordered Fort Reno, Fort Phil Kearney, Fort C. F. Smith to be dismantled and abandoned. Bridger was employed as guide for the wagon trains sent to remove Government property from the forts. The whole business was concluded in one trip. . . .

In that year of 1868 the Government signed a treaty with the Sioux, the only treaty ever signed by the United States in which nothing was asked of the other power except peace.

The Sioux got everything they asked for. After all that bloodshed and hardship, the cussed Injuns had come out on top—sassier than ever!

After Bridger and the troops moved out of Fort Phil Kearney, a Cheyenne chief, Old Little Wolf, set it on fire.

At Fort D. A. Russell near Cheyenne, Wyoming, Bridger was paid off and discharged. He had made his last scout for the Army.

XXIX
THE END
OF THE TRAIL

Taking his discharge, July 21, Bridger went home to Missouri—as he thought, for the last time.

There he learned that General Phil Sheridan was planning a winter campaign against the hostiles on the Southern Plains. Sheridan believed it useless to attack Indians in summer when their ponies were fat and full of ginger, able to carry the warriors out of the way of the plodding troops. The time to strike was in winter, when the ponies would be half-starved and the grass covered by snow. Then troops, he thought, could raid the villages, destroy the Indian's supplies, and force him to come in and surrender.

When Old Gabe heard that, he felt it his duty to go out to Fort Hays and let the General know what he was heading into.

It was a long trip for an old and ailing man, but Jim had never spared himself when duty called.

At Fort Hays he found a lot of new scouts, led by California Joe, employed to guide the troops. He must have felt a slight twinge of professional jealousy—not to say scorn— at having to give way to these younger and much less experienced men. If they knowed their business, Jim Bridger wouldn't have to go traipsin' clear out to western Kansas to warn the General.

Jim tried to talk Sheridan out of his winter campaign, and shook his head over the General's stubborn determination to pitch into the cussed Indians in the blizzard season. But it war no use. Sheridan insisted that soldiers, so much better fed and clothed and equipped than the Indians, would have all the advantage, and that—if all the different columns moved with energy and speed—one short campaign would do the job.

But General Sheridan, to say nothing of many of his officers, could not but be impressed by Bridger's earnestness. So, in order to show that he would not send anyone where he would not go himself, Sheridan moved out from Fort Hays on November 15, 1868, with the main column.

The first night out a blizzard struck the command and whisked away their tents. The sixty-mile wind was so violent they could not put the tents up again. Wet snow and rain drenched them to the skin. Sheridan reports, "Shivering from wet and cold, I took refuge under a wagon, and there spent such a miserable night that, when at last morning came, the gloomy predictions of old man Bridger . . . rose up before me with greatly increased force." [1]

That morning the command labored on through sleet and snow, losing many animals along the way as the mules played out. Fortunately their next stop was Fort Dodge and not the Cheyenne villages. . . .

By good luck and good reconnaissance, General Custer struck the allied camps on the Washita River soon after, burned one of these, and, though not without loss, managed to bring his command safely back again, together with a number of Indian prisoners.

Meanwhile, Old Jim, heading back to Missouri, began to

worry about his claim to Fort Bridger. The ten-year term of his lease of the fort to the United States Government had now elapsed without payment of one cent to Bridger, and now the land had been declared a military reservation by the President. Jim employed an attorney and made some effort to collect the money due him. But his ill health and his inability to establish a clear title kept the matter hanging fire. Jim needed that money, but it was never paid during his lifetime.

He suffered a good deal from his goiter, from an old rupture, from rheumatism; and then, as time passed, his sight began to fail. This was the greatest cross of all. As his vision dimmed, Bridger would often say, "I wish I war back thar among the mountains agin. A man kin see so much farther in that country." Before long he could only recognize people by their voices, and by 1875 was wholly blind.

Still, though his domain had shrunk from half a continent to a small farm, the old man kept up his heart. He tried to run a little store,[2] only to find he was too feeble to tend it. He took great pride in his orchard. But at times, overcome by restlessness, he grew so nervous that his daughter Virginia had to lead him around, he so wanted to be on the go.

She writes: "I got father a good old gentle horse, so that he could ride around and to have something to pass away time, so one day he named his old horse 'Ruff.' We also had a dog that went with father; he named this old, faithful dog 'Sultan.' Sometimes father would call me and say: 'I wish you would go and saddle old Ruff for me; I feel like riding around the farm,' and the faithful old dog would go along. Father could not see very well, but the old faithful horse would guide him along, but at times father would draw the lines wrong, and the horse would go wrong, and then they would get lost in the woods. The strange part of it was the old faithful dog, Sultan, would come home and let us know that father was lost. The dog would bark and whine until I would go out and look for him, and lead him and the old horse home on the main road. Sometimes father wanted to take a walk out to the fields with old Sultan by his side, and cane in hand to guide his way out to the wheat field, would want to know how high the wheat was, and then father would go down on his knees and reach out his hands to feel for the wheat, and that was the way he passed away his time.

"Father at times wished that he could see, and only have his eyesight back again, so that he could go back out to see the mountains. I know he at times would feel lonesome, and long to see some of his old mountain friends to have a good chat of olden times away back in the fifties. . . ."[3]

As his world contracted, Bridger took more and more pleasure in visitors. His son William could play the fiddle, his daughters were good dancers, and Bridger always enjoyed having young people in for a dance. He was also fond of children, who reveled in his wonderful tales. One of their favorites was, naturally enough, his own.[4] When the youngsters gathered round him, he would tell them how five Indians had surprised him and gave chase on their fleet ponies. He spurred his horse and rode for his life. He was armed only with a six-shooter in which, of course, he carried only five cartridges. The first Injun closed up on him. Jim turned in his saddle and picked the cussed redskin off. One after another they overtook him; one after another he shot them down. He saved that last bullet for the right time. The cussed Injun kept on and would not be shaken off.

"We war nearing the edge of a deep and wide gorge. No horse could leap over that awful chasm, and a fall to the bottom meant sartin death. I turned my horse suddint and the Injun was upon me. We both fired to once, and both horses war killed. Then we engaged in a hand-to-hand conflict with butcher knives. He war a powerful Injun—the biggest I ever see. It war a long, hard fight. One minute he had the best of it; next minute I did. At last—"

Here Bridger always paused, as if to get his breath.

Inevitably one of his breathless listeners would cry out anxiously, "What happened then?"

Poker-faced and deliberate, Bridger would solemnly reply, "Why, then the Injun *killed* me!"

But in spite of the new friends about him, the old man sometimes grew very lonely. He longed to talk to some of his comrades of the beaver trail, the soldiers and explorers he had known, and particularly General Grenville M. Dodge. Said he, "I would give anything in the world if I could see some of the old Army officers once more, and have a talk with them of olden times. But I know I will not be able to see any of my oldtime mountain friends any more. I know that my time is near. I feel that my health is failing me very fast and see that I am not the same man I used to be." [5]

But, as many an Injun well knew, Jim Bridger was hard to kill. He was long a-dying. So, old and blind and poor, he sat on his porch with sightless eyes towards the West, with his square face and close-cropped beard, which reminded visitors of President Grant—with his tall, lank frame and the shawl about his shoulders, which reminded people of President Lincoln—sat and waited for the end.

The journalists of those days seem to have been a peculiarly unenterprising lot of men. For thirteen years Jim Bridger, the greatest American explorer living, a good talker with a wonderful memory, sat lonely and eager to talk on his porch within four miles of Kansas City. In that town and in many another within easy reach, newspapermen continued to write and publish their ephemeral essays, their silly political twaddle, their insipid lyrics, stale jokes, and unreliable news stories while any one of them, in a few hours' time, might have made an imperishable record by taking down what Jim Bridger had to tell him. None of them so much as went out to take a photograph of Old Jim. Only his old friend, General Dodge, had interest enough to prepare a short biographical sketch of the old scout after his death —July 17, 1881—and to erect in Kansas City above his grave in Mount Washington Cemetery, the memorial monument which—below his portrait in relief—bears the following inscription:[6]

1804—JAMES BRIDGER—1881
Celebrated as a hunter, trapper, fur trader and guide.
Discovered Great Salt Lake 1824, the South Pass
1827. Visited Yellowstone Lake and Geysers 1830.
Founded Fort Bridger 1843. Opened Overland
Route by Bridger's Pass to Great Salt Lake.
Was a guide for U. S. exploring expeditions, Albert Sidney Johnston's army in
1857, and G. M. Dodge in U. P. surveys and Indian campaigns 1865-66.

But the record of Jim Bridger's work and character lies written in the trails he laid out and the towns and farms and cities which have sprung up where he camped. He performed a great service to our nation, and his character set a standard to which Americans are proud to point. For his sake, we may hope that there are mountains in heaven.

APPENDIX

ACKNOWLEDGMENTS

EVERYONE who writes of Jim Bridger must gratefully acknowledge his debt to Major General Grenville M. Dodge, author of the first authentic biographical sketch of Bridger; to J. Cecil Alter, compiler and interpreter of most of the available published records of Bridger's career; to Mrs. Frances Fuller Victor for her record of racy anecdotes; to Captain Hiram M. Chittenden for his voluminous information about Bridger's part in the development of the fur trade; to the three Carringtons—Margaret, Frances, and J. B.—for intimate pictures of Bridger in his last years of active service; and to Dr. Grace Raymond Hebard and Mr. E. A. Brininstool for their book, *The Bozeman Trail*.

In addition, I wish to express my hearty thanks to the following individuals: William C. Almquist, of Miles City, Montana; Donald Deer Nose, of the Crows; Guy Hobgood, Superintendent, Cheyenne-Arapaho Agency; Reginald Laubin; F. H. McBride, Superintendent, Wind River Agency; Warren L. O'Harra, Superintendent, Crow Agency; Chief Henry Oscar One Bull, of the Sioux; Mrs. Lucille H. Pendell, War Records Department, the National Archives; Mrs. Clyde Porter; J. L. Rader, Librarian, University of Oklahoma; Professor Carl Coke Rister, University of Oklahoma; Professor Elmo Scott Watson; Chief Joseph White Bull, of the Sioux; C. C. Wright, Superintendent, Flathead Agency; Tom Yellowtail, of the Crows; Frank Zahn, the Upper Missouri Interpreter; to Guy M. Steele, Jr., Oklahoma Geological Survey, who prepared the small maps used in this book; and Mrs. Elinore Zaruba, my secretary.

I am indebted as well to the Bureau of American Ethnology, the Library of Congress, the National Archives, the New York Public Library, the Frank Phillips Collection at the University of Oklahoma, the historical collections of Montana, Wyoming, North Dakota, South Dakota, Colorado, Nebraska, Kansas, Missouri, and Oklahoma, and to the Yale University Library for permission to consult Chambers' *History of Fort Bridger* and Brackett's *History of Fort Bridger* (Coe MSS, Nos. 18 and 28).

I am also happy to express my gratitude to the publishers listed below for their permission to reprint passages from their books, as follows:

To the Arthur H. Clark Company for quotations from *The Bozeman Trail*, by Grace Raymond Hebard and E. A. Brininstool, and *Two Great Scouts and Their Pawnee Battalion*, by George Bird Grinnell.

To Lathrop C. Harper, Publishers, for quotations from *Life, Letters and Travels of Pierre Jean De Smet, S.J.*, by Hiram M. Chittenden and Alfred T. Richardson.

To Lathrop C. Harper for quotations from *Forty Years a Fur Trader*, by Charles Larpenteur.

To the Historical Society of Montana for quotations from *"Bonneville and Bridger,"* by William S. Brackett.

To the Houghton Mifflin Company for passages quoted from *Mountain Men*, by Stanley Vestal.

To the J. B. Lippincott Company for quotations from *My Army Life and the Fort Phil. Kearney Massacre*, by Frances C. Carrington.

To Unz & Company, Publishers, for quotations from *A Biographical Sketch of James Bridger: Mountaineer, Trapper and Guide*, by Major General Grenville M. Dodge.

BIBLIOGRAPHY

ALTER, J. CECIL. James Bridger. Salt Lake City, 1925.

BANCROFT, H. H., History of Utah. San Francisco, 1889.

BOARDMAN, JOHN. Journal, MS. (Mrs. W. B. Dods, Salt Lake City).

BONNER, T. D. The Life and Adventures of James P. Beckwourth. London, 1892.

BRACKETT, WILLIAM S. "Bonneville and Bridger." Historical Society of Montana Contributions. Vol. III. 1900.

BRISBIN, JAMES S. Belden, the White Chief. New York, 1870.

BROWN, JAMES S. Life of a Pioneer. Salt Lake City, 1900.

BRYANT, EDWIN. What I Saw in California (or Rocky Mountain Adventures).

BURTON, RICHARD F. The City of the Saints. London, 1862.

CANNON, MILES. Waiilatpu. Boise, Idaho, 1915.

CARRINGTON, FRANCES C. Army Life on the Plains. Philadelphia, 1911.

CARRINGTON, J. B. Across the Plains with Bridger as Guide. facsim. Scrib. M. 85:66-71 Ja. '29.

CARRINGTON, MARGARET I. Ab-Sa-Ra-Ka, the Land of Massacre. Philadelphia, 1879.

CHANDLESS, WILLIAM. A visit to Salt Lake. London, 1857.

CHAPMAN, A. Master Trapper and Trail Maker. Outing. 47:431-4 Ja. '06.

CHITTENDEN, CAPT. HIRAM M. History of the American Fur Trade of the Far West. 3 vols. New York, 1902.

CHITTENDEN, CAPT. HIRAM M. The Yellowstone Park. Cincinnati, 1920.

CLAMPITT, JOHN W. Echoes from the Rocky Mountains. Chicago, 1888.

CLAYTON, WILLIAM. Journal. Salt Lake City, 1921.

CONNELLEY, W. E. Doniphan's Expedition (Moorhead's Narrative). Topeka, 1907.

Cooke, P. St. George. Scenes and Adventures in the U. S. Army. Philadelphia, 1859.

Coutant, C. G. History of Wyoming. Laramie, 1899.

Dale, Harrison C. The Ashley-Smith Explorations. Cleveland, 1918.

Dellenbaugh, F. S. Frémont and 49. New York, 1914.

Dellenbaugh, F. S. The Romance of the Colorado River. New York, 1906.

De Smet, Father Pierre Jean. Life, Letters and Travels by Chittenden and Richardson. New York, 1905.

Dodge, Maj.-Gen. Grenville M. Biographical Sketch of James Bridger, New York, 1905.

Dodge, Col. Richard I. Our Wild Indians. Hartford, 1883.

Drannan, Capt. Wm. F. Thirty-One Years on the Plains and in the Mountains; and the sequel, Chief of Scouts, Piloting Emigrants Across the Plains, 1900.

Egan, Howard. Pioneering in the West. Salt Lake City, 1917.

Elliott, T. C. Biography and Journals of Peter Skene Ogden, in Oregon Historical Society Quarterlies. Portland, 1909-1910.

Executive Document No. 45, Thirty-ninth Congress, Second Session.

Executive Document No. 77, Fortieth Congress, First Session.

Ferris, Mrs. B. G. Life Among the Mormons. New York, 1855.

Frémont, John Charles. Memoirs of My Life.

Gottfredson, Peter. Indian Depredations in Utah. Salt Lake City, 1919.

Grinnell, George Bird. Two Great Scouts and Their Pawnee Battalion. Cleveland, 1928.

Grinnell, George Bird. The Fighting Cheyennes. New York, 1915.

Gunnison, J. W. History of the Mormons. Philadelphia, 1852.

Handbook of Reference (Mormon). Salt Lake City, 1884.

Hebard, Dr. Grace Raymond and Brininstool, E. A. The Bozeman Trail. Cleveland, 1922.

Hickman, Wm. A. Brigham's Destroying Angel, etc. Salt Lake City, 1904.

Hough, Emerson. The Covered Wagon. New York, 1922.

HOUGHTON, ELIZA P. DONNER. The Expedition of the Donner Party. Los Angeles, 1920.

HOWE, HENRY. Historical Collections of the Great West. Cincinnati, 1852.

HUMFREVILLE, J. LEE. Twenty Years Among Our Savage Indians. Hartford, Conn., 1897.

INMAN, COL. HENRY. The Old Santa Fe Trail. New York, 1897.

IRVING, WASHINGTON. The Adventures of Captain Bonneville.

JENSEN, J. MARINUS. Early History of Provo, Utah. Provo, 1924.

JOHNSTON, W. P. Life of Gen. Albert Sidney Johnston. New York, 1878.

JOHNSTON, WM. G. Experiences of a Forty-Niner. Pittsburgh, 1892.

Kansas City Star, news story. January 18, 1924.

KELLY, WILLIAM. An Excursion to California, Etc.

LANGFORD, N. P. The Discovery of Yellowstone Park. St. Paul, 1923.

LARPENTEUR, CHARLES. Forty Years a Fur Trader, Edited by Eliott Coues. New York, 1898. 2 vols.

LINFORTH, JAMES (and Frederick Piercy). Route from Liverpool to Great Salt Lake Valley. Liverpool, 1855.

LINN, W. A. The Story of the Mormons. New York, 1902.

LITTLE, JAMES A. From Kirtland to Salt Lake City. Salt Lake City, 1890.

LOWE, PERCIVAL G. Five Years a Dragoon ('49 to '54) and Other Adventures on the Great Plains. Kansas City, Mo., 1906.

MANLY, W. L. Death Valley in '49. San Jose, 1894.

MARCY, R. B. Thirty Years of Army Life. New York, 1874.

McGLASHAN, C. F. History of the Donner Party. Sacramento, 1907.

MILES, NELSON A. Personal Recollections. New York, 1896.

Missouri Historical Society, Collections. St. Louis, Mo.

National Republican. 19:28 N. '31. (Portrait of Jim Bridger).

Nebraska State Historical Society. Vol. XX. Lincoln, 1922. Historical news items from *Missouri Republican* and *Missouri Intelligencer.*

Nebraska State Historical Society Transactions. Vol. II. Lincoln, 1887.

NEIHARDT, JOHN G. The Song of Hugh Glass. New York, 1915.

OSTRANDER, MAJ. ALSON B. An Army Boy of the Sixties. New York, 1924.

PALMER, CAPT. H. E. History of Powder River Indian Expedition of 1865. Nebraska State Historical Society. Vol. II. Lincoln, 1887.

PALMER, JOEL. Journal of Travels Over the Rocky Mountains. In Early Western Travels, edited by R. G. Thwaites. Cleveland, 1906.

PARKER, REV. SAMUEL. Journal of an Exploring Tour Beyond the Rocky Mountains. Auburn, 1846.

PARKMAN, FRANCIS. The Oregon Trail, Sketches of Prairie and Rocky Mountain Life. 1849.

POND, FRED E. The Life and Adventures of "Ned Buntline." New York, 1919.

POWELL, J. W. Exploration of the Colorado River of the West. Washington, 1878.

RAYNOLDS, CAPT. W. F. Report on the Exploration of the Yellowstone River. Executive Document No. 77, Fortieth Congress, First Session.

ROOT, FRANK A. (and W. E. CONNELLEY). The Overland Stage to California. Topeka, 1901.

RUSLING, JAMES T. Across America. New York, 1874.

SABIN, EDWIN L. Building the Pacific Railway.

———. Kit Carson Days. Chicago, 1919.

SAGE, RUFUS B. Rocky Mountain Life. New York, 1887. (Also same as Scenes in the Rocky Mountains.)

Senate Report No. 625, Fifty-Second Congress, First Session.

SHERIDAN, GEN. P. H. Personal Memoirs. 2 vols. New York, 1888.

SHOTWELL, A. J. Articles in Freeport, O., *Press*, May 3, 1916.

SIMPSON, CAPT. J. H. Explorations across the Great Basin of the Territory of Utah. Washington, 1876.

SMITH, MARY ETTIE V. Fifteen Years Among the Mormons. Hartford, 1887.

STANSBURY, HOWARD. Exploration and Survey of the Valley of the Great Salt Lake of Utah. Philadelphia, 1855.

STENHOUSE, T. B. H. Rocky Mountain Saints. New York, 1873.

THOMAS, D. K. Wild Life in the Rocky Mountains, 1917.

TOPPING, E. S. Chronicles of the Yellowstone. St. Paul, Minn., 1888.

TOWNSEND, JOHN K. Narrative, in Early Western Travels, Edited by R. G. Thwaites. Cleveland, Ohio, 1905.

TRIPLETT, COL. FRANK. Conquering the Wilderness. Minneapolis, 1888.

TULLIDGE, E. W. History of Salt Lake City. Salt Lake City, 1886.

VICTOR, MRS. FRANCES F. The River of the West. Hartford, 1870.

VESTAL, STANLEY. Kit Carson. Boston, 1928.

——. Sitting Bull. Boston, 1932.

——. Warpath. Boston, 1933.

——. New Sources of Indian History. Norman, Oklahoma, 1934.

——. Mountain Men. Boston, 1937.

——. Old Santa Fe Trail. Boston, 1939.

——. Missouri, The. New York, 1945.

WHEELER, OLIN D. The Trail of Lewis and Clark.

WHITNEY, O. F. History of Utah, 4 vols. Salt Lake City, 1892.

——. Life of Heber C. Kimball. Salt Lake City, 1888.

WISLIZENUS, F. A. A Journey to the Rocky Mountains in 1839. St. Louis, 1912.

WOODRUFF, WILFORD. Journal and Life History, edited by M. F. Cowley. Salt Lake City, 1909.

WYETH, N. J. Correspondence and Journals, Oregon Historical Society. Eugene, Oregon, 1899.

Wyoming Historical Department files.

NOTES

PART 1: TRAPPER

CHAPTER V

1. The preceding paragraphs describing the adventures of Hugh Glass with the bear first appeared in *Mountain Men* by Stanley Vestal, Boston, 1937, pages 48 to 53, and are reprinted here by courtesy of the Houghton Mifflin Company.

2. Our authority for identifying this young fellow with Jim Bridger is that of Captain La Barge. See *The American Fur Trade of the Far West* by Hiram M. Chittenden. New York, 1902. p. 704. Captain La Barge was one of the great men of the Old West, and his single statement must carry great weight—if only the weight of tradition. It has been objected that Bridger's behavior in deserting Hugh Glass is not in character with his later life. True, it is not; but that only makes his behavior the more probable—for this early mistake affords the most satisfying explanation of his later splendid character and achievements.

3. The five preceding paragraphs are here reprinted by courtesy of Houghton Mifflin Company from *Mountain Men* by Stanley Vestal. Boston, 1937. pp. 53-54.

4. Hiram M. Chittenden, in his book *The American Fur Trade of the Far West,* page 953, describes Fort Kiowa as being situated on the right bank of the Missouri "some 10 miles above where Chamberlain, South Dakota, now stands." On page 701, he describes Fort Kiowa as being distant from the place where Glass was abandoned "a hundred miles." But even the mouth of Grand River, the nearest point, is fully 200 miles from Fort Kiowa, and Glass was wounded near the forks of the Grand five days' march above the mouth. If Glass followed a straight line between these points, he would strike the Missouri directly at the mouth of Cheyenne River.

PART 2: BOOSHWAY

CHAPTER VI

1. See St. Louis *Weekly Reveille,* March 1, 1847. Article "Fitzpatrick, the Discoverer of the South Pass." Files of Missouri Historical Society, St. Louis, Missouri. The Astorians in 1812 appear to have missed the trail over South Pass, passing around the headwaters of the Sweetwater.

2. See *The River of the West* by Frances Fuller Victor. Hartford, 1870. pp. 95-96.

3. According to Joe Meek the name *Casapy* means Blanket Chief, and—if so—is apparently a corruption or abbreviation of the Crow word *chaopétsabatsótse,* from the words *chaopétsa,* blanket, and *batsótse,* chief.

Possibly *Casapy* is derived from a Crow word *bikasopia,* meaning *cloth.* The Indian used the term "chief" here much as we use the word "master" or "boss," as in "wagon master" or "wagon boss"— a man in charge of wagons.

CHAPTER VII

1. The preceding paragraphs describing the Rendezvous and Battle of Pierre's Hole first appeared (somewhat altered) in *Mountain Men* by Stanley Vestal, Boston, 1937, pages 106 to 121, and are reprinted here by courtesy of the Houghton Mifflin Co.

2. *Captain Bonneville* by Washington Irving. G. P. Putnam's Sons, 1895. p. 85.

CHAPTER VIII

1. Washington Irving, in *Adventures of Captain Bonneville,* (Chap. XI).

2. Irving, *op. cit.*

3. The thirteen paragraphs preceding first appeared in *Mountain Men* by Stanley Vestal, Boston, 1937, pages 136-139, and are here reprinted by courtesy of the Houghton Mifflin Co.

CHAPTER IX

1. This scrape is narrated in detail in *Kit Carson* by Stanley Vestal, (Chapter VIII).

2. See *Kit Carson,* by Stanley Vestal, Boston, 1928. p. 145.

3. According to Chittenden. See *The American Fur Trade of the Far West* by Hiram M. Chittenden. Vol. I, p. 302. New York, 1902.

4. See *Life in the Far West* by George Frederick Ruxton. Blackwood's magazine, 1848.

5. See *The River of the West.* Life and Adventure in the Rocky Mountains and Oregon. By Mrs. Frances Fuller Victor. R. W. Bliss and Company, Newark, N. J., 1870. pp. 235-236.

CHAPTER X

1. See Chittenden, *The American Fur Trade in the Far West.* New York, 1902. pp. 305-07.

2. "Whereas, a dissolution of partnership having taken place by mutual consent between Thomas Fitzpatrick, Milton G. Sublette, Henry Fraeb, John Baptiste Gervais and James Bridger, members of the Rocky Mountain Fur Company, all persons having demands against said company are requested to come forward and receive payment; those indebted to said firm are desired to call and make immediate payment, as they are anxious to close the business of the concern.

"Hams Fork, June 20, 1834.

"(Signed) Thos. Fitzpatrick,

M. G. Sublette,
(In different ink as if at a later date)
Henry Fraeb,
J. B. Gervais,
James (his x mark) Bridger.

"Witness: Wm. L. Sublette for Bridger and Fitzpatrick.

"Witness: J. P. Risley for Fraeb and Gervais.

"The public are hereby notified that the business will in future be conducted by Thomas Fitzpatrick, Milton G. Sublette and James Bridger, under the style and firm of Fitzpatrick, Sublette and Bridger.

"Hams Fork, June 20, 1834.

"(Signed) Thos. Fitzpatrick,

M. G. Sublette,

(In different ink as above)

James (his x mark) Bridger.

"Witness: Wm. L. Sublette." *

* *American Fur Trade* by Hiram Martin Chittenden. Vol. II. New York, 1902. p. 864.

3. See *Kit Carson* by Stanley Vestal. Chapter X.

CHAPTER XI

1. This incident may be found in *The River of the West* by Mrs. Frances Fuller Victor. Hartford, 1870. Chapter XIV. The Indian words which Meek or his biographer, Mrs. Victor, puts in the mouth of the Crow chief, have puzzled most of the Crows and white interpreters to whom I have submitted them for interpretation. The best they can make of it is that *Shiam* is a corruption of the English word *Cheyenne,* and that the second word *Shaspusia* is a misspelling of the Crow name for Cheyennes—*His-Arrow-Feathers-Are-Striped.*

CHAPTER XII

1. *The River of the West.* Life and Adventure in the Rocky Mountains and Oregon. By Mrs. Frances Fuller Victor. Hartford, 1870. pp. 229-230.

2. Ibid. p. 230. *Crede* Mrs. Victor.

3. Ibid. p. 231.

CHAPTER XIII

1. See *The River of the West,* by F. F. Victor, Hartford, 1870. p. 238.

2. Dr. F. A. Wislizenus has left us a detailed account of what he saw at this famous rendezvous. See Bibliography.

3. See *Life, Letters and Travels of Father Pierre-Jean De Smet, S.J.,* 1801-1873, by Hiram Martin Chittenden and Alfred Talbot Richardson. New York, 1905. Vol. III, p. 1012.

4. See Denver *Tribune-Republican,* July 10, 1886. See also *Exploration and Survey of the Valley of the Great Salt Lake of Utah* by Howard Stansbury. Washington, D. C., 1853. pp. 239-240. For details of Frapp's (Fraeb's) battle, see *Mountain Men* by Stanley Vestal, Boston, 1937, Chapter XVII, and the article by LeRoy R. Hafen in *The Colorado Magazine,* Vol. VII, No. 3 (May, 1930), pp. 97-101.

PART 3: TRADER

CHAPTER XIV

1. See *The Oregon Trail* by Francis Parkman. Chapter IX "Scenes at Fort Laramie."

2. *Biographical Sketch of James Bridger* by Maj. Gen. Grenville M. Dodge. New York, 1905.

CHAPTER XV

1. *Forty Years a Fur Trader on the Upper Missouri* by Charles Larpenteur. Edited by Elliott Coues. Vol. I, New York, 1898. pp. 211-215. Quoted here by permission of Lathrop C. Harper.

2. Wilford Woodruff, *Journal.* Quoted by J. Cecil Alter; see his *James Bridger.* Salt Lake City, 1925. p. 198.

3. Woodruff, quoted by Alter, *op. cit.,* p. 198.

4. See Wilford Woodruff's *Journal,* quoted in Alter, *op. cit.,* p. 198.

5. See Alter, *op. cit.,* p. 189, quoting the MS History of Brigham Young, 1847, p. 95.

6. For a complete account of the variants see Alter, *op. cit.,* Chapter XXX.

CHAPTER XVI

1. *Twenty Years Among Our Savage Indians* by J. Lee Humfreville. Hartford, Conn., 1897. p. 573.

2. *Experiences of a Forty-Niner* by William G. Johnston. Pittsburgh, 1892.

3. *Exploration and Survey of the Valley of the Great Salt Lake of Utah,* by Howard Stansbury. Philadelphia, 1855.

CHAPTER XVII

1. *Five Years a Dragoon* ('49 to '54) And Other Adventures on the Great Plains. By Percival G. Lowe. Kansas City, Missouri, 1906.

2. *Life, Letters and Travels of Father Pierre-Jean De Smet, S.J.,* 1801-1873. By Hiram Martin Chittenden and Alfred Talbot Richardson. Four Volumes—Vol. II. New York, 1905. p. 682.

3. Ibid. Vol. I. New York, 1905. pp. 679-680.

4. St. Louis (Mo.) *Republican,* October 26, 1851.

5. The reputation of Jim Bridger at this time was recorded by the editor of the *Missouri Republican* of St. Louis in the issue of October 24, 1851, in the following terms:

"In addition the Commissioners had the assistance of Mr. James Bridger, the owner and founder of Bridger's Fort, in the mountains, This man is a perfect original. . . . He has traversed the mountains East and West, and from the Northern boundary of the United States to the Gila River. He is not an educated man, but seems to have an intuitive knowledge of the topography of the country, the courses of streams, the direction of mountains, and is never lost, wherever he may be. It is stated by those who have had him in their employ, that in the midst of the mountains, when the party of trappers wished to move from one stream to another, or cross a mountain to any stream or place, or when lost or uncertain of the proper direction, they would always appeal to Bridger. He would throw his gun carelessly over his shoulder, survey the country awhile with his eye, and then strike out on a course, and never fail to reach the place, although he had several hundred miles to traverse over a country which he never had traveled, and to places he had never seen."

6. St. Louis (Mo.) *Republican,* October 26, 1851.

7. *Five Years a Dragoon* ('49 to '54) and Other Adventures on the Great Plains. By Percival G. Lowe. Kansas City, Missouri, 1906.

8. Ibid.

CHAPTER XVIII

1. See *The Mormons at Home* by Mrs. Benjamin G. Ferris. 1856.

2. A detailed account of all this business—largely from the Mormon point of view—may be found in the excellent biography *James Bridger* by J. Cecil Alter. Chapters 36, 37, and 38.

3. See *Fifteen Years Among the Mormons* by Mary Ettie V. Smith. Hartford, 1887.

4. Ibid.

5. See *Thirty Years of Army Life* by R. B. Marcy. New York, 1874.

6. See Senate Report No. 625, Fifty-Second Congress, First Session.

PART 4: GUIDE

CHAPTER XIX

1. Parkman writes: "I cannot take leave of the reader without adding a word of the guide who had served us throughout with such zeal and fidelity. Indeed his services had far surpassed the terms of his engagement. Yet whoever had been his employers, or to whatever closeness of intercourse they might have thought fit to admit him, he would never have changed the bearing of quiet respect which he considered due to his bourgeois. If sincerity and honor, a boundless generosity of spirit, a delicate regard to the feelings of others, and a nice perception of what was due to him, are the essential characteristics of a gentleman, then Henry Chatillon deserves the title. He could not write his own name, and he had spent his life among savages. In him sprang up spontaneously those qualities which all the

refinements of life, and intercourse with the highest and best of the better part of mankind, fail to awaken in the brutish nature of some men. In spite of his bloody calling, Henry was always humane and merciful; he was gentle as a woman, though braver than a lion. He acted aright from the free impulses of his large and generous nature. A certain species of selfishness is essential to the sternness of spirit which bears down opposition and subjects the will of others to its own. Henry's character was of an opposite stamp. His easy good-nature almost amounted to weakness; yet while it unfitted him for any position of command, it secured the esteem and good-will of all those who were not jealous of his skill and reputation."

2. See F. Geo. Heldt, *Contributions,* Montana Historical Society, Volume I, 1876.

3. Marcy, R. B., *Thirty Years of Army Life.* New York, 1874.

CHAPTER XX

1. See *Rocky Mountain Saints* by T. B. H. Stenhouse. New York, 1873.

2. Stenhouse, *op. cit.*

CHAPTER XXI

1. See *Bonneville and Bridger* by William S. Brackett. Historical Society of Montana Contributions, Vol. I, 1900.

2. *The Yellowstone Park* by Hiram Martin Chittenden. Cincinnati, 1920.

3. Ibid.

4. *The Old Santa Fe Trail* by Colonel Henry Inman. New York, 1897.

5. See *Bonneville and Bridger* by William S. Brackett. Historical Society of Montana Contributions, Vol. I, 1900.

6. Through courtesy of Mr. E. G. Campbell, Director, War Records Office, The National Archives, Washington, D.C., I am enabled to give the following data:

Service of James Bridger as a Guide in the Employ of the Quartermaster Department

The records of the War Department in the National Archives show that James Bridger was employed by Captain J. H. Dickerson as a guide at Camp Scott, June 12-30, 1858; at Camp Floyd, July 1-2, 1858; in the field, July 16-20, 1858. He was paid at the rate of $150.00 a month for this service. The date of entry into service given on each report is July 16, 1857. And entry in the remarks column for the record of June 12-30 states that Bridger was employed continuously during that period. An entry in the remarks column for the record July 16-20 states "Discharged, certificate given."

Correspondence of the Army of Utah contains a few references to Bridger which indicate that he was serving as a guide with the Army in 1858, but no details of his services are given.

Hired at Fort Laramie by Lt. O. S. Glenn, Acting Asst. Quartermaster, U.S. Army

FILE NO.	POSITION	DATE	RATE OF PAY	REMARKS
1863-421 1864-732	Guide	October 1, 1863- April 30, 1864	$5.00 a day	Discharged on April 30.

Hired at Fort Laramie by Lt. H. E. Averill, Acting Asst. Quartermaster, U.S. Army

1864-207	Guide	August 3-31, 1864	$5.00 a day	Discharged

Hired at Fort Laramie by Capt. S. D. Childs, Asst. Quartermaster, U.S. Army

1865-428	Chief Guide	July 6-September 30,1865	$10.00 a day	Guide for the Indian Expedition
	Chief Guide	October 1-November 30, 1865	$10.00 a day	Retained by order of General Wheaton as Guide for Post Headquarters. Discharged.
1866-178	Chief Guide	January 25-31, 1866	$10.00 a day	Guide for Headquarters, West Subdistrict of Nebraska, employed by order of Col. H. E. Maynadier, Commanding.
1866-178	Guide	March 5-May 31, 1866	$5.00 a day	Same as above.
	Guide	June 1-15, 1866	$5.00 a day	Guide for Headquarters, District of the Platte, by order of Col. H. E. Maynadier, Commanding.

Hired at Fort Philip Kearney by Lt. F. H. Brown, Acting Asst. Quartermaster, U.S. Army

1866-119	Chief Guide	June 16-August 31, 1866	$10.00 a day	

Hired at Fort Philip Kearney by Lt. W. S. Watson, Quartermaster, U.S. Army

1866-551	Chief Guide	October 14-December 31, 1866	$10.00 a day	Note: There is a notation that Bridger was transferred by Lt. Brown to Lt. Watson on October 13, 1866, which indicates that he was employed by Lt. Brown from June 16 to October 13, 1866. Lt. Brown's records for September and October, 1866, appear to be missing.

Hired at Fort Philip Kearney by Bvt. Brig. Gen. G. B. Dandy, Quartermaster, U.S. Army

| 1867-172 | Chief Guide | January 1-September 23, 1867 | $10.00 a day | Discharged. |

Hired at Fort Laramie by Major E. B. Grimes, Quartermaster, U.S. Army

| 1868-312 | Guide | May 15-22, 1868 | $5.00 a day |

Hired at Fort Laramie by Lt. P. P. Barnard, Acting Asst. Quartermaster, U.S. Army

| 1868-582 | Guide | May 23-July 21, 1868 | $5.00 a day |

7. See also *James Bridger* by J. Cecil Alter. Salt Lake City, 1925. pp. 400-401.

8. *Twenty Years Among Our Savage Indians* by J. Lee Humfreville. Hartford, Conn., 1897. pp. 566-567.

PART 5: CHIEF OF SCOUTS

CHAPTER XXII

1. Reprinted by permission of the Publishers, The Arthur H. Clark Company, from *Two Great Scouts and Their Pawnee Battalion,* George Bird Grinnell. See p. 91.

2. History of the Powder River Expedition of 1865. By H. E. Palmer, Late Captain Company A, Eleventh Kansas Volunteer Corps. Taken from *Transactions and Reports of the Nebraska State Historical Society,* Vol. II. Lincoln, Nebraska, 1887.

3. Reprinted by permission of the Publishers, the Arthur H. Clark Company, from *Two Great Scouts and Their Pawnee Battalion,* George Bird Grinnell. See p. 91.

4. History of the Powder River Expedition of 1865. By H. E. Palmer, Late Captain Company A, Eleventh Kansas Volunteer Corps. Taken from *Transactions and Reports of the Nebraska State Historical Society,* Vol. II. Lincoln, Nebraska, 1887.

5. See A. J. Shotwell, Freeport, Ohio, *Press,* May 3, 1916. Shotwell also declares "Bridger was a prince among men and the uncrowned king of all the Rocky Mountain scouts."

6. My friend, Mr. Frank Zahn, the Upper Missouri Interpreter,

writes: "According to my grand-mother (*Uncage-wakan-win*—Holy
Generation) the "medicine" wolf's warning of impending disaster
was not the ordinary howl that wolves give; but was identical with
that of the Sioux woman's death lament."

CHAPTER XXIII

1. See A. J. Shotwell, Free Port, Ohio, *Press*. May 3, 1916.

2. See the *Kearney Herald,* Fort Kearny, N. T., January 6, 1866,
reprinted in "Across the Plains with Jim Bridger as Guide" by
James B. Carrington, *Scribner's Magazine,* Vol. LXXXV. January-
June, 1929. pp. 68-69.

3. *Twenty Years Among Our Savage Indians* by J. Lee Humfreville. Hartford, Conn., 1897. pp. 573.

CHAPTER XXIV

1. See Margaret Irvin Carrington's *Ab-Sa-Ra-Ka,* Land of Massacre: Being the Experience of an Officer's Wife on the Plains.
Philadelphia, 1878. Chapter XII.

CHAPTER XXV

1. Mrs. Louis Gazzeau.

2. Mr. Frank Zahn, the Upper Missouri Interpreter, states that the
Sioux, in punishing a member of their own tribe, used the same expressions as when counting *coup* upon an enemy. The man who first
struck shouted *"Onhey."* The second to strike shouted *"Okihe-
wakte"*—I kill him second." The third, *"Iyamini-wakte*—I kill him
third." The fourth warrior shouted in like manner in his turn. I
have been unable to find any old warrior who had heard the Sioux
yell *"Coo"* or *"Coup"* on such an occasion.

3. Mr. Frank Zahn, the Upper Missouri Interpreter, informs me
that his father, William Presley Zahn (Company G, 17th US Infantry) who served on four expeditions against the Sioux (1869-
1876) told him that while marching with Custer, he saw skulls showing Indian drawings as here illustrated. Custer's Indian scouts explained that the marks meant that the Sioux would attack and defeat the Crows. When white troops were indicated, a broken gun
was substituted for the broken arrow.

The drawing of the weapon representing the Sioux was always placed on the right side of the skull facing with the buffalo, or on the left of the beholder facing the skull.

It is surmised that the location of the coming fight might be indicated by the direction in which the skull faced on the trail, or by a drawing showing the forks of a river and the figure of a crazy woman. In Sioux picture writing, anything supernatural or crazy was indicated by wavy lines extending upward from the mouth or head of the creature to be indicated as crazy. Such drawings may be found in Garrick Mallery's "Picture Writing of the American Indians" page 462 ff., U.S. Bureau of American Ethnology, Tenth Annual Report, 1888-89.

Mr. Zahn suggests that the time of the fight might be indicated by a single rising sun, "that day," and the invitation to Indians to join the fray might be indicated by a row of tipis below the arrow and the broken gun.

Such a drawing would tell every Indian who saw it that the fight was to be on the Crazy Woman's Fork. Hoof prints crossing the stream might be added to indicate the trail.

4. This incident is recorded by Frances C. Carrington in *My Army Life and the Fort Phil Kearney Massacre*. Philadelphia, 1910.

5. See "Items of Indian Service" by Brigadier General William H. Bisbee, U.S.A., Retired, in *Proceedings of the annual Meeting and Dinner of the Order of Indian Wars of the United States*. 1928. p. 23 ff.

6. *Ab-Sa-Ra-Ka*, Land of Massacre by Mrs. Margaret Irvin Carrington. Philadelphia, 1878. p. 151.

CHAPTER XXVI

1. The signals in use at the fort may be found recorded in the unpublished notebook of George A. Boehmer, (page 61), No. 2066 in the files of the Bureau of American Ethnology, Smithsonian Institution, Washington, D.C., entitled "Crow or Absaroka Dictionary." Boehmer also lists engagements, with losses from the "massacre," until the treaty in 1868, and a list of "game" killed (the bag in-

cludes five "common Indians!")—and wounded!,—at the fort during the last months of 1867. The signals follow:

FORT PHIL KEARNEY INDIAN SIGNALS

Flag Out of sight	"all quiet."
Flag Raised and still	"attention."
Flag Waved, three times from vertical to right	"small party on Reno Road."
Flag Waved, three times from vertical to left	"small party on Big Horn Road."
Flag Waved, five times from vertical to right	"large party on Reno Road."
Flag Waved, five times from vertical to left	"large party on Big Horn Road."
Flag Waved, three times from right to left	"Indians."
Flag Waved, around the head	"Train attacked."
Flag Raised and carried in a vertical position around the picket defense	"The Attack."

(Signals to be repeated three times, with intervals of three minutes between signals).

2. Proceedings of the Annual Meeting and Dinner of the Order of Indian Wars of the United States. January 19, 1928. p. 29.

CHAPTER XXVII

1. On this matter of Carrington's orders, the reader may consult (1) *The Bozeman Trail* by Grace Raymond Hebard and E. A. Brininstool, Cleveland, 1922. Vol. I, pp. 332-338; and (2) "Items of Indian Service" by Brigadier General William H. Bisbee, U.S. Army, Retired, in *Proceedings of the Annual Meeting and Dinner of the Order of Indian Wars of the United States,* Jan. 28, 1928. pp. 30-32.

2. The only eye-witness accounts of the battle are those of Indian participants. For the Cheyenne account, see *The Fighting Cheyennes* by George Bird Grinnell. New York, 1915. Chapter XVIII. For the Sioux account, see *Warpath, the True Story of the Fighting Sioux Told in a Biography of Chief White Bull* by Stanley Vestal. Boston, 1934. Chapter VI.

CHAPTER XXVIII

1. The *St. Louis Republican's* special correspondent, reporting what the investigating Commissioners had learned from the Sioux about the massacre, was quoted by Horace Greeley's *New York Semi-Weekly Tribune,* April 2, 1867: "The bravery of our bugler was much spoken of, he having killed several indians by beating them over the head with his bugle." A much-battered copper bugle was picked up on the field, and is now in the collection made by Mr.

T. J. Gatchell, of Buffalo, Wyoming. The most complete account of this bugler was syndicated by Professor Elmo Scott Watson of Northwestern University, and may be found reprinted in *Old Travois Trails, A Magazine Devoted to the History and Literature of the West,* published bi-monthly at the restored portion of old Fort Phil Kearney, Banner, Wyoming, by Charles D. Schreibeis. March-April, 1941 issue; Vol. I, No. 6, pp. 21-24. It is also referred to very briefly in George P. Belden's *Belden, the White Chief,* Robert W. David's *Malcolm Campbell, Sheriff,* etc., etc.

2. *The Old Santa Fe Trail* by Colonel Henry Inman. New York, 1897.

3. Reprinted by permission of the Publishers, The Arthur H. Clark Company, from *The Bozeman Trail,* Grace Raymond Hebard and E. A. Brininstool, Vol. II. See pp. 232-233.

CHAPTER XXIX

1. *Personal Memoirs of Philip Henry Sheridan.* New York, 1904. Vol. II, p. 308.

2. *The Kansas City Star,* January 18, 1924.

3. *Biographical Sketch of James Bridger* by Maj. Gen'l Grenville M. Dodge. New York, 1905.

4. *Twenty Years Among Our Savage Indians* by J. Lee Humfreville. Hartford, Conn., 1897. pp. 572-573.

5. Grenville M. Dodge, *op. cit.*

6. The date given for the discovery of South Pass in this inscription should be 1823.

INDEX

325